THE

LIFE

OF

WILLIAM HUTTON, F. A. S. S.

&c. &c.

Thomas Ransom sculpt.

WILLIAM HUTTON, F.A.S.S.

at the Age of Eighty.

Published by Baldwin Cradock & Joy, July 1816.

THE LIFE

OF

WILLIAM HUTTON, F.A.S.S.

INCLUDING

A PARTICULAR ACCOUNT OF

𝕿𝖍𝖊 𝕽𝖎𝖔𝖙𝖘 𝖆𝖙 𝕭𝖎𝖗𝖒𝖎𝖓𝖌𝖍𝖆𝖒 𝖎𝖓 1791,

TO WHICH IS SUBJOINED,

THE HISTORY OF HIS FAMILY,

WRITTEN BY HIMSELF,

AND PUBLISHED BY HIS DAUGHTER,

CATHERINE HUTTON.

LONDON:

PRINTED FOR BALDWIN, CRADOCK, AND JOY,
PATERNOSTER ROW;
AND BEILBY AND KNOTTS, BIRMINGHAM.

1816.

PREFACE.

NONE is so able to write a Life as the person who is the subject; because his thoughts, his motives, and his private transactions, are open to him alone. But none is so unfit; for his hand, biassed in his favour, will omit, or disguise simple truth, hold out false colours, and deceive all but the writer. I have endeavoured to divest myself of this prejudice.

I must apologize to the world, should this ever come under its eye, for presenting it with a life of insignificance. I have no manœuvres, no state tricks, no public transactions, nor adventures of moment, to lay before my Readers. I have only the history of an individual, struggling, unsupported, up a mountain of difficulties. And yet some of the circumstances are so very uncommon, as barely to merit belief. A similar mode of a man ushering himself into life, perhaps, cannot be met with.

If I tell unnecessary things, they are not told in unnecessary words. I have avoided prolixity.

A man cannot speak of himself without running into egotism; but I have adhered to facts.

Some writers, in speaking of themselves, appear in the third person: as, "*the Author,* "*the Recorder,* or *the Writer of this Narra-* "*tive;*" which seems rather far-fetched. I can see no reason why a man may not speak in the first, and use the simple letter *I*.

But without entering into the propriety of these methods, I have adopted the last. If I speak *of* myself, why not *from* myself? A rareeshow-man may be allowed to speak through a puppet, but it is needless in an Author.

It may seem singular that I should, at seventy-five, and without any preparation, be so very circumstantial in date and incident, with only the assistance of memory; which is, in a double sense, carrying my life in my head. Those who know me are not surprized. There is not a statement either false or coloured.

WILLIAM HUTTON.

Aug. 29, 1798.

THE HISTORY

OF THE LIFE OF

WILLIAM HUTTON.

IF I pretend to write from memory, how can I pretend to write things which happened near the time of my birth? Yet this must be granted me. Till the child can walk, he is allowed the hand of another. Whether I tell of myself, or another tells for me, truth shall never quit the page.

I was born September 30, 1723, which will bear the name of the last day in summer, on Wednesday, at a quarter before five in the evening, at the bottom of Full Street, in Derby; upon premises on the Banks of the Derwent, now occupied by Mr. Upton, an Attorney.

There were no prognostications prior to my birth, except that my father, the day before, was chosen Constable. But a circumstance occurred which, I believe, never did before or after — the purchase of a Cheshire cheese, price half a guinea; so large, as to merit a wheel-barrow to convey it. Perhaps this was the last *whole* cheese ever bought during my stay. A good painter may seem to give many insignificant strokes, which, to the observer, amount to nothing; but, taken in the aggregate, they may form a complete picture and a just likeness. As I must have been very little at this time, the Reader will excuse me if I talk of little things; though my mother observed, "I was the largest child she ever had, but so very " ordinary (a softer word for ugly), she was " afraid she should never love me." But whatever were her parental affections then, I had no cause to complain during the nine remaining years of her life.

At an early period I had given me, while sitting on my mother's knee, a large hollow brass drop, such as were the furniture of our old-fashioned chests of drawers, to amuse me while she was engaged in conversation. The discourse ended; the drop was missing! After diligent search, to no purpose, it was concluded that I must have swallowed it, for it had been observed at my mouth. Consternation ensued! The discharge was attended to, for one day, when all their fears subsided; the brazen bolus had found its way, without doing injury. This incident I do not remember, but have heard my mother repeat it.

1725.

Memory now comes in to aid the pen: for this year I recollect many incidents; one, playing upon the verge of the Derwent, with older children, where, I am surprized, they suffered a child of two years old to remain. Another, playing with my uncle's whip, who had just come from Mountsorrel to see us, and, to close the farce, putting it in the fire, and burning the lash. A third was a dangerous adventure. We infants were playing at the fire, which was large; and, though the least of the flock, I was not the least active. My sister had given me a piece of cap paper, plaited in the form of a fan; in lighting which, I set fire to my petticoats, frock, and bib. My cries brought my mother from the next room, who put an end to the tragi-comedy. My mother afterwards took me with her on a visit to Mountsorrel. While the waggon was crossing the Trent in a barge, a pleasure boat in view, with the people in it, seemed gradually to sink under water, and rise up alternately. This shews how very delusive is the sight of an infant of two years old. The weather was serene, the water clear, and, though deep, the pebbles at the bottom were visible.

1726.

Every class of the animal world associates with its like. An old couple, Moses Simpson and his wife, who lived at the next door, took great notice of me, but I shunned them with horror; had they been young, I should probably have sought *them*, but I was fully persuaded they would kill me. I stood at the top of a flight of stairs, and this woman at the bottom, coaxing me to come to her. She might as well have intreated the moon. I instantly tumbled to the bottom. She took me in her arms, endeavoured to pacify me, dandled me on the knee, and I was surprized that I escaped with life.

A few weeks after I saw my mother in the pangs of labour of my brother George; the mid-wife and assistants about her. I being the only male in the room, was ordered out. A woman carried me. I afterwards saw the child asleep; my mother took me by the hand and led me away, lest I should awake him.

1727.

At Mountsorrel I had an uncle who was a Grocer, and a bachelor; also a grand-mother who kept his house; and at Swithland, two miles distant, three crabbed aunts, all single, who resided together as Grocers, Milliners, Mercers, and School-mistresses. My family being distressed I was sent over, and I resided alternately with my uncle and my aunts fifteen months. Here I was put into breeches, at the age of four: here I was an interloper, and treated with much ill-nature. Nothing is more common than for people, particularly young women, to be fond of children. I can recollect numberless instances of insult, but not one civil thing they ever said. " You are an ugly " lad: you are like your father. Your brother " is a pretty lad: he is like his mother" (she was their sister). I was unable to return an answer. They might have considered that this, and other evils, were out of my power to remove.

It is curious to observe the ideas of infants. One of my aunts taking me from Mountsorrel to Swithland, entered a house at the skirts of the town, where I saw several men rather noisy, and could not conceive they were of the family. I observed also the shelves abound with crockery-ware, and could not imagine the use. The woman of the house took us into a back room, where she and my aunt seemed very familiar.

We passed on without resting; and my aunt, during this little journey, fell down, perhaps, twenty times, and generally at a stile; often lay a minute or two, and bade me look if any person was coming. I answered, "No," but the answer was needless; for I was scarcely able to look over a blade of grass. No damage ensued, except my being terrified.

Many years elapsed before I could unravel this mystery, which was no more than my aunt entering a public house. The crocks were the drinking cups; and, in the private room, she got so completely drunk, she could neither stand nor walk.

In the corner of my aunt's garden stood a hive of bees. I one day watched them, with great attention, at their own door, and thought their proceedings curious; when, like a child with a plaything, which he first admires and then destroys, I gave them a blow with my hat, and ran away. A party was instantly detached in pursuit of me, which being swifter of wing than I of foot, settled in my neck. I roared as well as ran. My timorous aunts durst not touch them, but sent for a neighbour, while I continued in agonies. After committing great depredations the enemy was reduced: I was put under cure, but never forgot who was the aggressor.

Standing at the hob by the fire, at supper, with the spoon in my left hand, my uncle asked me, "Which was my right?" Without knowing, I instantly stretched out the right, "This:" Though meant as a reproof, which I did not comprehend, yet for many years, when it was necessary to know which was the right or left hand, imagination placed me at the hob, which instantly informed me.

Another incident that occurred was the adventures of a frog. An humble member of the croaking society happening to hop out, to take the evening air, approached the door where our three heroines stood, and I near them. They darted in, terribly frightened, shut the door, and handed a broom through the window, with orders for me to kill the frog. I was pleased that I could be useful. But while fumbling with the broom, which I was not much used to handle, the condemned animal escaped; I lost a little credit and got more blame, as having left an enemy in ambush.

My eldest aunt, an ingenious, prudent, ill-tempered woman, was taken sick, and I saw her breathe her last, without having the least knowledge of that momentous event.

1728.

My mother, unknown to me, came to Mountsorrel to fetch me home. The maid took me out of bed naked, except my shirt, and, having her left hand employed, could only spare the right, with which she dangled me down stairs by the arm, as a man does a new-purchased goose, her knee thumping against my back every step. I was exceedingly ashamed to appear before my mother, then a stranger, in that indecent state.

My uncle, the next day, carried her behind him on horseback, and me before, upon a pillow, to meet the Derby waggon at Loughborough. My father, who had not seen me for fifteen months, received me with only two words, and those marked with indifference, " So, Bill."

Being four years and a half old, and dressed in my best suit, a cocked hat, and walking-stick, my sister took me by the hand to Gilbert Bridge's, for the evening's milk, which was, in future, to be my errand. One of his buxom daughters, in a gay mood, snatched off my hat, and laughed at me, as one who wins. I gave her a blow with the knob end of my stick; she returned the hat in a more serious tone, with, " The young rogue has hurt me," and from thence gave me the name of *Smiler*.

I now went to school to Mr. Thomas Meat, of harsh memory, who often took occasion to beat my head against the wall, holding it by the hair, but never could beat any learning into it; I hated all books but those of pictures.

Now a brother John was born, but soon left us, by which he escaped that distress which awaited me.

1729.

My father worked from home; and when my mother was out, the care of the family, two brothers and myself, devolved upon me, though not the eldest. My mother ordered me, when breakfast was ready, " to pour out each his " portion of milk-porridge, and take my father " his, before I eat mine." I served a mess to each, rejoiced at the excellent measure, and fell to.

During the pleasure of eating, I recollected I had forgotten my father. Astonishment seized me; I proposed that each of us should contribute to make good the deficiency. My eldest brother refused. I, therefore, took a little from the youngest, and all my own, to cure the evil. My father, at noon, remarked, *Bill* had rather pinched him. Thus I began housekeeping early, but began with a blunder.

My father had borrowed two Newspapers. I was sent to return them. I lost both. The price of each was only three halfpence, but I was as much harassed as if I had committed a crime of magnitude.

Consultations were held about fixing me in some employment, for the benefit of the family.

Winding quills for the weaver, was mentioned; but died away. Stripping tobacco for the grocer, in which I was to earn fourpence a week, was proposed; but it was at last concluded that I was too young for any employment.

1730.

This Summer my sister Ann was born; and, as I was considered the most active of the children, the nursing was committed to me. I wished to see her in leading strings, like other children; but, being too poor to buy, I procured a packthread string, which I placed under her arms, but the dear little thing informed me, by her cries, that I hurt her.

Now we lost my dear brother George, a lovely child, three years and a half old. It had been my office to take him by the hand, to play. My father expressed great sorrow.

My days of play were now drawing to an end. The Silk-mill was proposed. One of the clerks remarked to the person who took me there, that the offer was needless, I was too young. However, the offer was made; and, as hands were wanted, in the infant state of this work, I was accepted. It was found, upon trial, that nature had not given me length sufficient to reach the engine, for, out of three hundred persons employed in the mill, I was by far the least and the youngest.

It is happy for man that invention supplies the place of want. The superintendents wisely thought, if they could lengthen one end it would affect both. A pair of high pattens were therefore fabricated, and tied fast about my feet, to make them steady companions. They were clumsy companions, which I dragged about one year, and with pleasure delivered up.

I had now to rise at five every morning during seven years; submit to the cane whenever convenient to the master; be the constant companion of the most rude and vulgar of the human race, never taught by nature, nor ever wishing to be taught. A lad, let his mind be in what state it would, must be as impudent as they, or be hunted down. I could not consider this place in any other light than that of a complete bear-garden.

1731.

March the eleventh, was born, quite unknown to me, at Aston upon Trent, six miles east of Derby, a female child, who, twenty-four years after, was to become my wife; be my faithful and dear companion, and love me better than herself. I was to possess this inestimable treasure forty years, then to lose it, and mourn its loss every future day of my life.

There does not exist in man a thankfulness proportionate to the long enjoyment of a valuable favour; but there does exist a regret at the loss equal to its magnitude.

I became a favourite of two of the clerks, and many of the children, owing, perhaps, to my being the least infant among infants.

We were the only family of Dissenters connected with the Silk-mill. One of the clerks wished to make me a convert to the established church, and threw out the lure of a halfpenny every Sunday I should attend divine service there. This purchased me; and my father, who was a moderate man, winked at the purchase. This proves an assertion of Sir Robert Walpole, "That every man has his price." None could be much lower than mine.

One Sunday I was discovered in a remote pew, playing at push-pin. My patron, the next morning, had too much good nature to punish me, or withhold his favour, but he applied a more effectual remedy. He played at push-pin under my own eye, and with a tolerable share of grimace; which brought the laugh of the whole room upon me.

Entering the gates of the mill, at noon, a strong wind blew off my hat, which rolled before me into the Derwent. I could have gone swifter than the hat, but knew I should acquire a velocity that would have run me into the river, which, being deep, I had lost my life. In distress, I travelled by its side, the whole length of the building, but it continued just out of my reach. I mourned its loss the whole afternoon, as well as dreaded the consequence.

My master informed the chief Governor, who ordered him to take me to a hatter, and purchase another. I was asked whether I would have a plain band, or one with a silver tassel? What child refuses finery? I chose the latter, and became the envy of the mill.

Christmas holidays were attended with snow, followed by a sharp frost. A thaw came on, in the afternoon of the 27th, but in the night the ground was again caught by a frost, which glazed the streets. I did not awake, the next morning, till daylight seemed to appear. I rose in tears, for fear of punishment, and went to my father's bed-side, to ask what was o'clock? "He believed six;" I darted out in agonies, and, from the bottom of Full street, to the top of Silkmill lane, not 200 yards, I fell nine times! Observing no lights in the mill, I knew it was an early hour, and that the reflection of the snow had deceived me. Returning, it struck two. As I now went with care, I fell but twice.

Remarkably fond of fruit, but unable to purchase it, my mother was obliged to conceal her stock, for fear of depredation. She had bought a quantity of apples, and hid them, as she thought, out of the reach of my ken; but few eyes are more watchful than those of a longing child. Opening her store for use, when a few days had elapsed, she was astonished to find they had all vanished except two small ones! Her good nature, however, excused and concealed the fault, which my father's remembrance of a similar fault of his own would not have induced him to pardon, had he been apprized of it.

1732.

Going to the execution of Hewett and Rosamond (see the History of Derby), I could not get over the steps at the brook, and the crowd was more inclined to push me in than help me.

My father accidentally came, handed me over, and moralized upon the melancholy subject.

I assisted in the rejoicings at the Silk-mill, owing to Government granting Sir Thomas Lombe £.14,000 in consideration of their not renewing his patent.

In pouring some bobbins out of one box into another, the cogs of an engine caught the box in my hand. The works in all the five rooms began to thunder, crack and break to pieces; a universal cry of " Stop mills" ensued; all the violent powers of nature operated within me. With the strength of a madman I wrenched the box from the wheel; but, alas, the mischief was done. I durst not shew my face, nor retreat to dinner till every soul was gone. Pity in distress was not found within those walls.

It is uncommon for depression to continue upon an infant mind. In my way home I saw a man intoxicated, playing a variety of most foolish tricks, highly diverting to the company. Had my spirits been but moderately affected, I should have laughed most heartily; but they were too far sunk. Sorrow operated against rejoicing.

I saw the wonderful feats performed by *Cadman*, in flying from the top of All-saints steeple to the bottom of St. Michael's (see the History of Derby.)

During the Christmas holidays, my mother sent me for some tobacco. In the joyous airs of childhood, I tossed up the halfpenny till I lost it beyond redemption. Returning, my mother upbraided me, when I imprudently replied, with a careless air, " You should not " have sent me." That word proved my bane; she informed my father, who gave me the most severe thrashing I ever received from him. He broke his walking-stick, the fragments of which, after the battle was over, I began to splice together with a string for my own use.

1733.

The year began to increase, and my calamities with it. My mother brought forth a son, Samuel: during her lying-in, being hurt at seeing the nurse unhandy, she would do the work herself, and rinsing clothes in cold water brought her to the grave five weeks after her delivery, at the age of forty-one. I returned from the mill at noon, on Friday, March the ninth, when Nanny Ease, my mother's friend, accosted me with, " Your mother is gone." I burst into tears. " Don't cry, you will go yourself soon." This remark did not add to my comfort. My

father said, " You have lost an excellent mo-
" ther, and I a wife."

A few days after her death, as I have related in my history of the family, he declined house-keeping, sold up, and spent the money, took lodgings for himself and three children, with a widow, who had four of her own.

My mother gone, my father at the ale-house, and I among strangers, my life was forlorn. I was almost without a home, nearly without clothes, and experienced a scanty cupboard. At one time, I fasted from breakfast one day, till noon the next, and even then, dined upon only flour and water boiled into an hasty pudding. I was also afflicted with the chin-cough and with biles.

In August I saw, upon Sinfin-moor, a horse-race for the first time.

Though my father was neither young, being forty-two, nor handsome, having lost an eye, nor sober, for he spent all he could get in liquor, nor clean, for his trade was oily, nor without shackles, for he had five children, yet women of various descriptions courted his smiles, and were much inclined to pull caps for him.

On my birthday at night my father treated us with a quart of twopenny beer; and observed, that the life of man was divided into seven stages of ten years each, and that I had now completed the first.

1734.

This year kindled a violent election flame, which burnt vehemently in the county of Derby. Drinking, fighting, cursing, injuring, animosity, and murder, were the result; nor is it a wonder that ten thousand evils should arise, when the process of any plan of moment is radically bad. The contending parties were, Sir Nathaniel Curzon, father to the present Lord Scarsdale; John Harper, son to the then baronet, and grand-father to the present, on one side; and Lord Charles Cavendish on the other. Cavendish and Curzon were the successful candidates.

In October, my sister, whom we had not seen for five years, paid us a visit from Swithland. She was drawing towards fifteen, and appeared a tall, handsome, straight girl. I was struck with the singularity of her departure. She was to attend the Leicester waggon at five in the morning; my father called her to his bed side, gave her a kiss, and two shillings towards her journey, wished her well, never stirred a foot to conduct her, but suffered her to go alone, though the morning was dark.

The rage for flying had continued two years in full force; I caught that rage, but not being able to procure a rope, I and my companions laid hold of a scaffold pole in the absence of the workmen, who were erecting a house in Amen corner, south of Allsaints. We placed one end in the churchyard, and the other in the chamber window, and flew over the wall. We soon made the pole as bright as a looking-glass, but reduced our raiment to rags. To this day I never pass the place without a glance at the window.

A few young men, adepts in the art of flying, procured the consent of Sir Nathaniel Curzon, to perform at Keddleston for the amusement of the family. They fastened one end of the rope to the top of the hall, the other in the park; but the unlucky performer, instead of flying *over* the river, fell *in*, blasted his character, and instead of regaling upon beef and ale, the whole bevy sneaked off privately. This gave a check to the art; but when the man, boy, wheelbarrow, and ass flew down, the tragedy put an end to the art of flying. See my History of Derby, page 247.

1735.

This summer was so dry that the water would scarcely turn the wheels; which, giving us children leisure, was very agreeable.

I visited Bredsall-moor, as all the country did, a warren, and on fire for many weeks. I frequently went to Mackworth, to see my little brother, who, being prudently attended, became a charming boy.

The colony of Georgia, in its infant state, invited many emigrants under General Oglethorpe. They produced Organzine silk, and sent it to England. It was good, but of a bad colour. The General, Sir Thomas Lombe, and the Trustees, waited upon Queen *Caroline* with a specimen, who ordered a gown and petticoat. It was sent to Derby, and I was one employed in the manufactory. Thus an insignificant animal, nearly naked himself, assisted in cloathing a queen.

1736.

I was now turned twelve. Life began to open. My situation at the mill was very unfavourable. Richard Porter, my master, had made a wound on my back with his cane. It grew worse. In a succeeding punishment, the point of his cane struck the wound, which brought it into such a state, that a mortification was apprehended. My father was advised to bathe me in Keddleston water. A cure was effected, and I yet carry the scar.

An agreeable old woman of the name of Gell, from Wirksworth, came to lodge where we did. She had been a school-mistress. She made many entertaining remarks, and promised us lads we should be the better for her coming; nor did she disappoint us.

My uncle and aunt Fletcher paid a visit, from Herefordshire, to my uncle at Nottingham; and, on Friday in Whitsun week, my father, brother, and I, met them there, and returned on Monday.

Nothing could equal the pleasure of this journey. I brought home such a description as could not be expected from my age. Every auditor looked up to me, and I took the lead in conversation. This was the only time I saw my aunt. I thought her handsome, proud, and sensible. "*Billy*," said she, " it is not " good manners to sit in the house with your "hat on." I felt the reproof, and neve forgot it.

1737.

I was now in the last year of my servitude at the Silk-mill, and was advancing towards fourteen. It, therefore, became requisite to point out some mode of future life. My father had often declared, that none of his sons should ever be brought up to the wool-combing business, his own; or to the stocking-frame, his brother's. As I knew his dilatory temper, I was afraid, when the time came, I should have a trade to seek. I chose that of a Gardener. This he encouraged. Time still advanced, but nothing was done. A Stocking-maker in Derby solicited to have me. My father replied, " I have " refused my own brother."

Nicholas Richardson, an old honest Scotsman, intimate with both father and uncle, took me aside in August, and used all his rhetoric to induce me to serve my uncle. *He*, however, was serving him. At the same time my father assured me, " Gardening was a slavish trade ;" that is, he had no inclination to stir. I was induced to consent to the proposal of Nicholas.

I cut, with a pen-knife, upon one of the top rails of the seventh mill above, W. H. 1737, which I saw in 1790, fifty-three years after *.

Christmas arrived when I must quit that place, for which I had a sovereign contempt: which many hundreds had quitted during my stay, but not one with regret: a place most curious and pleasing to the eye, but which gave me a seven years' heart-ache. No friendships are formed there, but such as the parties are willing to break. The attendants are children of nature, corrupted by art. What they learn *in* the Mill, they ought to unlearn *out*.

1738.

I now quitted my occupation, my father, brothers, friends, connexions, and place of nativity, for every thing new at Nottingham, where a scene opens for thirteen years. I found a generous friendly uncle, a mean sneaking aunt: he seriously religious; she as serious a hypocrite: two apprentices; one a rogue, the other a greater.

I had just finished one seven years' servitude, and was entering upon another. In the former

* And again in 1808.

I was welcome to the food I ate, provided I could get it; but now that it was more plentiful, I was to be grudged every meal I tasted. My aunt kept a constant eye upon the food and the feeder. This curb galled my mouth to that degree, that to this day I do not eat at another's table without fear. The impressions received in early life are astonishing.

This loving couple agreed admirably well. The reason was plain: he submitted.

I was too young to have any concern in the terms of servitude, and my father too poor to lend assistance. A burden was therefore laid upon me, which I afterwards found intolerable: that my over-work, without knowing whether I should get any, must find me clothes.

My task was to earn five shillings and tenpence a week. The first week I could reach this sum I was to be gratified with sixpence; but ever after, should I fall short, or go beyond it, the loss or profit was to be my own. I found it was the general practice of apprentices to be under the mark.

Things went on smiling, as all new concerns will, till Whitsuntide; when my uncle took me to Derby to see my friends. A week prior to this I had arrived at my task, got the sixpence, and puffed away like a young winner.

My brother, who was then sixteen, had not found a trade, nor had there been any attempts to find one for him. He must either be a despicable stockinger, or nothing. He followed us; and now my uncle had got two of the three sons.

He who stretches his utmost powers to accomplish a point in one week, will probably fall short the next. This was my case. Instead of earning apparel with over-work, I ran in arrears. At Christmas we took another trip to Derby, but my uncle had not the good fortune to pick up another lad.

1739.

I now got into what was called the fine frame, and my weekly task was six shillings and ninepence. Clothes came as sluggishly as food. I was arriving at that age when the two sexes begin to look at each other, consequently wish to please; and a powerful mode to win is that of dress. This is a passport to the heart, a key to unlock the passions, and guide them in our favour. My resources were cut off; my sun was eclipsed. Youth is the time to dress; the time in which it is not only excusable, but laudable. I envied every new coat: I had the wish to earn one, but not the power.

Perhaps there is not a human being but sooner or later feels, in some degree, the passion of love. I was struck with a girl, watched her wherever I could, and peeped through the chink of the window-shutter at night. She lay near my heart eleven years; but I never spoke to her in my whole life, nor was she ever apprized of my passion.

My uncle and his friends being religious men, and the doctrine of the Trinity, which had employed the public tongue and the pen for seven years, not being determined, I was witness to many disputes upon this dark point. Scripture, the source of argument, seemed to support both sides; for each drew his artillery from thence; consequently the dispute might be carried on *ad infinitum,* and both find themselves where they set out, only with this difference, that controversy disjoints society, and produces a shyness among friends. I could easily perceive the contenders were willing to send each other to the Devil. Besides, if a man wins, he gains nothing by winning, as dispute forms no part of Christian practice. It may, in some measure, disguise truth; for, if I endeavour to persuade a man into my opinion, either in religion or politics, it tends to confirm him in his own. He instantly makes a side against me; nay, it even confirms him in what he only doubted before. The utmost length allowable is to state reasons.

The lesser rogue of an apprentice ran away, and was heard of no more; and the greater was sold, and ruined his master.

1740

Was ushered in with the *hard frost*. Two or three frosts have since occurred, which the world has thought as cold, or nearly; but I remember them well, and can assure the reader there has been nothing like it for severity. That frost was not followed by a thaw, but continued till the spring gradually wore it away. We are not, however, to suppose the *whole* of the time intensely cold; the greater part resembled other frosts.

On New-year's day fell a moderate snow, perhaps three inches in depth; and no more fell during the winter. Some of this I saw in March. Many persons remarked that their breath was frozen on the sheet. Mine was not; for I lay wholly covered all night, which

I never could do before or since. At the beginning of the frost, which was the severest part, I wore a thin waistcoat, without a lining, and no coat.

The inclement season was not the sole wonder of the day. My uncle and his wife had a violent quarrel; the only one in my time. I understood that she had struck him, which provoked him beyond bounds. He made an attempt to punish her. I stepped in by way of prevention, and, with gentle soothings, effected a peace. He afterwards seemed pleased, and she, in plain terms, acknowledged the kindness. He was mild as a lamb, but, when once irritated, observed no bounds.

My uncle thought it necessary to keep up the succession of apprentices; and, as two were gone, a boy from Draycott, ten miles distant, was recommended. My uncle brought him on Saturday night; but, by Monday morning, the boy's mother could not rest, because he was either kidnapped or murdered; and sent the father, with positive orders, to bring him back, alive or dead, if above ground. The father entered the house, with sounds like the roarings of a Bull; and, in the Derbyshire dialect, cried, " Where's th' lad ? I mun tak " him bak! I've lond ith' feeld wo'th fifty paund.

"I've thutty paund by ma, an I dunna owe th' wo'ld a shilling!"

My uncle looked disappointed; thought the fellow a fool; and gave up the lad with a promise of his return, after having shewn the booby to his mother. The promise was never fulfilled.

Another apprentice, Roper, was brought from Derby. He proved surly and overbearing; ran away himself, and taught me. He returned again; then went into the army, and so good bye.

The frost, followed by an untoward summer, brought on a rise of provisions. It was considered by the mistress as almost a sin to eat. I should have been an acceptable servant, could I have subsisted without eating.

1741.

What the mind is bent upon obtaining, the hand seldom fails in accomplishing. I detested the frame, as totally unsuitable to my temper; therefore, I produced no more profit than necessity demanded. I made shift, however, with a little over-work, and a little credit, to raise a genteel suit of clothes, fully adequate to the sphere in which I moved. The girls eyed me with some attention; nay, I eyed myself as much as any of them.

My sister came, whom I had not seen for seven years; handsome, keen, and sensible. Her manner commanded respect.

Thus matters went on prosperously. I was rising into notice: a foundation was laid for a brighter day, when an unhappy quarrel between my uncle and me, upon a mere trifle, caused me to run away, blasted my views, sunk me in the dust, and placed me in a degraded point of view, from which I did not recover for five years. This I have faithfully related in *The History of a Week*, (a quarto manuscript in my son's library,) written from memory thirty-eight years after the event, which I shall literally transcribe.

THE HISTORY OF A WEEK.

The week of the races is an idle one among Stockingers at Nottingham. It was so with me. Five days had passed, and I had done little more than the work of four.

My uncle, who always judged from the present moment, supposed I should never return to industry. He was angry at my neglect, and observed, on Saturday morning, that if I did not perform my task that day, he would thrash me at night. Idleness, which had hovered over me five days, did not choose to leave me the sixth. Night came. I wanted one hour's work. I hoped my former conduct would atone for the present. But he had passed his word, and a man does not wish to break it. " You have not done the task I ordered!" I was silent. " Was it in your power to have " done it?" Still silent. He repeated again, " Could you have done it?" As I ever detested lying, I could not think of covering myself, even from a rising storm, by so mean a subterfuge; for we both knew I had done near twice as much. I therefore answered in a low meek voice, " *I could.*" This fatal word, innocent in itself, and founded upon truth, proved my destruction. " Then," says he, " I'll make " you." He immediately brought a birchbroom handle, of white-hazel, and holding it by the small end, repeated his blows till I thought he would have broken me to pieces. The windows were open, the evening calm, the sky serene, and every thing mild but my uncle and me. The sound of the roar, and the stick, penetrated the air to a great distance.

The neighbourhood turned out to inquire the cause; when, after some investigation, it was said to be, "Only Hutton thrashing one of his lads." Whether the crime and the punishment were adequate, I leave to the reader to determine. He afterwards told my father that he should not have quarreled with me, but for that word. But let me ask, what word could I have substituted in its room, unless I had meant to equivocate?

I was drawing towards eighteen, held some rank among my acquaintance, made a small figure in dress, and was taken notice of by the fair sex: therefore, though I was greatly hurt in body, I was much more hurt in mind. Pride takes a very early root in the heart, and never leaves us but with life. How should I face those whom I had often laughed at, and whipped with the rod of satire?

The next day, July 12, 1741, I went to Meeting in the morning as usual. My uncle seemed sorry for what had passed, and inclined to make matters up. At noon he sent me for some fruit, and asked me to partake. I thanked him with a sullen *no*. My wounds were too deep to be healed with cherries.

Standing by the palisades of the house, in a gloomy posture, a female acquaintance passed by, and turning, with a pointed sneer, said, "You were *licked* last night." The remark stung me to the quick. I had rather she had broken my head.

My fellow apprentice, Roper, was bigger and older than I, though he came two years after me. This opake body of ill-nature centered between my uncle and myself, and eclipsed that affection which gave pleasure to both. He staid with us three years. The two years of my servitude, before he came, were spent in great friendship with my uncle; and after he left, the same friendship returned, and continued for life.

This lad had often solicited me to run away with him; but I considered that my leaving my uncle would be a loss to him, for which I should be very sorry; and that, if I told Roper my design, he would insist upon going with me, which would double that loss. I could not bear the thought: therefore resolved to go alone, for which Roper afterwards blamed me.

I put on my hat, as if going to Meeting, but privately slipped up stairs till the family were gone. The whole house was now open to my inspection. Upon examining a glass in the beaufet, I found ten shillings. I took two, and left eight.

After packing up my small stock of moveables, I was at a loss how to get out of the house. There was but one door, which was locked, and my uncle had the key. I contrived, therefore, to get my chattels upon a wall, eight feet high, in a small back yard; climb up myself, drop them on the other side, and jump down after them.

While this was transacting, an acquaintance passed by. I imparted my design to him, because it was impossible to hide it, and enjoined him secrecy. He seemed to rejoice at my scheme, or rather at my fall; for if I commit an error and he does not, he is the best of the two.

Figure to yourself a lad of seventeen, not elegantly dressed, nearly five feet high, rather Dutch built, with a long narrow bag of brown leather, that would hold about a bushel, in which was neatly packed up a new suit of clothes; also, a white linen bag, which would hold about half as much, containing a sixpenny loaf of coarse blencorn bread, a bit of butter, wrapped in the leaves of an old copy-book; a new bible, value three shillings; one shirt; a pair of stockings; a sun-dial; my best wig, carefully folded and laid at top, that, by lying in the hollow of the bag, it might not be crushed. The ends of the two bags being tied together, I slung them over my left shoulder, rather in the style of a cock-fighter. My best hat, not being properly calculated for a bag, I hung to the button of my coat. I had only two shillings in my pocket; a spacious world before me, and no plan of operations.

I cast back many a melancholy look, while every step set me at a greater distance; and took, what I thought, an everlasting farewel of Nottingham.

I carried neither a light heart, nor a light load; nay, there was nothing light about me but the sun in the heavens, and the money in my pocket. I considered myself an out-cast, an exuberance in the creation, a being now fitted to no purpose. At ten, I arrived at Derby. The inhabitants were gone to bed, as if retreating from my society.

I took a view of my father's house, where, I supposed, all were at rest; but before I was aware, I perceived the door open, and heard his foot not three yards from me. I retreated with precipitation. How ill calculated are we to judge of events! I was running from the last hand that could have saved me!

Adjoining the town is a field called Abbey-barns, the scene of my childish amusements.

Here I took up my abode upon the cold grass, in a damp place, after a day's fatigue, with the sky over my head, and the bags by my side. I need not say I was a boy, this rash action proves it. The place was full of cattle. The full breath of the cows half asleep, the jingling of the chains at the horses' feet, and a mind agitated, were ill calculated for rest.

I rose at four, July 13, starved, sore, and stiff; deposited my bags under the fourth tree, covering them with leaves, while I waited upon Warburgh's bridge for my brother Samuel, who I knew would go to the Silk-mills before five. I told him that I had differed with my uncle, had left him, and intended to go to Ireland; that he must remember me to my father, whom I should probably see no more. I had all the discourse to myself, for my brother did not utter one word.

I arrived at Burton the same morning, having travelled twenty-eight miles, and spent nothing. I was an economist from my cradle, and the character never forsook me. To this I in some measure owe my present situation.

I ever had an inclination to examine fresh places. Leaving my bags at a public-house, I took a view of the town, and, breaking into my first shilling, I spent one penny as a recompence for the care of them.

Arriving the same evening within the precincts of Lichfield, I approached a barn, where I intended to lodge; but, finding the door shut, I opened my parcels in the fields, dressed, hid my bags near a hedge, and took a view of the city for about two hours, though very sore-footed.

Returning to the spot about nine, I undressed, bagged up my things in decent order, and prepared for rest; but alas! I had a bed to seek. About a stone's cast from the place stood another barn, which, perhaps, might furnish me with a lodging. I thought it needless to take the bags while I examined the place, as my stay would be very short.

The second barn yielding no relief, I returned in about ten minutes. But what was my surprise when I perceived the bags were gone! Terror seized me. I roared after the rascal, but might as well have been silent, for thieves seldom come at a call. Running, raving, and lamenting about the fields and roads, employed some time. I was too much immersed in distress to find relief in tears. They refused to flow. I described the bags, and told the affair to all I met. I found pity, or seeming pity, from all, but redress from none. I saw my hearers dwindle with the twilight; and, by eleven o'clock, found myself in the open street, left to tell my mournful tale to the silent night.

It is not easy to place a human being in a more distressed situation. My finances were nothing; a stranger to the world, and the world to me; no employ, nor likely to procure any; no food to eat, or place to rest: all the little property I had upon earth taken from me: nay, even *hope*, that last and constant friend of the unfortunate, forsook me. I was in a more wretched condition than he who has nothing to lose. An eye may roll over these lines when the hand that writes them shall be still. May that eye move without a tear! I sought repose in the street, upon a butcher's block.

July 14, I inquired, early in the morning, after my property, but to as little purpose as the night before. Among others, I accosted a gentleman in a wrought night-cap, plaid gown, and morocco slippers. I told him my distress, and begged he would point out some mode of employ, that might enable me to exist. He was touched with compassion. I found it was easy to penetrate his heart, but not his pocket. " It is market-day at Walsall," said he, " yon- " der people are going there; your attendance " upon them may be successful." I instantly put his advice in practice, and found myself in the company of a man and his servant with a waggon load of carrots; and, also, of an old fellow and his grandson with a horse-load of cherries. We continued together to the end of the journey; but I cannot say that either pity or success were of our party.

As my feet were not used to travel, they became extremely blistered; I, therefore, rubbed them with a little beef fat begged of a Walsall butcher, and found instant relief.

Upon application to a man who sold stockings in the market, I could learn that there were no frames in Walsall, but many in Birmingham; that he would recommend me to an acquaintance; and, if I should not succeed, there was Worcester, a little to the right, had some frames; and Coventry, a little to the left, would bring me into the stocking country.

Addison says, " There is not a *Woman* in " England; that every one of the British fair " has a right to the appellation of *Lady*." I wondered, in my way from Walsall to Birmingham to see so many blacksmiths' shops; in many of them one, and sometimes two *Ladies* at work; all with smutty faces, thundering at the anvil. Struck with the novelty, I asked if the ladies in this country shod horses? but was answered, " They are nailers."

Upon Handsworth heath, I had a view of Birmingham. St. Philip's Church appeared first, uncrowded with houses, (for there were none to the North, New Hall excepted) untarnished with smoke, and illuminated with a Western sun. It appeared in all the pride of modern architecture. I was charmed with its beauty, and thought it then, as I do now, the credit of the place.

I had never seen more than five towns; Nottingham, Derby, Burton, Lichfield, and Walsall. The last three I had not known more than two days. The out-skirts of these, and, I supposed, of others, were composed of wretched dwellings, visibly stamped with dirt and poverty. But the buildings in the exterior of Birmingham rose in a style of elegance. Thatch, so plentiful in other places, was not to be met with in this. It did not occur to my thoughts, that nine years after I should become a resident here, and thirty-nine years after should write its history!

I was surprized at the place, but more at the people. They possessed a vivacity I had never beheld. I had been among dreamers, but now I saw men awake. Their very step along the street shewed alacrity. Every man seemed to know what he was about. The town was large, and full of inhabitants, and these inhabitants full of industry. The faces of other men seemed tinctured with an idle gloom; but here, with a pleasing alertness. Their appearance was strongly marked with the modes of civil life.

How far commerce influences the habits of men is worthy the pen of the philosopher. The weather was extremely fine, which gave a lustre to the whole; the people seemed happy; and I the only animal out of use.

There appeared to be three stocking-makers in Birmingham. *Evans*, the old Quaker, yet in being, was the principal. I asked him, with great humility, for employ? " You are an ap-
" prentice." "Sir, I am not, but am come with " the recommendation of your friend, Mr. " Such-a-one, of Walsall." " Go about your " business, I tell you, you are a run-away " 'prentice." I retreated, sincerely wishing I had business to go about.

I waited upon *Holmes*, in Dale-end; at that moment a customer entering, he gave me a penny to get rid of me.

The third was *Francis Grace*, at the Gateway, entering New-street. This man was a native of Derby, and knew my family. Fourteen years after, he bestowed upon me a valuable wife, his niece; and sixteen years after, he died, leaving me in possession of his premises and fortune, paying some legacies.

I made the same request to Mr. Grace that I had done to others, and with the same effect. He asked after his brother at Derby. I answered readily, as if I knew. One lie often produces a second. He examined me closely; and, though a man of no shining talents, quickly set me fast. I was obliged to tell three or four lies to patch up a lame tale, which I plainly saw would hardly pass.

I appeared a trembling stranger in that house, over which, sixteen years after, I should preside. I stood like a dejected culprit by that counter, upon which, thirty-eight years after, I should record the story. I thought, though his name was Grace, his heart was rugged; and I left the shop with this severe reflection, that I had told several lies, and without the least advantage. I am sorry to digress, but must beg leave to break the thread of my narrative while I make two short remarks.

I acquired a high character for honesty, by stealing two shillings! Not altogether because I took two out of ten, but because I left the other eight. A thief is seldom known to leave *part* of his booty. If I had had money, I should not have taken any; and if I had found none, I should not have run away. The reader will think that two shillings was a very moderate sum to carry me to Ireland.

The other is, whether lying is not laudable? If I could have consented to tell one lie to my uncle, I should not only have saved my back, my character, and my property, but also prevented about ten lies which I was obliged to tell in the course of the following week. But that Supreme Being, who directs immensity, whether he judges with an angry eye according to some Christians, or with a benign one, according to others, will ever distinguish between an act of necessity and an act of choice.

It was now about seven in the evening, Tuesday, July 14, 1741. I sat to rest upon the North side of the Old Cross, near Philip street; the poorest of all the poor belonging to that great parish, of which, twenty-seven years after, I should be overseer. I sat under that roof, a silent, oppressed object, where, thirty-one years after, I should sit to determine differences between man and man. Why did not some kind agent comfort me with the distant prospect?

About ten yards from me, near the corner of Philip Street, I perceived two men in aprons eye me with some attention. They approached

near. "You seem," says one, "by your me-
"lancholy situation, and dusty shoes, a forlorn
"traveller, without money, and without friends."
I assured him it was exactly my case. "If you
"choose to accept of a pint of ale, it is at your
"service. I know what it is myself to be a
"distressed traveller." "I shall receive any
"favour with thankfulness."

They took me to the Bell in Philip Street,
and gave me what bread, cheese, and beer, I
chose. They also procured a lodging for me
in the neighbourhood, where I slept for three
half-pence.

I did not meet with this treatment twenty-
nine years after, at Market Bosworth, though
I appeared rather like a gentleman. The inhabitants set their dogs at me merely because I
was a stranger. Surrounded with impassable
roads, no intercourse with man to humanize
the mind, no commerce to smooth their rugged
manners, they continue the boors of nature.

Wednesday, July 15. I could not prevail
with myself to leave Birmingham, the seat of
civility; but was determined to endeavour to
forget my misfortunes, and myself, for one
day, and take a nearer view of this happy abode
of the smiling Arts.

Thursday 16. I arrived early in the day at Coventry, but could get no prospect of employment. The streets seemed narrow, ill paved; the Cross, a beautiful little piece of architecture, but composed of wretched materials. The city was populous; the houses had a gloomy air of antiquity; the upper story projecting over the lower, designed, no doubt, by the Architect, to answer two valuable purposes; those of shooting off the wet, and shaking hands out of the garret windows. But he forgot three evils arising from this improvement of art; the stagnation of air, the dark rooms, and the dirty streets.

I slept at the Star Inn, not as a chamber guest, but a hay-chamber one.

Friday 17. I reached Nun-Eaton, and found I had again entered the dominions of Sleep. That active spirit which marks the commercial race, did not exist here. The inhabitants seemed to creep along, as if afraid the street should be seen empty. However, they had sense enough to ring the word *'prentice* in my ears, which I not only denied, but used every figure in rhetoric I was master of, to establish my argument; yet was not able to persuade them out of their penetration. They still called me a boy. I thought it hard to perish because I could not convince people I was a man. I left the place without a smile, and without a dinner: perhaps it is not very apt to produce either. I arrived at Hinckley about four in the afternoon. The first question usually put was, " Where " do you come from?" My constant answer was, " Derby." " There is a country-man of " yours," said the person, " in such a street, " his name is Millward." I applied, and found I had been a neighbour to his family. He also knew something of mine. He set up the same objection that others had done, and I made the same unsuccessful reply.

He set me to work till night, about two hours, in which time I earned two-pence. He then asked me into the house, entered into conversation with me, told me he was certain I was a run-away apprentice, and begged I would inform him ingenuously. I replied with tears that I was; and that an unhappy difference with my uncle was the cause of my leaving his service.

He said, if I would set out on my return in the morning, I should be welcome to a bed that night. I told him that I had no objection to the service of my uncle, but that I could not submit to any punishment; and if I were not received upon equitable terms, I would immediately return to my own liberty.

He asked if I had any money? I answered, "Enough to carry me home." He was amazed, and threw out hints of crimination. I assured him he might rest satisfied upon that head, for I had brought two shillings from Nottingham. He exclaimed with emotion, "Two shillings!" This confirmed his suspicions.

Wrapped in my own innocence, I did not think my honesty worth vindicating; therefore, did not throw away one argument upon it. Truth is persuasive, and will often make its way to the heart, in its native simplicity, better than a varnished lie.

Extreme frugality, especially in the prospect of distress, composes a part of my character.

Saturday, the 18th, I thanked my friend Millward for his kindness, received nothing for my work, nor he for his civility, and we parted the friends of an hour. At noon I saw Ashby-de-la-Zouch. It was market day. I had eight pence remaining of my two shillings. My reader will ask, with Millward, "How I lived?" As he could not. Moralists say, " Keep desire "low, and nature is satisfied with little." A turnip-field has supplied the place of a cook's shop; a spring, that of a public-house; and, while at Birmingham, I knew by repeated experience, that cherries were a half-penny a pound.

I arrived at Derby at nine in the evening. My father gladly received me, and dropped a tear for my misfortunes. We agreed that he should send for my uncle early in the morning, who would probably be with us by four in the evening.

Sunday 19. My father told me that I could not have appeared before him in a more disadvantageous light, if I had said I was out of a jail: that he should think of this disagreeable circumstance every future day of his life, and that I must allow him to reprove me before my uncle.

As the time approached, he seemed greatly cast down, and invited two of my uncle's old friends to step in, and soften matters between us. But I considered that my uncle was naturally of a good temper, passion excepted; that I had left him suing for peace; that I had returned a volunteer, which carried the idea of repentance; that he must be conscious he had injured me; that he considered my service as a treasure, which he had been deprived of, and which, being found, he would rejoice at, just in proportion as he had grieved at the loss.

The two friends forgot to come. About nine my uncle entered, and shook hands with my father, for the two brothers were fond of each other. While their hands were united, my uncle turned to me, with a look of benignity, superficially covered with anger, and said, "Are not you to blame?" I was silent.

The remainder of the evening was spent agreeably; and, in the course of it, my uncle said, that if my father would make up one half of my loss, he would make up the other. My father received the proposal joyfully, and they ratified the agreement by a second shake of the hand. But, I am sorry to observe, it was thought of no more by either. I considered it peculiarly hard, that the promise to punish me was remembered, but the promise to reward me forgotten.

This unhappy ramble damped my rising spirit. I could not forbear viewing myself in the light of a fugitive. It sunk me in the eye of my acquaintance, and I did not recover my former balance for two years. It also ruined me in point of dress, for I was not able to re-assume my former appearance for five years. It ran me in debt, out of which I have never been to this day. Nov. 21, 1779.

THE END OF THE WEEK.

An old gentleman of the name of Webb, who had passed a life in London, brought £.3000 into business, lived in genteel life, and had filled many offices, but was reduced, came to reside with us. He was one of the most sensible and best of men, completely formed for an instructor of youth. It was my fortune to attend him, sleep with him, and love him. I treated him as a father, a monitor, and endeavoured to profit by him. He had many acquaintance, all men of sense, to whose conversation I listened by the hour.

I began this year with an old remark—let me close it with another: "One evil seldom comes " alone." In addition to the distress arising from running away, I was long and sorely afflicted with the ague, which still impeded a rising spirit.

1742.

There was a contested election, March 6, at Derby, between Lord Duncannon, who had married the daughter of the Duke of Devonshire, and Germon Pole of Radburn. My uncle being a burgess, was gone to vote. My brother, Roper, and I, his three apprentices, being Derby lads, set out, or ran away if you please, to see the election. My uncle was very angry: he could not stir a foot but we must follow! My father undertook our excuse, succeeded, and the next day my uncle gave us sixpence to carry us back.

Monday, July 18, my worthy friend Mr. Webb complained he had had an uncomfortable night. He grew worse till Friday morning, the 22d, when he died. I saw him expire, assisted in bearing him to the grave, and need not observe, I mourned his loss. His friends declined their visits, which added to that loss.

I had many agreeable acquaintances, with whom I spent my evenings in athletic exercises, which, in some measure, counterbalanced the dull life of the frame. I was deemed the second in the class.

1743.

I began to make a small figure in dress, but much inferior to that two years ago. However, a young woman chose to fall in love with me, daily sought me out, drew me for her Valentine, talked of matrimony, lamented that I had two years to serve, mentioned several such-a-ones who solicited her hand, and with what eagerness she had said *no.* I never answered any of these remarks. At length she asked me to marry her, in plain terms. Thus she took a liberty totally forbidden to her sex, however unreasonably. I asked her "What prospect there could be of future life?" She replied, in the low phrase of her sex, "I will please my eye, if I plague my heart."

My uncle fixed upon the son of Joseph Knowles of Mackworth for an apprentice; hired a horse, fixed me upon him, and his wife behind, to perform this journey of nineteen miles, and employ the arts of solicitation. Whether this was a prudent step, is doubtful. I had never ridden a mile, therefore could guide a horse about as well as a ship; neither did he know much more of the matter. Our family are not naturally equestrians. He advised me to keep a tight rein. I obeyed, and the horse took it for granted he must stand still. I held my legs close, for fear of falling. He danced. I was in agonies, and held by the mane. The beholders cried, "Take your spurs out of his sides!" I did not know they were in.

We jogged on with fear and trembling. I held the bridle with the right, and the pommel with the left hand, which soon wore a hole in the hand. My hat blew off. I slipped down before to recover it, but could not mount again. I walked with the bridle in hand, and my aunt upon the pillion, to find a place to rise. The horse went too slow. To quicken his pace, I gave him a jerk. He started from under his burthen, and left her in the dirt.

We were both frightened, but not hurt, and came home safe, wind and limb. My uncle, when he paid for the hire, blamed the horse; but the owner, with a smile, said, " Was there " no defect in the rider ?"

At Whitsuntide I went to see my father, but upon a safer bottom, my feet, and was favourably received by my acquaintance. One of them played upon the bell-harp. I was charmed with the sound, and agreed for the price, when I could raise the sum, half a crown.

I found that *love*, like a common flower in the garden, would spring into existence, rise to maturity, and die away. My father yet resided with the widow; they had courted each other ten years, and their love, having had its day, was withered, and had died of old age. He had sought another woman, and she a man. His marriage was brought forth in a few weeks, but hers proved still-born. My brother Samuel, ten years old, went with us. So now my uncle had all the three sons.

At Michaelmas I went to Derby, to pay for, and bring back, my bell-harp, whose sounds I thought seraphic. This opened a scene of pleasure which continued many years. Music was my daily study and delight. But, perhaps, I laboured under greater difficulties than any one had done before me. I could not afford an instructor. I had no books, nor could I borrow, or buy; neither had I a friend to give me the least hint, or put my instrument in tune.

Thus was I in the situation of a first inventor, left to grope in the dark, to find out something. I had first my ear to bring into tune, before I could tune the instrument; for the ear is the foundation of all music. That is the best tune, which best pleases the ear; and he keeps the best time, who draws the most music from his tune.

For six months did I use every effort to bring a tune out of an instrument, which was so dreadfully out, it had no tune in it. Assiduity never forsook me. I was encouraged by a couplet I had seen in Dyche's Spelling-book:

> Despair of nothing that you would attain,
> Unwearied diligence your point will gain.

When I was able to lay a foundation, the improvement, and the pleasure, were progressive. Wishing to rise, I borrowed a dulcimer, made one by it, then learned to play upon it. But in the fabrication of this instrument, I had neither timber to work upon, tools to work with, nor money to purchase either. It is said, " Necessity is the mother of invention." I pulled a large trunk to pieces, one of the relics of my family, but formerly the property of *Thomas Parker*, the first Earl of Macclesfield. And as to tools, I considered that the hammer-key and the plyers, belonging to the stocking-frame, would supply the place of hammer and pincers. My pocket knife was all the edge-tools I could raise; and a fork, with one limb, was made to act in the double capacity of sprig-awl and gimlet.

I quickly was master of this piece of music; for if a man can play upon one instrument, he may soon learn upon any.

A young man, apprentice to a Baker, happening to see the dulcimer, asked if I could perform upon it? Struck with the sound, and with seeing me play with, what he thought, great ease, he asked if I would part with the instrument, and at what price? I answered in the affirmative, and, for sixteen shillings. He gave it.

I told him, " If he wanted advice, or his " instrument wanted tuning, I would assist " him." " O no, there's not a doubt but I shall " do." I bought a coat with the money, and constructed a better instrument.

Seeing him a short time after, "Well, how "do you succeed?" "O rarely well. I can "play part of *Over the hills and far away.*" This excited a smile of satisfaction in both.

Our next meeting produced the same question, to which he replied, " O damn the music, " I could not make it do; which provoked me "so much, that I took a broom-stick, and "*whacked* the strings till I broke them; then "knocked the body to pieces, and burned it in " the oven."

1744.

This year was ushered in and ushered out with the same pursuit after music. The relish increased with the knowledge. I wished to soar, but poverty clipped my wings.

The Corporation, attended by the Waits, went in solemn procession to declare war against France. I marched close by the music with great attention and pleasure.

At Christmas my servitude expired. I must now launch into the world upon my own bottom. I had hitherto been under the care of others; but now I must attend to the compass myself, and steer the vessel. The thought crossed me with anxiety.

I had served two seven years to two trades, neither of which I could subsist upon. During this servitude, I had earned about seven pounds over-work, which, with a debt I had contracted to my uncle, of thirty shillings, had frugally furnished me with apparel.

1745.

I continued a journeyman with my uncle. I had a particular acquaintance, William Martin, who was extremely attached to me. We never parted without, " When shall I see you " again?" His parents also wished my company. I spent every Sunday evening at least at their house, and was their main oracle.

He courted Miss Woolley, who resided with an old aunt. As I could perform upon the dulcimer, I was led there. Late in the evening, the old lady, half tipsy, followed me into the yard; used all the rhetoric of the tongue, sometimes laid her right hand on my left shoulder, and once uttered, " I love thee. If I " was but as young as thou, I would have thee, " if thou wouldst but marry me." Had she attempted a salute, I must, for once, have run away from the embraces of a woman. How will liquor expose what folly prompts!

My uncle took notice of me. I attended him in his walks and his visits; had some knowledge of history, and could speak tolerably well.

The Rebellion broke out, which produced sufficient matter for inquiry and conversation. I could not relish the thought of being a journeyman for life; and, should I let youth pass by, all would be over. I asked my uncle to permit me to set a frame in his work-room, paying the usual price; in which case I would hire one, and work for a warehouse. This would make me a master, though of the very lowest order. He cheerfully consented. I mentioned the affair, in conversation, a few days after, when he refused me in anger, saying, " I would sooner eat hay with a horse." I knew this last sentiment was not his own; his wife was the prompter. The matter and my ambition fell together. I loved him, and was unwilling to leave him. The terms were common, and anywhere would have been accepted. I thought it rather ungenerous to nip an opening bud.

I finished the year with a visit to my father at Derby, and seemed extremely acceptable to my friends.

1746.

The year, and the disagreement between my sister and her husband, opened together. This caused me to take many journeys to Mountsorrel, but to no purpose, except for the pleasure of seeing her. Her husband, to win my favour, offered to lend me ten pounds to purchase a frame. I accepted it; but, when the moment arrived, he chose to charge it with interest.

My sister and he parted, as may be seen in her life. The husband gave it out that I should break, and he should lose his money; and as she, while in service, had saved that sum, and lent it to a person in prosperity, he requested her to exchange the securities. She, unwilling a brother should be stigmatized, consented. It happened, a few years after, that I paid my ten pounds; the other person broke, and never paid a shilling.

Here again the husband was dissatisfied; and, to content him, she gave him ten pounds of her own money.

An inclination for books began to expand; but here, as in music and dress, money was wanting. The first article of purchase was three Volumes of the Gentleman's Magazine,

1742, 3, and 4. As I could not afford to pay for binding, I fastened them together in a most cobbled style. These afforded me a treat.

I could only raise books of small value, and these in worn-out bindings. I learnt to patch, procured paste, varnish, &c. and brought them into tolerable order; erected shelves, and arranged them in the best manner I was able.

If I purchased shabby books, it is no wonder that I dealt with a shabby bookseller who kept his working apparatus in his shop. It is no wonder too, if by repeated visits I became acquainted with this shabby bookseller, and often saw him at work; but it is a wonder and a fact that I never saw him perform one act but I could perform it myself, so strong was the desire to attain the art.

I made no secret of my progress, and the bookseller rather encouraged me, and that for two reasons: I bought such rubbish as nobody else would; and he had often an opportunity of selling me a cast-off tool for a shilling, not worth a penny. As I was below every degree of opposition, a rivalship was out of the question.

The first book I bound was a very small one, Shakspeare's Venus and Adonis. I shewed it to the bookseller. He seemed surprized. I could see jealousy in his eye. However, he recovered in a moment, and observed, that though he had sold me the books and tools *remarkably cheap*, he could not think of giving so much for them again. He had no doubt but I should break.

He offered me a worn-down press for two shillings, which no man could use, and which was laid by for the fire. I considered the nature of its construction; bought it, and paid the two shillings. I then asked him to favour me with a hammer and a pin, which he brought with half a conquering smile, and half a sneer. I drove out the garter-pin, which, being galled, prevented the press from working, and turned another square, which perfectly cured the press. He said, in anger, " If I had known, you should " not have had it." However, I could see he consoled himself with the idea that all must return in the end. This proved for 42 years my best binding press.

I now purchased a tolerably genteel suit of clothes, and was so careful of them, lest I should not be able to procure another, that they continued my best for five years.

My Uncle was indisposed; had frequent fits of the gravel; Nature seemed exhausted. On Wednesday, the 10th of September, I was told that he was taken ill in the garden. I darted in, and found him supporting himself against a pillar. He instantly fainted, and I caught him in my arms while falling. He had broken a blood-vessel, and threw up about a quart of blood.

The next day Michael Pare remarked that, as my uncle had discharged a load of blood from the stomach, he would soon be well. This was the judgment of a Quack. He forgot that a depraved system could not bear so great a loss; that straining again would open the wound; and that an internal fracture is hard to cure.

On Sunday several friends came to see my uncle. He conversed freely with them. A tender part of the conversation occasioned him to drop a tear. His strength was spent; I carried him up stairs to his room; he quitted it no more, but died five days after. I was present, and could not bear the shock. My sister was obliged to support me. I was ignorant how much I loved him till my sorrow for his death informed me.

The stocking-frame being my own, and trade being dead, the hosiers would not employ me. They could scarcely employ their own frames. I was advised to try Leicester, and took with me half a dozen pair of stockings to sell. I visited several warehouses; but, alas! all proved blank. They would neither employ me, nor give for my goods any thing near prime cost. As I stood like a culprit before a gentleman of the name of Bennet, I was so affected, that I burst into tears, to think that I should have served seven years to a trade at which I could not get bread.

My sister took a house; and, to soften the rent, my brother and I lodged with her.

1747.

It had been the pride of my life, ever since pride commenced, to wear a watch. I bought a silver one for thirty-five shillings. It went ill. I kept it four years, then gave *that* and a guinea for another, which went as ill. I afterwards exchanged this for a brass one, which going no better, I sold it for five shillings; and, to complete the watch farce, I gave the five shillings away, and went without a watch thirty years.

I had promised to visit my father on Whitsun eve, at Derby. Business detained me till it was eleven at night before I arrived. Expectation had, for some time, been upon the stretch, and was now giving way. My father, being elevated with liquor, and by my arrival, rose in extasy, and gave me the first kiss, and, I believe, the last, he ever gave me.

This year I began to dip into rhime. The stream was pleasant, though I doubt whether it flowed from Helicon. Many little pieces were the produce of my pen, which, perhaps, pleased : however, they gave no offence, for they slept upon my shelf till the rioters burnt them in 1791.

1748.

It is difficult for a young man to live without love. I was intimate with a young widow, but never touched upon the word Marriage. She frequently dragged me to the test; but I observed, that I was between two trades,—one of them, it was clear, I could not live by; and the other, at best, was uncertain. She replied, she did not wish to be a burthen; but if she was sure of me, I might take my own course, and we might live separate till better times, hinting that it might be as well to pursue my own trade. I asked, if she ever knew two young people, who loved each other, live asunder out of choice? I made no remark upon her advice, of " following my own trade;" but I felt it.

As I would neither marry, nor promise, and as she did not chuse to live single, she accepted another, who followed her three or four years, then left her; and she never married.

Every soul who knew me, scoffed at the idea of my turning bookbinder, except my sister, who encouraged and aided me; otherwise I must have sunk under it. I considered that I was naturally of a frugal temper; that I could watch every penny; live upon a little; that I hated stocking-making, but not bookbinding; that, if I continued at the frame, I was certain to be poor; and if I ventured to leave it, I could but be so. My only fear was, lest I should draw in my friends; for I had nothing of my own.

I had frequently heard that every man had, some time or other in his life, an opportunity of rising. As this was a received opinion, I would not contradict it. I had, however, watched many years for the high tide of my affairs, but thought it never yet had reached me.

I still pursued the two trades. Hurt to see my three volumes of Magazines in so degraded a state, I took them to pieces, and clothed them in a superior dress.

1749.

I became acquainted with another girl; but we were so indifferent to each other, that it was easy to see love never cemented our hearts. When a man begins to change, he soon becomes a rover. I had observed such severe penury among the married stockingers, that the thoughts of a wife were horrid, unless I had been in a situation to support one.

A bookbinder, fostered by the stocking-frame, was such a novelty, that many people gave me a book to bind, that is, among my friends and their acquaintance; and I perceived two advantages attended my work. I chiefly served those who were not judges; consequently, that work passed with them which would not with a master. And, coming from the hands of a stockinger, it carried a merit, because no stockinger could produce its equal.

Hitherto I had only used the wretched tools, and the materials for binding, which my bookseller chose to sell me; but I found there were many things wanting, which were only to be had in London; besides, I wished to fix a correspondence for what I wanted, without purchasing at second hand. There was a necessity to take this journey; but an obstacle arose,—I had no money.

My dear sister raised three guineas; sewed them in my shirt collar, for there was no doubt but I should be robbed; and put eleven shillings in my pocket, for it was needful to have a sop, to satisfy the rogues when they made the attack.

From the diminutive sum I took, it may reasonably be supposed I could have nothing left for purchase.

On Monday morning, at three, April 8, I set out. Not being used to walk, my feet were blistered with the first ten miles. I must not, however, sink under the fatigue, but endeavour to proceed, as if all were well; for much depended on this journey. Aided by resolution, I marched on. Stopping at Leicester, I unfortunately left my knife, and did not discover the loss till I had proceeded eleven miles. I grieved because it was the only keep-sake I had of my worthy friend Mr. Webb. Ten times its value could not have purchased it. I had marked it with W. H. July 22, 1742.

A mile beyond Leicester I overtook a traveller, with his head bound. "How far are you

" going?" he asked. "To London," replied I. "So am I. When do you expect to arrive?" demanded he. "On Wednesday night." "So "do I." "What is the matter with your " head?" said I, "have you been fighting?" He returned an equivocal answer, which convinced me of the affirmative. I did not half like my companion, especially as he took care to walk behind me; but, when I understood he was a tailor, my fears rather subsided.

Determined upon a separation, I walked apace for half an hour. "Do you mean to " hold this pace?" said he. "It is best to use " day-light, while we have it." I found I could match him at walking, whatever I might do at fighting. In half an hour more, we came to a public-house, when he gave up the contest. "Will you step in and drink?" asked my companion? "No, I shall be moving on; you may " overtake me."

I stopped at Brixworth, having walked fifty-one miles: and my whole expence for the day was fivepence.

The next day, Tuesday the 9th, I rested at Dunstable. Passing over Finchley common, on the third day, I overtook a carter, who told me I might be well accommodated at the Horns, in St. John's street, Smithfield, by making use of his name. But it happened, in the eagerness of talking, and the sound of his noisy cart, that he forgot to tell his name, and I to ask it.

I arrived at the Horns at five; described my director, whom they could not recollect; however, I was admitted an inmate. I ordered a mutton chop and porter; but alas, I was jaded. I had fasted too long; my appetite was gone, and the chop nearly useless.

This meal, if it might be called a meal, was the only one during my stay; and, I think, the only time I ever ate under a roof. I did not know one soul in London; therefore, could have no invitations. Nature is supported with a little, which was well for me, because I had but little to give her. If a man has any money, he will see stalls enough in London which will supply him with something to eat; and it rests with him to lay out his money to the best advantage. If he cannot afford butter, he must eat his bread without. This will tend to keep up an appetite, which always gives a relish to food, though mean; and the scantiness will add to that relish.

The next morning I breakfasted in Smithfield, upon furmity, at a wheelbarrow. Sometimes I had a halfpenny-worth of soup, and another of bread. At other times bread and cheese. When nature called, I must answer. I ate to live.

If a man goes to *receive* money, it may take him a long time to transact his business. If to *pay* money, it will take him less; and if he has but a *little* to pay, still less. My errand fell under the third class. I only wanted three alphabets of letters, a set of figures, and some ornamental tools for gilding books; with leather, and boards, for binding.

I wished to see a number of curiosities, but my shallow pocket forbade. One penny, to see Bedlam, was all I could spare. Here I met with a variety of curious anecdotes; for I found conversation with a multitude of characters. All the public buildings fell under my eye, and were attentively examined; nor was I wanting in my inquiries. Pass where I would, I never was out of the way of entertainment. It is reasonable to suppose that every thing in London would be new and wonderful to a youth who was fond of inquiry, but who had scarcely seen any thing. Westminster-abbey, St. Paul's, Guild-hall, Westminster-hall, &c. were open to view; also both Houses of Parliament, for they were sitting. As I had always applied deification to great men, I was surprised to see a hawker cram her twopenny pamphlet into a Member's face; and that he, instead of caning her, took not the least notice.

I joined a youth who had business in the Tower, in hopes of gaining admission. But the Warders, hearing a Northern voice, came out of their lodge; and, seeing dust upon my shoes, reasonably concluded I had nothing to give; therefore, with an air of authority, they ordered me back.

The Royal Exchange, the Mansion-house, the Monument, the Gates, the Churches, many of which are very beautiful, the bridges, river, vessels, &c. afforded a fund of entertainment. I attended at Leicester-house, the residence of Frederick Prince of Wales; scraped acquaintance with the sentinels, who told me, had I been half an hour sooner, I should have seen the Prince and his family enter the coach for an airing.

Though I had walked 125 miles to London, I was upon my feet all the three days I was there. I spent half a day in viewing the West end of the town, the squares, the park, the beautiful building for the fire-works, erected in the Green Park, to celebrate the peace of Aix la Chapelle. At St. James's I accosted the guard at the bottom of the stairs, and rather attempted to advance; but one of them put forward the butt-end of his piece, to prevent me from stepping over. At St. James's too, I had my pocket picked of a handkerchief; so that I went home rather lighter than I came. The people at St. James's are apt to fill their own pockets at the expence of others.

Seeing in one of the squares the figure of a man on horse-back, I modestly asked a by-stander whom it represented? He answered, in a surly tone, "It 's strange you could see no-"body else to ask, without troubling me: it 's "George the First."

I could not forbear mentioning at night to my landlord at the Horns, the curiosities I had seen, which greatly surprised him. He replied, "I like such a traveller as you. The strangers "that come here cannot stir a foot without me, "which plagues me to that degree I had rather be "without their custom. But you, of yourself, "find out more curiosities than they can see, "or I can shew them."

On Saturday evening, April 13, I set out with four shillings for Nottingham, and stopped at St. Alban's. Rising the next morning, April 14, I met in the street the Tailor with the muffled head, whom I had left near Leicester. "Ah! my friend, what are you still

" fighting your way up? Perhaps you will " reach London by *next* Wednesday. You " guessed within one week the first time!" He said but little, looked ashamed, and passed on.

This was a melancholy day: I fell lame, owing to the sinews of my leg being over-strained with hard labour. I was far from home, wholly among strangers, with only the remnant of four shillings. The idea occasioned tears!

I stopped at Newport-Pagnell. My landlord told me my shoes were not fit for travelling: however I had no others, and, like my blistered feet, I must try to bear them. The next day, Monday the 15th, I slept at Market Harborough, and on the 16th, called at Leicester. The landlady had carefully secured my knife, with a view to return it should I ever come that way. I reached Nottingham in the afternoon, having walked 40 miles.

I had been out nearly nine days, three in going, which cost three and eightpence; three in London, which cost about the same; and three returning, nearly the same. Out of the whole eleven shillings, I brought fourpence back.

London surprised me; so did the people, for the few with whom I formed a connexion deceived me, by promising what they never performed. This journey furnished vast matter for detail among my friends.

It was now time to look out for a future place of residence. A large town must be the mark, or there would be no room for exertion. London was thought of, between my sister and me, for I had no soul else to consult. This was rejected for two reasons. I could not venture into such a place without a capital, and my work was not likely to pass among a crowd of judges.

My plan was to fix upon some market-town, within a stage of Nottingham; and open shop there on the market-day, till I should be better prepared to begin the world at Birmingham.

I fixed upon Southwell, as the first step of elevation. It was fourteen miles distant, and the town as despicable as the road to it. I went over at Michaelmas, took a shop at the rate of twenty-shillings a year, sent a few boards for shelves, a few tools, and about two hundred weight of *trash*, which might be dignified with the name of *books*, and worth, perhaps, a year's rent of my shop. I was my own joiner, put up the shelves and their furniture, and in one day became the most eminent bookseller in the place.

During this rainy winter, I set out at five every Saturday morning, carried a burthen of from three pounds weight to thirty, opened shop at ten, starved in it all day upon bread, cheese, and half a pint of ale, took from one to six shillings, shut up at four, and, by trudging through the solitary night and the deep roads five hours more, I arrived at Nottingham by nine; where I always found a mess of milk porridge by the fire, prepared by my valuable sister.

Nothing short of a surprizing resolution and rigid economy, could have carried me through this scene.

In one of these early morning journeys, I met upon Sherwood Forest, four deer-stealers, returning with a buck. This put me in fear, lest I should be knocked on the head to keep silence. I did not know them, but was afterwards informed that they knew me.

1750.

I took a journey to Birmingham in February, to pass a judgment on the probability of my future success.

I found three eminent booksellers for mental improvement, *Aris*, *Warren*, and *Wollaston*. I considered the town was crowded with inhabitants, and perhaps I might mingle in that crowd unnoticed by three great men, for an ant is not worth destroying. I must again confess, I was pleased with the active spirit of the people.

Wishing to take Swithland in my return to Nottingham, to visit my two aunts, I was directed through Tamworth, where I spent one penny; then through a few villages, with blind roads, to Charnwood Forest; over which were five miles of uncultivated waste without *any* road. To all this I was a stranger.

Passing through a village in the dusk of the evening, I determined to stop at the next public house; but, to my surprize, I instantly found myself upon the Forest. It began to rain; it was dark; I was in no road, nor was any dwelling near. I was among hills, rocks, and precipices, and so bewildered I could not retreat. I considered my situation as desperate, and must confess I lost the fortitude of a man.

I wandered slowly, though in the rain, for fear of destruction, and hollowed with all my powers, but met with no return. I was about two hours in this cruel state, when I thought the indistinct form of a roof appeared against the sky. My vociferations continued, but to no purpose. I concluded it must be a lonely barn; but, had it been the receptacle of ghosts, it would have been desirable.

At length I heard the sound of a man's voice, which, though one of the most terrific, gave me pleasure. I continued advancing, perhaps, thirty yards, using the soft persuasives of distress, for admission, even under any roof, but could not prevail. The man replied, that all his out-buildings had been destroyed by a mob of freeholders, as standing upon the waste. He seemed to be six feet high, strong built, and, by the sound of his voice, upwards of fifty.

I could not, as my life was at stake, give up the contest; but thought, if I could once get under his roof, I should not easily be discharged. Though his manner was repelling as the rain, and his appearance horrid as the night, yet I would not part from him, but insensibly, at length, wormed myself in.

I was now in a small room, dignified with the name of a house, totally dark, except a glow of fire, which would barely have roasted a potatoe, had it been deposited in the centre. In this dismal abode I heard two female voices, one, that of an old aunt, the other, of a young wife.

We all sat close to this handful of fire, as every one must who sat in the room. We soon became familiarized by conversation, and I found my host agreeable. He apologized for not having treated me with more civility; he pitied my case, but had not conveniences for accommodation.

Hints were now given for retiring to rest. "I will thank you," said I, "for something to "eat; I have had nothing since morning when "at Birmingham." "We should have asked "you, but we have nothing in the house." "I shall be satisfied with any thing." "We "have no eatables whatever, except some pease "porridge, which is rather thin, only pease "and water, and which we are ashamed to "offer." "It will be acceptable to a hungry "man."

He gave me to understand that he had buried a wife, by whom he had children grown up. Being inclined to marry again, he did not choose to venture upon a widow, for fear of marrying her debts; he therefore had married a girl thirty years younger than himself, by whom he had two small children, then in bed. This I considered as an excuse for misconduct.

While supper was *warming*, for *hot* it could not be, a light was necessary; but alas the premises afforded no candle. To supply the place, a leaf was torn from a shattered book, twisted round, kindled, and shook in the hand to improve the blaze. By this momentary light, I perceived the aunt, who sat opposite, had a hair-shorn lip, which, in the action of eating, so affected me, that I was obliged to give up my supper.

By another lighted leaf, we marched up to bed. I could perceive the whole premisses consisted of two rooms, house, and chamber. In the latter was one bed, and two pair of bedsteads. The husband, wife, aunt, and two children, occupied the first; and the bedstead, whose head butted against their bedside, was appropriated for me. But now another difficulty arose. There were no bed clothes to cover me. Upon diligent inquiry, nothing could be procured but the wife's petticoat; and I could learn that she robbed her own bed to supply mine. I heard the rain patter upon the thatch during the night, and rejoiced it did not patter upon me.

By the light of the next morning, I had a view of all the family faces, except the aunt's, which was covered with a slouched hat. The husband seemed to have been formed in one of Nature's largest and coarsest moulds. His hands retained the accumulated filth of the last three months, garnished with half a dozen scabs; both, perhaps, the result of idleness. The wife was young, handsome, ragged, and good-natured.

The whole household, I apprehend, could have cast a willing eye upon breakfast; but there seemed a small embarrassment in the expectants. The wife, however, went to her next neighbour's, about a mile, and in an hour returned with a jug of skimmed milk and a piece of a loaf, perhaps two pounds, both of which, I have reason to think, were begged; for money, I believe, was as scarce as candle. Having no fire, we ate it cold, and with a relish.

When I left the house, I saw the devastations made by the rioters, a horde of monsters I have since had reason to dread.

My host went with me half a mile, to bring me into something like a track; when I gave him a shake of the hand, a sixpence, and my sincere good wishes. We parted upon the most friendly terms.

Though I seemingly received but little, yet a favour is great or small, according to the need of the receiver.

I had seen poverty in various shapes; but this was the most complete. There appeared, however, in that lowest degree, a considerable share of content. The man might have married a widow and her debts with safety; for no creditor durst have sued him. Neither need he have dreaded a jail, except from the loss of liberty, for he would have risen in point of luxury.

I had also seen various degrees of idleness; but none surpassed this. Those wants cannot merit pity, which idleness might, but will not, prevent.

Returning to Nottingham, I gave warning to quit at Southwell, and prepared for a total change of life.

On the 10th of April, I entered Birmingham, for the third time, to try if I could be accommodated with a small shop. If I could procure any situation, I should be in the way of procuring a better. On the 11th, I traversed the streets of Birmingham; agreed with Mrs. Dix, for the lesser half of her shop, No. 6, in Bull-street, at one shilling a week; and slept at Lichfield, in my way back to Nottingham.

On May 13th, Mr. Rudsdall, a dissenting minister of Gainsborough, with whom my sister had lived as a servant, travelling from Nottingham to Stamford, requested my company, and offered to pay my expences, and give me eighteen pence a day for my time. The afternoon was wet in the extreme. He asked why I did not bring my great coat? Shame forbade an answer, or I could have said I had none. The water completely soaked through my cloaths, but not being able to penetrate the skin, it filled my boots. Arriving at the inn, every traveller, I found, was wet; and every one procured a change of apparel but me. I was left out, because the house could produce no more. I was obliged to sit the whole evening in my drenched garments, and to put them on nearly as wet on my return the next morning! What could I expect but destruction? Fortunately I sustained no injury.

It happened that Mr. Rudsdall now declined housekeeping, his wife being dead. He told my sister that he should part with the refuse of his library, and would sell it to me. She replied, " He has no money." " We will not " differ about that. Let him come to Gains- " borough; he shall have the books at his own " price." I walked to Gainsborough on the 15th May, stayed there the 16th, and came back on the 17th.

The books were about two hundred pounds weight. Mr. Rudsdall gave me his corn chest for their deposit; and, for payment, drew the following note, which I signed.

"I promise to pay to Ambrose Rudsdall, "one pound seven shillings, when I am able."

Mr. Rudsdall observed, "you never need "pay this note, if you only say you are not "able." The books made a better shew, and were more valuable, than all I possessed beside.

I had now a most severe trial to undergo; parting with my friends, and residing wholly among strangers. May 23, I left Nottingham, and I arrived at Birmingham on the 25th. Having little to do but look into the street, it seemed singular to see thousands of faces pass, and not one that I knew. I had entered a new world, in which I led a melancholy life; a life of silence and tears. Though a young man, and rather of a cheerful turn, it was remarked, "that I was never seen to smile." The rude family into which I was cast added to the load of melancholy.

My brother came to see me about six weeks after my arrival, to whom I observed, that the trade had fully supported me. Five shillings a week covered every expence; as food, rent, washing, lodging, &c. Thus a solitary year rolled round, when a few young men of elevated character and sense took notice of me. I had saved about twenty pounds, and was become more reconciled to my situation. The first who took a fancy to me was Samuel Salte, a Mercer's apprentice, who, five years after, resided in London, where he acquired 100,000*l*. He died in 1797. Our intimate friendship lasted his life.

In this first opening of prosperity, an unfortunate circumstance occurred, which gave me great uneasiness, as it threatened totally to eclipse the small prospect before me. The Overseers, fearful I should become chargeable to the parish, examined me with regard to my settlement; and, with the voice of authority, ordered me to procure a certificate, or they would remove me. Terrified, I wrote to my father, who returned for answer, " That All-" Saints, in Derby, never granted certifi-" cates."

I was hunted by ill nature two years. I repeatedly offered to pay the levies, which was refused. A succeeding Overseer, a draper, of whom I had purchased two suits of clothes, value 10*l*. consented to take them. The scruple exhibited a short sight, a narrow principle, and the exultations of power over the defenceless.

1751.

Among others who wished to serve me, I had two friends, Mr. Dowler, a Surgeon, who resided opposite me; and Mr. Grace, a Hosier, at the Gate-way, in the High-street, mentioned in the year 1741. Great consequences often arise from small things. The house adjoining that of Mr. Grace's, was to be let. My friends both urged me to take it. I was frightened at the rent, eight pounds. However, one drew, and the other pushed, till they placed me there. A small house is too large for a man without furniture; and a small rent may be too large for an income which has nothing certain in it but the smallness. Having felt the extreme of poverty, I dreaded nothing so much; but I believed I had seized the tide, and I was unwilling to stop.

Here I pursued business in a more elevated style, and with more success. In August, my sister came to see me, and brought a young lady, as an intended wife. They staid a few days. She was tolerably handsome, and appeared agreeable. But love is a delicate and shy bird, not always caught at first sight; besides, every thing formal operates against it. We behaved with civility, but neither of us taking fire, the matter died away.

I had been nearly a year in Birmingham, and had not indulged myself with any new clothes. My best coat now had been my best coat five years. Frederic Prince of Wales dying in March, I dressed in a suit of mourning. My new cloaths introduced me to some new acquaintance; among others, to William Ryland, one of the worthiest of men, with whom I contracted a close and intimate friendship, which has continued 46 years, and is only to be broken by death.

1752.

I had now a smiling trade, to which I closely attended; and a happy set of acquaintances, whose society gave me pleasure. As I hired out books, the fair sex did not neglect the shop. Some of them were so obliging, as to shew an inclination to share with me the troubles of the world.

Placed at ease, I again addressed the Muses; and, as I thought, properly applied my talent, and with better success than five years before.

Some of my productions crept into the Magazines, and other periodical papers; but all plunged into the fire at the riots.

Attention enabled me to abstract a small sum from trade, and I frequently amused myself with marshalling, in battalia, fifty bright guineas; a sight I had not been accustomed to.

I was taken ill of a fever, and was attended by my friend Mr. Dowler, who seemed to be alarmed at my situation, and who alarmed me, by inquiring whether I had any relations, and whether I had made a will?

As capital increased, I wished to extend the trade. Tuesday being a leisure day, I thought it might be beneficial to open a shop at Bromsgrove, where it was market-day. I put the plan in practice; followed it one year and three quarters; but finding I lost nearly as much abroad, as I got at home, I declined it.

I also took a female servant, which proved less profitable; for, when I was absent, she sold the books for what they would bring, left the shop, and got completely drunk with the money. An instant separation was requisite.

In November, my friend, and next door neighbour, Mr. Grace, being a widower, took his niece, Miss Sarah Cock, from Aston, near Derby, to keep his house. I saw her the night she arrived, and thought her a little, neat, delicate creature, and rather handsome. It was impossible, situated as we were, to avoid an intercourse. Without my having the least idea of courtship, she seemed to dislike me, which caused a shyness on my side, and kept us at a distance. The intercourse continued; for, as I had no house-keeper, I dined with Mr. Grace at a fixed price. A young woman of my acquaintance, who had a lover whom she affected to despise, repeatedly solicited me to begin a sham courtship, " to plague him." " No," said I, " you know how to plague him suffici- "ently, without my assistance." The man who plays with edge-tools may, by chance, cut his fingers. Courtship may begin in jest, and end in earnest. She afterwards married her lover.

1754.

I ventured upon another female servant; for business called me out. She was recommended by the minister of the congregation, who assured me that she would not cheat me, for she feared the Lord. He might be right; but she cheated my dumplings one Sunday, by setting them to boil without water. When we returned from Meeting, they were burned to a cinder. I found her totally unable to conduct a family even of two persons, and much inferior to a shop.

Michaelmas arrived. Miss Cock and I had not, of late, looked quite so shy upon each other. Mr. Grace was gone to Worcester market to buy hops. It was nine o'clock, he not come, and she alone. The night was dark; we stood together at the door expecting him. I thought she seemed to wish I would not leave her. She kept me in conversation, and I was not displeased to be kept. As he rode my horse, I also was interested in his return. This did not diminish our acquaintance.

I had been introduced to an amiable family at Bromsgrove, situated within five yards of the shop I kept, in which were two agreeable daughters. While the first year was rolling round, I frequently stepped in, enjoyed a friendly chat, and thought myself a favourite; nor was I displeased when informed that the father had told a friend of his privately, "that I was welcome to either of his daughters."

I usually mounted my horse to return home at four; but business, one night in October, detaining me till seven, I called at the house of my friend, and found that daughter alone whom I liked best, though she was not the handsomest. In our conversation I said, "I will "stop in Bromsgrove to-night, if you will "favour me with your company?" "I never "will," she replied, "keep company with any "one, without my father's consent." This remark struck me dumb, though I could easily have replied to it. I consider a parent's consent requisite; yet it is but a secondary step. How could I tell whether our tempers would unite? Whether my stock of prudence, or manner of life, were suited to her taste; whether they were likely to gain and keep her affections; and the same with regard to myself.

It is time enough to ask when the young couple see a fair prospect. That trifling remark, I really believe, broke a match. A few insignificant words ensued, I took my leave, returned home, and never renewed the attempt. There is something extremely delicate in the first approaches of love. Like an infant, it is easily thrown down; and, like that, too weak to raise itself up.

While conversing with my next-door neighbour, Miss Cock, in November, I remarked that I perceived a growing affection for her, and should take no pains to check it. She did not receive this short declaration with the least disrespect. Our intimacy increased.

By the time Christmas arrived, our hearts had united without efforts on either side. Time had given numberless opportunities of observing each other's actions, and trying the tenor of conduct by the touch-stone of prudence. Courtship is often a disguise. We had seen each other when disguise was useless. Besides, nature had given to few women a less portion of deceit.

I never courted her, nor she me; yet we, by the close union with which we were cemented, were travelling towards the Temple of Hymen, without conversing upon the subject. Such are the happy effects of reciprocal love.

1755.

Although there was no formal courtship between Miss Cock and myself, nor did we ever spend one evening together past ten, nor *that* without company, yet Mr. Grace began to suspect us. As the affair opened, his anger kindled. He tried at a separation; complained of ill-treatment; had given up the thoughts of marriage, because suited with a house-keeper whom he was likely to lose in so short a space as fifteen months.

Though money has been in circulation many thousand years, and its properties often examined, yet those properties are not fully known. Mr. Grace had a doubtful debt, owing at Moseley, of about seven pounds. He asked me to accompany him to solicit payment. I consented. He was very cross, and treated me with scolding language all the way, expressive of his aversion to the match. I was silent.

Unexpectedly he received the money, which gave an instant turn to his temper; and from that moment he became good-humoured, and promoted the marriage. Such are the wonderful effects of money. He hinted, at the same time, that I had been apt to change, but hoped I would not use Sarah ill. I assured him I had too much love for her to injure her.

Our courtship now went on publicly, though always a *day-light* courtship.

March 21, Mr. Grace and I went to Aston to treat with the parents of Miss Cock. As I ever detested being a beggar, I wished to have, in the first instance, as much as they chose to give, for I knew I should never ask after. I answered faithfully whatever questions were asked, and shewed the progressive state of my circumstances, which was now an accumulation of two hundred pounds. They offered one hundred. I replied, "It is rather too little." "You cannot," said her mother with mildness, for she was one of the best women that ever lived, "desire more than we can give."

Struck with this reasonable reply, I could not call in one word to object. If she had offered me nothing, I could not have given up my dear girl. She asked, what settlement? The father was a yeoman, who farmed his own estate, and the mother had a settlement. I said a settlement was useless, for her daughter had one hundred pounds, and I had two; so that she would be certain of her thirds, let what would happen. The mother asked me next morning, what were my sentiments of the match? "I would consider of it." She little suspected how near that living treasure lay to my heart.

The next day I rode to Derby to see my father, and some acquaintance, and the next to Nottingham, to see my sister, whom I had not seen for four years. I told her my errand, and rather regretted that the fortune was small. She replied, "A fortune is a trifle; what is the "woman?" "To my wish." "Then she has "a fortune within her."

During our intimacy, two young men came from Derbyshire, who had been lovers, to renew their efforts, but in vain. No offers, however advantageous, I believe, could have detached one from the other. Thus was that pure flame kindled which, forty-one years after, gave rise to the following remarks: three months before her death, when she was so afflicted with an asthma that she could neither walk, stand, sit, or lie; but, while on a chair, I was obliged to support her head, I told her that she had never approached me without diffusing a ray of pleasure over the mind, except when any little disagreement had happened between us. She replied, " I can say more " than that. You never appeared in my sight, " even *in* anger, without that sight giving " me pleasure." I received the dear remark, as I now write it, with tears.

I parted with my dull house-keeper, gave notice to quit at Bromsgrove, sold my horse, and ate at the table of Mr. Grace with my dear love, without any plan for the future.

June 23, I awoke before seven, and ruminating on the first object of my life, I thought to myself, " What am I waiting for? I have no- " thing to expect, no end to answer, by delay. " That which *must* be done, may as well be

"done *now*. I will rise, and tell my love she
"must be no longer single. Fixing a future
"day, without some reason, is only fixing a
"shackle."

Mr. Grace and she received the information as a thing unexpected. We applied for a licence, and went through the marriage ceremony at St. Philip's Church. While her hand was in mine, I pressed it, almost unknown to myself; she told me, afterwards, the pressure revived her spirits.

Thus I experienced another important change, and one I never wished to unchange.

No event in a man's life is more consequential than marriage; nor is any more uncertain. Upon this die his sum of happiness depends. Pleasing views arise, which vanish as a cloud; because, like that, they have no foundation. Circumstances change, and tempers with them. Let a man's prior judgment be ever so sound, he cannot foresee a change; therefore he is liable to deception. I was deceived myself, but thanks to my kind fate, it was on the right side. I found in my wife more than ever I expected to find in woman. Just in proportion as I loved her, I must regret her loss. If my father, with whom I only lived fourteen years, who loved me less, and has been gone forty, never is a day out of my thoughts, what must be those thoughts towards her, who loved me as herself, and with whom I resided an age!

1756.

My dear wife brought me a little daughter, who has been the pleasure of my life to this day. We had now a delightful plaything for both.

Robert Bage, an old and intimate friend, and a paper-maker, took me to his inn, where we spent the evening. He proposed that I should sell paper for him, which I might either buy on my own account, or sell on his by commission. As I could spare one or two hundred pounds, I chose to purchase; therefore appropriated a room for the reception of goods, and hung out a sign: THE PAPER WAREHOUSE. From this small hint I followed the stroke forty years, and acquired an ample fortune.

It appeared that, during the first year after marriage, I had accumulated eighty pounds. In May, Mr. Grace thought his breath short, and sent for a surgeon, who opened a vein, and made an orifice as wide as a water-cock. Two basons were filled in about two minutes. A fainting fit ensued. This brought on a dropsy. A physician was called in, who prescribed a medicine, which drew off the water.

Supposing health returned, and discontented with his situation, on the 20th October he took a wife. As the power of the medicine declined, the disorder increased.

1757.

Mr. Grace grew worse, and February the first departed, after having been married fourteen weeks. The use of his property he left to his wife; and, at her death, it was partly to be divided into legacies among his relations, and the other part came to me, in right of his niece, as residuary legatee.

As all his property was personalty, I judged it precarious; but the widow, perfectly honest, agreed to assign all to me for an annuity, for which I gave security. She enjoyed it only one year and a half, when she was called away. I paid the legacies, and then my wife might be said to have brought in three, to my two, hundred pounds.

Feb. 17, she brought me a son.

Attention will increase business; and it was not possible to avoid attention; for the pleasure of providing for a beloved family is inconceivable. As room was wanted, I kept both houses in my own hands, resided in Mr. Grace's, and converted mine into a warehouse.

1758.

I perceived more profit would arise from the new trade than the old; that blank paper would speak in fairer language than printed; that one could only furnish the head, but the other would furnish the pocket; and that the fat kine would, in time, devour the lean. These larger profits, however, could only arise from larger returns, and these would demand a larger capital.

Few men can bear prosperity. It requires a considerable share of knowledge to know when we are well; for it often happens that he who is well, in attempting to be better, becomes worse. It requires resolution to *keep* well. If there was a profit to the *seller*, I concluded there must be one to the *maker*. I wished to have both. Upon this erroneous principle I longed for a paper-mill.

I procured all the intelligence I could relative to the fabrication of paper; engaged an artist to make me a model of a mill; attended to business; and nursed my children; while the year ran round. On the 2nd of July, Mrs. Hutton brought me another son, so that I had now three to nurse; all of whom I frequently carried together in my arms. This I could not do without a smile; while he who had none, would view the act with envy.

Dec. 13, my father died.

1759.

Perfectly mill-mad, I continued to mature this airy scheme. I ought to have been contented with my present lot; for, upon taking stock at Midsummer, we had saved in the past year, exclusive of all expences, one hundred and thirty-seven pounds. It pleased us both, and sufficiently rewarded the hand which had kept a steady stroke.

At Midsummer too, I took a lease of two acres of waste land upon Handsworth heath, of Mr. Wyrley, for ninety-nine years at twenty shillings *per annum*, and began to build a mill. Till now I had known what I was doing. My property then, exclusive of furniture, &c. was seven hundred and seventy-seven pounds.

1760.

Wanting a horse, I applied to a neighbour who had one to dispose of. After the usual askings and biddings, I offered six guineas: "No, he is worth ten. I will take him to "Stourbridge fair." Being refused, I went to Stourbridge fair, saw the horse, and bid the same money again; was refused, and came back without him. He returned unsold. The next day the owner offered him at my price, and I closed.

We now enter a melancholy year. It is not possible to be connected with the world without tasting its bitters; but sometimes they are administered in large draughts, which overcome and cast down the individual.

My dear wife, while pregnant of her fourth child, was afflicted with the jaundice, which baffled remedies, and brought her low. Her life was despaired of, and I unhappy.

One of our sons was taken ill; continued so four weeks, and on the 19th of May we lost him.

The next day, my dear love was delivered of another son. Soon after, my eldest son was taken with the measles, then with the small pox.

Before he recovered, my daughter fell ill of both, and was reduced to great danger. Then the infant was attacked.

Extreme grief for the loss of my son brought the jaundice upon me; which kept me long between life and death. Among other remedies, my physician prescribed a bolus of such magnitude, that I could not attempt to swallow it till it was cut in pieces. It produced seventeen large pills. Many a tear did my dear wife shed, for fear of losing me; and, to preserve my life, ran the utmost hazard of her own.

I got on horseback as soon as I was able; but I did not return to health till Michaelmas, when a journey to Nottingham recovered me. In one of my airings, a pompous, unfeeling man, who thought himself my superior, called out, "So! you are going to the devil I see!"

1761.

I still pursued the mill scheme, till lost in a labyrinth. The workmen saw my ignorance, and bit me as they pleased. " Let us fleece " Hutton, he has money." I discharged them all, let the work stand, and left myself at rest.

To confirm the health of my wife, entertain my daughter a delightful prattler, and son just put into breeches, I treated them all with a journey to Aston and Nottingham, where they made a stay of some weeks. This induced me to make during that time six journeys. In the first of these I saw the transit of Venus over the Sun's disk. She appeared a small black spot, the size of a large fly or bee, moving over the face of the sun. I think it was the 6th of June.

It appeared plain, though *I* could not see it, that the mill-wrights would not suffer me to rest while my property lasted. One of them was set on to persuade me, as I had given up the paper-mill, at what a small expence it might be converted into a corn-mill, and what amazing profit would attend it! while I, unwilling it should lie dormant, and still a dupe, was caught in the lure.

1762.

In March Mrs. Hutton was delivered of a still-born son. Her health was hurt, which induced me to take her to Aston. We went in a chaise, at sixpence a mile, the first time we either of us had ridden in one.

I found that, as a miller, I was cheated on all sides, which induced me again to discharge the people, and suffer the mill to stand, with a determination never to move it again. I also sold my horse for four guineas, resolving to keep no more.

Mr. Honeyborn thought the mill would answer his purpose, in polishing brass nails; and, after much *pro* and *con*, I consented to sell it for eighty guineas, and take his bond bearing interest.

Upon examining my accounts, for they were very minute, I found I had lost in cash, *two hundred and twenty-nine pounds!* Add to this the loss of three years of the prime part of my life, when trade was prosperous, and at a time when I had no opponent; I considered myself a sufferer of, at least, £.1000.

I was so provoked at my folly, that I followed up my business with redoubled spirit; cast up stock every quarter, and could not rest till I had brought my affairs into a successful line. The first quarter after the sale, which was from Midsummer to Michaelmas, I augmented my fortune twenty-nine pounds.

For all my inconsiderate follies, my dear wife never once upbraided me; but I could not forbear upbraiding myself. There is no need to accuse the man who accuses himself. I had drained the trade so much, to feed the mill, that I had but few goods to sell; the consequence was, I lost the customers.

1763.

We took several pleasurable journeys; among others, one to Aston, and in a superior style to what we had done before. This is the peculiar privilege of us Birmingham men: if ever we acquire five pounds extraordinary, we take care to shew it.

Business was prosperous, I had no rival, and I struck the nail that would drive. I began to doubt whether the mill had been any loss; for the disappointment had raised that commercial spirit which would not have been raised without it.

I never could bear the thought of living to the extent of my income; never omitted to take stock, or regulate my annual expences so as to meet casualties and misfortunes.

1764.

Every man has his hobby-horse, and it is no disgrace prudently to ride him. He is the prudent man who can introduce cheap pleasure without impeding business.

About ten of us, intimate friends, amused ourselves with playing at tennis. Entertained with the diversion, we erected a tennis-court, and met on fine evenings for amusement, without expence. I was constituted steward of our little fraternity.

My family continued their journeys, and were in a prosperous state.

1765.

When life glides smoothly on, incident is not to be expected. The man who sleeps in peace, has no tale to tell.

I was summoned upon the low bailiff's jury, which was my first step towards public life.

With our friends, we made a party of pleasure to Dosthill Spa; held various conversations; played at various games; boated on the river; went a fishing; visited the neighbouring curiosities, and drew much pleasure into a small compass of time.

Our Derbyshire journeys continued.

1766.

There is nothing more common than for a man to be discontented with his state. Something is always wanting; and that want, though a trifle, becomes a balance, in his own esteem, against the many things he enjoys, though any one of them is equal to the thing wanted. By good fortune, this was not my case: I, my wife, two dear sons, and one daughter, were in health, and they acted to my wish. Trade was successful; we enjoyed our little pleasures, and lived happily. Dress, the tennis-court, and our excursions, came of course.

Ever since I was eight years old, I had shewn a fondness for land; often made inquiries about it; and wished to call some my own. This ardent desire after dirt never forsook me; but the want of money had hitherto prevented me from gratifying my wish. Nothing makes a man poorer, except gaming. And, to buy land without money, is often followed with ruin.

My trade would spare none. Yet this did not expel the desire, particularly as the prospect drew nearer.

A paper-maker at Alfrick, in Worcestershire, with whom I dealt, told me that a small farm adjoining his own was upon sale. He wanted land, and urged me to purchase. I gave him a commission to buy it for £.250, agreed to let it him for £.20 *per annum*, and I borrowed all the money to pay for it. Thus I ventured, and with success, upon a most hazardous undertaking.

1767.

This year opened with the purchase of another estate, near Birmingham, copyhold, six acres, for two hundred pounds. The same person who advanced money for the last purchase, was to advance it for this. My attorney, an honest loggerhead, raised a dispute between the lord of the manor and me. This, upon the day of admission, stopped the proceedings. The case was submitted to counsel, who gave it against me. The lord threatened revenge. I made the best apology I was able, which rather softened his resentment; and, when the scale begins to turn, it subsides apace. He and his son passing by the door, I invited them in. They became tipsy; we instantly agreed, and I was admitted. By this delay, I was able to pay the money without borrowing. I let it for a brick-yard at £.18 *per annum*. The clay failing, I reduced it to £.13, and afterwards sold it for £.250, with a resolution never more to purchase copyholds.

In the beginning of this year I was taken ill; then Mrs. Hutton. We thought her under the hand of death, when the three babes and I mourned over her with tears. She recovered, but one of our sons was attacked with a fever. Through the ignorant treatment of the apothecary's man, he grew worse; languished from the 15th March to the 3d April, and then departed.

We were inconsolable for the loss of this lovely boy, which was followed by daily tears. I could observe thousands of faces pass by, which carried every mark of serenity; while my inward oppression was beyond bearing. Every article which had been his was carefully kept from our sight; nor durst my dear wife, nor I, ever mention him to each other during ten years, though he was not one day out of either of our thoughts.

1768.

I bought three acres of land at Handsworth, for £.156; paid one hundred guineas down, and gave my note, six months after date, for the remainder; let it for nine guineas, and afterwards sold it for £.250.

The day after this purchase, April 8th, I was chosen overseer of the poor, and thought myself elevated beyond my ancestors; for none, within the reach of tradition, had equalled it. They had rather been *the poor* than *overseers of* the poor. My property was then about £.2000.

Perhaps I was the first overseer in Birmingham that ever rejoiced at the office. When, in the evening, I met my five new brethren at the Castle, they were all affected; some provoked, and some cast down; while I kept up the joke, and brought them to a smile. Some of them afterwards acknowledged I did them a service.

In the course of the year they had still greater reason to thank me; for, by an active conduct, I did not only my own duty, but a considerable part of theirs. I kept the chair twenty-four weeks, though my time was only eight. The most irksome part of the office was collecting the levies. It grieved me to take people's last shilling, which was often the case. I found great pleasure in *giving* to distress; but then, it must be remembered, the money was not mine.

I acquired an amiable character among the dependant class; and my successor told me I was the favourite of all the old women.

The Lamp Act came upon the carpet. Great opposition arose, and more by my means than any other person's; and that for an obvious reason. I occupied two houses which formed the gate-way entering New Street, and they suited me. Both must come down if the Act passed. All the terms the opposition could obtain, and which were all I wanted, after many hundred pounds had been spent, were that the buildings should not come down, nor be included in the Act.

1769.

I bought half an acre of land at Bennett's Hill, near Washwood Heath, for £.40, with a view of erecting a house, which, twenty-nine years after, was to be the spot where I write this history. The land cost the seller £.12. This year I built my house. I now quitted the office of overseer, which had given me much pleasure, and returned to my private station.

I entered upon a gambling scheme in the purchase of land; for all uncertain bargains come under that description. I purchased the reversion of a small estate at Erdington of seven persons, for seventy-five guineas, and then agreed with the possessor for possession. It now lets for thirteen guineas.

I also made two purchases of Dr. Hinckley at Smethwick. One, the Shire Ash, thirteen acres, for £.250. I sold the timber for £.126, and let the land for thirteen guineas *.

The other, Spring Dale, eight acres, for which I gave £.100. This was under a lease of ninety-nine years, twenty-four of which were to come, at £.3 *per annum.* It now lets for ten guineas †.

The more attention a man pays to any undertaking, the more he is likely to succeed. The purchase of land was a delight, a study, and a profit. We saved this year £.479.

* This I sold, June 3, 1800, for £.500.
† I sold this, in May 1803, for £.400.

1770.

My worthy friend William Ryland, dreading the office of overseer, offered me twenty guineas to serve it for him. We went to Hampsted to ask Mr. Wyrley's consent, who gave it. And now I was reinstated in the office; but this second edition was unequal to the first, for then I assumed a real character, but now a borrowed one. Pride teaches a man to aspire, but I was sinking. Besides, the novelty was gone. My brethren, if it will bear the name, treated me with civility; but, as I was an interloper, and knew the pride of an overseer was rather great, they might, as I had no commission, have turned me out of the vestry. As it happened, I passed the year comfortably, and determined to be the tail-end of an overseer no more.

I erected the wings of my house at Bennett's Hill. I went to Nottingham races, and took my son upon a poney. When I surveyed the little man, and the little horse, the strong affection of a father taught me to think him the prettiest figure upon the race-ground.

We returned through Mountsorrel, and saw my aunt Jane, whom I remembered a beauty, and a haughty one, now a decrepid and dependant old woman; also, through Swithland, and saw my aunt Eyre, both for the last time. Then took our route through Market Bosworth, and surveyed the fatal field where Richard fell.

1771.

The year opened with the purchase of a farm at Stichford, £.780. I mortgaged it for £.400, paid the remainder, sold the timber for £.50, and let the land for forty guineas a year.

I planted the trees at Bennett's Hill, which, having been carried upon my shoulder, and planted by my hand, I have a thousand times viewed with the delight of adopted children.

I treated my family with a visit to Aston as usual. From thence, my son, daughter, and I, went to Nottingham races.

1772.

I purchased a farm called Hollymore, seven miles from Birmingham, seventy-four acres, £.850. It was already under mortgage for

£.800, which remained, and I paid the £.50. I set out early one morning, went over the grounds, marked and valued 600 trees, and returned home to breakfast, without tasting anything.

I sold the trees for £.220. The Commons were inclosing. I had an allotment of eight acres, worth £.100. I let the farm for fifty guineas, lost about half the rent, and then sold the place for nine hundred.

I had once resolved not to buy land without paying for it, which would have prevented me from running into debt; but the bent of mind was too strong for restraint. Every opening caused a longing. I could not pass by what I thought a bargain.

By an amendment of the Lamp Act, my houses were to come down. It happened, that the old house, on the spot where my son now resides, was upon sale. I durst not let the opportunity slip. I considered it as a tool by which I must carry on my trade. I purchased it for eight hundred and thirty-five guineas. It was then under mortgage for £.400. I was obliged to pay the residue; and, as these premises would be open to New Street if my two houses were removed, I now wished them down.

Thus purchase after purchase caused me to contract debts wholesale. I was now chosen a Commissioner of the Court of Requests, and it was prophesied I should make an active one.

It may fairly be concluded, that there cannot be a more useful service rendered to the public, than that of doing justice between man and man, giving every one his own in the mildest way, and composing differences. If a judge can keep clear of prejudice, as he is not interested, he will never decide wrong, except when misinformed. If he happens to relish the employment, it will be much in his favour, as well as in that of the public, because he will be master of the subject; and, if master, he will execute the task with propriety. Should he prove of a beneficent cast, he will never throw oil into the fire, but endeavour to extinguish the flame, which sets fire to two parties.

The Court of Requests soon became my favourite amusement. I paid a constant attendance, and quickly took the lead. Responsibility, I knew, must follow; for, standing in the front, I was obliged to take it myself, which excited caution. I had every party to watch, that fraud might not creep in.

The management of the Court engrossed nearly two days in a week of my time, including the trouble it gave me at my own house; and for this I never had the least emolument. That my government was not arbitrary will appear from two facts: I never had a quarrel with a suitor, nor the least difference with a Brother Commissioner.

I attended the Court nineteen years. During this time more than a hundred thousand causes passed through my hands! a number, possibly, beyond what ever passed the decision of any other man. I have had 250 in one day. Though I endeavoured after *right*, it cannot be supposed, in so large a number, they were *all* without error.

1773.

As far as I have proceeded in my history, it will easily be perceived, that my disposition was for active life. Ambition, and the idea of being useful, were the urging motives.

I was now chosen a Commissioner of the Lamp and Street Act. This also I relished, attended, and considered as a large field for reform. The whole of the inhabitants, I found, had been encroachers upon the public property, and that for ages. But this Act gave a fine opening to reduce things to order. My plan was to execute the Act with *firmness*, but with *mildness*. I would favour no man, but oblige all equally to conform.

But this plan, I found, could not be adopted. There were clashing interests among the Commissioners. Some wished to retain their own nuisances; others, to protect those of their friends; then, with what face could they vote down others? A rich man also was favoured beyond a poor one. The blame of some removals was charged upon me, because I was a speaker, an advocate for impartial reform, and not supported by my Brother Commissioners. I lost some friends, and declined attendance.

The waste lands in King's Norton were divided. As eight acres had fallen to my share, which lay some miles from Hollymoor farm, I purchased seven allotments, about fifty acres, from others; had them all laid together; built a house and barn; when, after sinking a considerable sum, I raised an estate of twenty-nine guineas a year. This was one of the blemishes in my *terra firma* conduct.

1774.

My son had a poney, which he had nursed with more care than sometimes a mother nurses her child. Now one year had run round, and he was two inches nearer a man, he chose a horse to look more *like* a man; and chose that another should have the care of him. This proved a family horse. He carried me to Warwick, being summoned upon the grand jury at the quarter sessions.

The waste lands upon Withall Heath employed much of my time, and more of my money. I perceived I had missed the mark in my calculations. The proprietors of land had their allotments laid near their farms; had every convenience at hand to improve them; and, being upon the spot, could watch and promote that improvement at a small expence. But I, who had no land near, no team to assist, or servants that could oversee, was obliged to hire all the work, and at a double price.

Every neighbour was my enemy; for " What " right had a tradesman to come among them?" Whatever property could be touched was stolen. Even the very fences which I had planted three times over were destroyed. I sowed the seeds, and found fourteen horses eating the crop. There is no law that will support a single man against a country.

Thus circumstanced, I was obliged to let it for a mere trifle, which was never paid. I afterwards granted a lease, at the low rent mentioned in 1773; and I did it with a determination never more to meddle with waste land.

My son and I went to Nottingham races, having omitted this delightful visit three years. The pleasure did not consist so much in the races, as in seeing a dear sister, who tenderly loved me.

As I had not seen my estate at Alfrick for seven years, I took Worcester races in the way; but, as I had no sister there, the race was a burthen.

1775.

Some years have glided on with pleasure, some with affliction, some with profit, some with disappointment, but this with fatigue.

I had now to take down the great old house purchased in 1772, and lay out, I was told, £.1200 in building; and yet my trade was unable to spare a shilling with propriety. All my neighbours, with whom I had lived in friendship, were to quarrel with me for supposed injuries; except a quarrelsome lawyer, with whom I never contracted a friendship. To rise above a friend, makes an enemy.

I have already remarked, that I purchased the house subject to a mortgage of £.400. As I knew I should want money, I asked the mortgagee to advance £.200 more. "Yes, if you "will add another estate to the security; for, "if you pull this house down, how do I know "you will build it up again?" Struck with the remark, I resolved to make no farther inquiries, but to try my own strength, and not call in assistance till necessity obliged me.

Now I had to undergo the hardest bodily labour I ever experienced. Up at four every morning, I set the people to work, watched *over* them, and laboured *with* them all day, and frequently charged myself with the meanest and most laborious parts of the employment.

It is amazing what a rapid progress may be made in any undertaking, when the proprietor conducts the work like a master, and labours like a servant.

This work was begun April 28, and covered in October 24. As I was obliged to quit my other house at Christmas, we resided at Bennett's hill till Whitsuntide; when my family, having paid a visit to Aston, entered the new house on their return.

As I was closely connected with the building the whole year, I have no incidents to fill the page, but dirty clothes, wounded fingers, bruised arms, waste of materials, drunken workmen, cheating carpenters, and daily duns.

1776.

The inside of my house yet demanded attention. This took me half the year to complete; and, being much larger than that I had left, it demanded additional furniture; and this required the other half.

My tenant at Stickford ran in arrears; and when bad, and getting worse, it is time to part. I took his stock; suffered him to take his household furniture, and we parted; with a loss on my side of fifty pounds.

Seized with a fond fit of farming, I took the place into my own hands; and, for two years and a half, paid the utmost attention to it. I also received much pleasure from it. But when business has no profitable returns, it soon ceases to be pleasure.

I paid my visits three or four times a week, though distant four or five miles, always on foot. I arrived there by five in the morning, and was back by breakfast. Thus I became a slave, in conducting what it was not in the power of man to conduct properly at so great a distance, and with the business consigned to unprincipled people.

My accounts told me, at the end of the above term, that I had lost exactly the rent, one hundred guineas. I let the place, with a resolution to farm no more.

I bought the manor and estate of Chadwich, for £.4,500 pounds, upon a promise, from an attorney, of supplying me with what money I should want. I let it for £.300 a year, and kept it one year; when it appeared that I could not fulfil my bargain, because my attorney had deceived me; nor the seller his, because in some places he had charged near twice as much land as there really was. He was pleased that I had procured a tenant at an advanced rent, and we mutually agreed to dissolve the contract.

My family rejoiced, but I lamented.

1777.

Although I could not borrow money, but had conducted the building and the farm by my own resources, yet I had so far impoverished the trade, that nothing but time could recover it from a consumption.

A person approached me, "Sir, I hear you "sometimes purchase land. There is a small "bit at Makeney, in Derbyshire, which is the "joint property of three cousins, of whom I "am one. I never saw it, nor can I give any "account of it, only I have heard it is three "acres, give me what you please for it. It has "been some ages in my family. My father is "lately dead, and the deeds are in the hands of "my mother."

If you can make me a freehold title, I will give you seven guineas. We instantly agreed, I drew the article, and gave one earnest. He procured the deeds, and I made the conveyance for a blind purchase, for I knew no more of the place than himself.

Not having seen my sister for three years, I went to Nottingham races, and took Makeney in my way. I saw the place of which I had purchased a third, and which *had been* three acres; but the proprietors having paid no attention to it, and the tenant having bought the adjoining land, he had filched one half. I could only accuse him of the fraud, for the remedy would have been a Chancery suit. I received my share of the rent, twenty-seven shillings; let the matter sleep twenty-one years; and sold my part to the tenant for seventy guineas, May 1, 1797.

1778.

The man who possesses any branch of useful knowledge, may have customers enough to partake of that knowledge, provided he distributes it *gratis*. A mercer in Birmingham, who had purchased the stock of a shopkeeper in Dudley, and had followed the various trades of bookseller, draper, haberdasher, and hosier, requested me to go over and value the stock. I consented, but did not receive even thanks.

One of my services met with a better return. A decent country woman came one market-day, and begged to speak with me. She told me, with an air of secrecy, that her husband behaved unkindly to her, and sought the company of other women; and that, knowing me to be a wise man, I could tell what would cure him.

The case was so common, I thought I might prescribe for it without losing my reputation as a conjurer. "The remedy is simple," said I, "*Always treat your husband with a smile.*" The woman thanked me, dropped a curtesy, and went away. A few months after, she came again, bringing a couple of fine fowls. She told me, with great satisfaction, that I had cured her husband; and she begged my acceptance of the fowls in return. I was pleased with the success of my prescription, but refused the fee.

It was Saturday, my son was gone to Nottingham races. I wished to follow, procured a horse, and set out the next morning. A soft wart had, for many years, been growing upon the verge of the left corner of the right eye. I had tried various remedies, but in vain. It was painful and alarming. At length I determined to try that dangerous remedy *Aqua fortis*. Meeting with a friend at Shenston, "What is "the matter with your eye?" "It is a painful "wart, which has been growing many years." "There is no wart!" Upon examination, I found it had tumbled out unknown to me, and left an empty socket that would have admitted a large pea. The cure was effected.

1779.

We now enter another year of misfortunes. The carpenter, while erecting my house, would never favour me with his account, but drew money occasionally, and managed matters in such a dextrous manner that it was impossible to keep a check against him. The man, who means fairly, will never hide his accounts. Thinking I had disbursed enough, I withheld payment. When his bill was delivered in, I considered myself overcharged. We agreed to leave it to reference. The referees appeared warm in his favour, for, being all of a trade, they might, like the lawyers, serve each other. I was awarded to pay, without being consulted, £.200 in one month. I remonstrated, and proved that they had charged, in many instances, fifteen *per cent.* more than was agreed upon. All was in vain, I was obliged to submit.

I had erected a house at Mill-pool hill. The brick-maker who had supplied me, and his man, quarrelling, the man informed me " that " he had, in every load, sent a deficient number "of bricks by order of his master." "Will you prove this, when you come face to face?" "I will." When the master came for payment, I remonstrated in gentle terms; was ignorant of the matter; wished to pay what was right; and begged he would wait till I could bring the man. He made no reply, but instantly served me with a writ; and, as I wished to avoid a suit, I paid the demand and expence.

A paper-maker sent me an invoice of 35 bundles of paper, value thirty pounds, which were sent off for me by Ashmore's waggon. I frequently, during the space of six weeks, inquired of the carrier if the goods were come, for they were wanted. The answer was always, "No." At the end of that time, the book-keeper told me I had received them. I was alarmed. Upon farther inquiry, neither the carrier, book-keeper, nor porters, knew where they were delivered; nay, the porters at first owned it. The carrier took his two porters to a master in Chancery, who then swore they delivered them on the 15th of April to me. I saw the evil that hung over me. I was not, in a court of law, allowed to prove a negative, though all my people were certain they never came to me. I proposed that the maker, carrier, and I, should equally share the loss. This the carrier alone refused. The maker brought his action for the money. I told the attorney, who served me with the writ, to desist; for I would pay the money. He *seemed* to consent, but, like a true lawyer, proceeded; and, to my surprise, served me with a second process, when I paid the debt and about ten pounds cost. We could all of us easily guess where the paper was delivered; but could bring no proof.

In addition to these evils my customers failed in my debt. Almost every week one fell.

This year too was the beginning of the worst of my afflictions, the indisposition of my dear wife, from which she never returned into health; but underwent a gradual increase of disorder for seventeen years, till Nature sunk under the weight.

One of my tenants broke, by which I lost several hundred pounds.

My daughter was taken ill of a nervous complaint, and struggled under great debility many years.

I had, a few years before, agreed with a bricklayer and carpenter, jointly, to erect a barn at Withall-heath for 70 pounds. When finished, I complained that they had pinched a little in every one of the dimensions. They did not deny the fact; but, to cover the defect, one of them said, they would each return me four shillings. This the other would not agree to; so the mover returned me his four, but no receipt passed. At this distant period of five years, the carpenter demanded a guinea, which he said was left unpaid. The bricklayer was dead. I treated the demand as a joke. However the man put me into the hands of *Freeman*, a notorious lawyer, which was deemed nearly equal to putting into the hands of Satan. I shewed a clear account, which *seemed* to satisfy Freeman; but the carpenter knew I could not produce a receipt; and, rather than dispute with a poor rogue, I paid the money. I must do Freeman the justice to say, he behaved like a gentleman.

In eating a sallad, a small stone wounded a tooth. Two days after, being at the play, a lady presented me with an orange. The moment the juice touched the wounded tooth, it gave me exquisite pain. The nerve being affected by the acidity, a swelling commenced in the gums. My teeth loosened, and some came out. An abscess formed in the throat, and a fever ensued. A surgeon was called in, then a physician. At length I broke out in boils. My wife and daughter were at Aston. My son attended me with the most filial care.

At a meeting of creditors, upon one of my insolvent customers, a person said, "I'll sell "you an estate." "No, I have no money." "I will not take much, for I have a mortgage "upon it for £.600, which shall lie at four "and a half *per cent.* as long as you please; I "shall not want it." I examined the estate; bought it for £.653; paid the fifty-three, and continued the mortgage. Having linked me fast, he said to me, six months after, "I can "make five *per cent.* of my money; you must "give me that, or pay in." I urged the unfairness of the measure, but in vain. When the second six months were elapsed, "You must "pay that money in, I want it." Unhappy is he who lies at the mercy of ungenerous men. He afterwards boasted in company how cleverly he had bit me. Some have supposed a fatality attends unjustifiable actions. He who exhibits one, has more in reserve. This man's fortune, by some means unknown to me, dwindled away. Riding through Bromsgrove, June 19, 1798, I saw him in old age, and in rags.

Several attorneys were applied to for the money. At length one agreed to supply me with it. Upon inquiry, he told me that the estate would not bear £.600, and that I must add another estate to secure the mortgagee. This I consented to; for, like Sterne's starling, "I was caught in a cage, and could not get out." Now the title to the added estate was defective. "Will you advance £.400, if I pay the other two?" "Yes." This was done; and he, like an honest lawyer, charged three times as much for transferring the mortgage as the conveyance had cost.

Thus I have gone through a year, replete with the largest number of calamities, though not the greatest, that ever occurred to me. I had lost so much money, and paid so much away, that I had bled the trade into a decline. I was determined to purchase no more land; but keep all the money I could in business, and attend to it in the best manner I was able. I had been draining it thirteen years, and had realized a considerable income.

1780.

I was distressed in the midst of plenty. My trade, like a man lamed, required time to recover; and I, like an attentive surgeon, applied the best remedies in my power. My efforts were successful.

During the last unfortunate year I had kept close at home; but now with my son I visited my sister and Nottingham races. We took Bradby in our way to see the place where the celebrated Lord Chesterfield was born and resided: Lord Chesterfield, whose genius will be had in repute when calumny shall cease.

We were treated with civility, told many anecdotes, shewn his sleeping and sitting rooms, his library, &c.; the horse too which he usually rode, and which was kept in the park to graze his last in peace.

The first nine months of this year were employed in writing the History of Birmingham. Fearing my ability, I wrote with dread. *Rollason* the printer was pleased with it, and shewed it to Dr. Withering, who pronounced it the " best topographical History he had ever " seen." I had for it seventy-five copies, the profit upon which amounted to about forty pounds. To venture into the world as an Author, without having had a previous education, was a daring attempt. It was setting my knowledge against that of the public: the balance very uneven. This was afterwards considered the best book I ever wrote. I considered it in a less favourable light.

Pleased as a fond parent with this History, as my first literary offspring, I may be said, while in manuscript, to have had the whole by heart. Had a line been quoted, I could have followed it up through the chapter. Frequently while awake in the night I have repeated it in silence for two or three hours together, without adding or missing a word. Perhaps the critic will say, " You were asleep and dreamed it." It corresponds however with an expression in the preface to the present work, that I wrote the history of my life with correctness of fact and of date from unpremeditated memory.

1781.

I supped Jan. 31, with a large company at the Bull and Gate. *Rollason* my bookseller was there, spoke highly of my History, and " made no doubt but the fine paper would, in " twenty years, sell for a guinea."

This year commenced with a new duty on paper; consequently an advance of price. Having no engagements upon my hands but business and the Court of Conscience, I made almost daily visits to a farm I had purchased near Sutton Coldfield; a walk that delighted me. These walks I always took very early in the morning or late in the evening, that more necessary pursuits might not be impeded. I also superintended the correcting, enlarging, and printing the History of Birmingham.

I attended Nottingham races as usual.

1782.

March 22, the History of Birmingham was published.

A man may live half a century, and not be acquainted with his own character. I did not know I was an Antiquary till the world informed me, from having read my History; but when told, I could see it myself. The Antiquarian Society at Edinburgh chose me a member; and sent me an authority to splice to my name, F. A. S. S. *Fellow of the Antiquarian Society of Scotland.*

During this Summer I made many visits to places of antiquity within fifteen miles of home; some of which were introduced into the second edition of the History of Birmingham, published the ensuing year.

1783.

The man in health ought not to be difficult in his choice of viands. If he wishes to relish his food, let him wait till he is hungry. February 8 I went to Wall, to examine the junction of the Watling Street, and the Icknield Street. I tasted nothing till noon. My landlord brought a homely dish upon the table, the gleanings of the cup-board, remnants of beef, pork, mutton, and potatoes, fried together. I relished this blended meal as much as the Lord Mayor his feast. On the 16th I went to Dudley after dinner, and returned to tea, near twenty miles, and found that tea as acceptable.

Rotten tradesmen are the bane of the industrious. One labours that the other may live. A person failed one hundred guineas in my debt. After waiting six years, a final dividend was squeezed out of the assignee. My share came to four guineas. Another failed, and owed me £.110. I received thirteen shillings in the pound. He afterwards had a fortune left him, when he did what the law could not have obliged him to do, paid twenty, which proves that we are not all rogues in Birmingham.

My family was thrown into the utmost distress, by my suffering under an inflammation in the bowels. On Sunday evening, Dec. 21, I began to feel slight pains, but was ignorant of the complaint. On Monday I took jalap, and grew worse. On Tuesday a conceited apothecary was sent for, who was as unacquainted with the disorder as myself. On Wednesday Dr. Ash was called in, and told me it was an inflammation in the bowels. He also informed my friends, that there was little hope; that my blood was as thick as a jelly, and as yellow as a guinea; but added, "We must not lose "him if we can help it, for he is a useful man." He saw the case desperate, and acted a bold part: bled me three times the first day, again the next, repeating it to six times. I underwent eight medical operations in one day, and was still worse. Thursday I was put into a warm bath. Friday the same. Death was expected. I had no sleep during three days and nights. A small symptom on Saturday, at midnight, took place in my favour. The doctor visited me on Sunday at noon, and holding the curtain in his hand, said, "You are as "safe as a bug in a rug."

I was so reduced, that the information gave me no pleasure; nor would it have made the least impression, had he told me I should depart the next hour. Life was nearly extinguished. No news, however important, could have affected me.

This taught me a lesson I could not have believed. The nearer the grave, the less the terror. Health is the season to dread death, not sickness. The world had lost every charm, and futurity every fear.

My affectionate wife, though ill herself, sat up with me three nights out of four.

1784.

Reduced as I had been to the last stage of existence, and even to the last inch of that stage, I continued in a debilitated state. The doctor told me I should never be the man I had been. But this proved the only point in which this worthy man was mistaken. He had exerted all his powers to save my life; a life, I am persuaded, I owe entirely to him. Whatever errors, therefore, I shall commit in future, let them, in return, be charged to him.

My son had, for some time, kept two horses, chiefly to graze in the field, for they were seldom out. The disorder, with which my dear wife was afflicted, was gaining ground. Riding was recommended. Our horses were incapable of carrying double. We frequently engaged a person to take her an hour's ride, which was of service.

April 27 her mother died, at the age of eighty-seven. She was, like her daughter, one of the best of women. Our visits to Aston were chiefly on her account.

I was subpœnaed, Dec. 1, as a witness upon a trial, which was to come on in London the next day. I was obliged to set out immediately, and I staid thirteen days.

1785.

Deeming the rides for my afflicted wife too short, I agreed with a person to hire me a horse, I finding a man, to go four or five miles, twice or thrice a week. I frequently attended in this service. Some benefit, we thought, was the result.

We now also extended our excursions; visited Buxton, and were much pleased with that gay place. Here we met with a variety of characters; and a man may draw pleasure or profit from all.

I took a ramble for one whole day, in which I visited the *Lover's Leap,* a romantic cliff; *Che Tor,* more romantic, said to be 365 feet high, which I doubt. I climbed a master mountain, in the centre of many, where the tops appeared level with each other, which had a most singular and beautiful appearance. They were all bare. I mounted the Castle-hill at Castleton, too steep for any attack. I examined the ruins of the Castle, Roman. The town below, and the adjacent views, were charming. I penetrated to the extremity of *Peak Hole,* under the Castle-hill, more tremendous than pleasant. I ascended *Mam Tor,* or the shivering mountain, said continually to moulder, but not diminish, which is totally untrue, as may be seen by every observer. The mountain has diminished one-third in size, and a considerable hill has been raised from the detached parts. It kept mouldering all the time I was there. This cannot amount to the smallest wonder, for every mountain will do the same which has a perpendicular side, composed of loose stones and a light soil. Upon the summit is an extensive camp, not very secure on one side. I returned by *Elden Hole,* a most terrific spectacle, a chasm lined with rock, thirty yards long, and five wide, guarded by a wall. I threw down many stones, which produced five or six sounds in their descent, owing to the various bends in the passage, which is not perpendicular. I got among the mines, and the miners; made enquiries, and paid money for making them. The Peak seemed inhabited by none but beggars. I could not ask a question, or even inquire my road, without, " Please, sir, to give me something." They seemed a tarnished, ragged, and happy people. I had a delightful walk, in my return, over Peak Forest; but was affected at a village called Dam, in the Forest, at the sight of a body of people carrying to his house a young man just killed in a mine. I returned in the evening much indisposed, with having taken liquors I was not used to drink.

My son and I went to Nottingham races this year, attended by a servant. Of all the journeys I ever undertook, this, of Nottingham races, was the most delightful. For though I knew nothing of the horses, the winners, or the company, nor was interested in the event, yet the body was at ease, the mind divested of care, every thing was new, pleasant, and, above all, I was accommodated by a sister whom I loved. This, since 1770, was my eleventh time of attending that gay scene, but, unknown to me, the last; for now my sister and I were to part for ever.

Mrs. Hutton remarked to me, in one of our rides, "That she was not likely, from the "growing state of her complaint, to continue "long; and pointed out a lady who would suit "me for her successor." I was affected, and only replied, "I could not entertain such an "idea, but should stay till I found her equal." If her dear shade should hover over me, and observe my action, it will never see another in those arms which have enfolded her. I have now, July 19, 1798, lost her two years and a half, and have never thought of offering that violence to her memory, or my own feelings. Can a cure be found for the man who has lost half of himself?

I had, in the preceding December, as I have already observed, been subpœnaed to London upon a trial. This gave me an opportunity of seeing many curiosities, which I this year gave an account of from memory, and printed it under the title of *The Journey to London*, being my second publication, price two shillings and six pence.

1786

Was ushered in with a melancholy event, the loss of my sister, Feb. 26; a woman of an extraordinary character, and as amiable as extraordinary. Her age was sixty-seven.

My tenant at Hollymoor not paying his rent, I went over to receive it; but, to my astonishment, I found the doors open, the furniture gone, the family fled, and not a hoof in the grounds. He owed me one hundred and fifty-eight pounds, and had left the farm in such a ruined state, that I could not let it except at a reduced rent. I lost the whole of what he owed me.

My brother and I were subpœnaed as witnesses upon a trial at Warwick. The attorney promised to reimburse the expence, the contenders being poor. My brother and myself went in a chaise. We won the cause. I was obliged to bear all the expence, and never received a shilling. So much for the faith of a lawyer.

I was subpœnaed to Worcester assizes to prove a person's hand-writing. I told the attorney I could do him no service, for I had never seen the person write. This would not satisfy him. I then told him that I had been bitten by two of his brethren, and that I would not stir unpaid. He paid me, I went, but was not called.

This year also we made a visit to Buxton. The country romantic and delightful, the company agreeable, and the journey attended with a small benefit to her I loved. In all our excursions, it was my happy province to take my family, and attend them on their return.

1787.

Being master of the rules in the Court of Requests, and wishing to instruct others, I wrote a full history of the process in octavo, with a variety of examples, some interesting, being my third publication.

As the health of my wife declined, the air of Birmingham became more unfavourable; and as my house at Bennett's Hill was not so commodious for a constant residence as we wished, an addition was requisite. I formed a plan, which perhaps might have cost eighty pounds; then altered the plan a first, second, and third time; till, when put in execution, it cost more than £.700. Mortar is rather apt to corrode the pocket.

I wished to try exercise for Mrs. Hutton upon a larger scale. In July, she, my daughter, and I, went in a chaise to Aberystwith, in hopes that change of scene, amusement, exercise, and sea-air, would have a desirable effect. The journey was a pleasure to all, and was performed in three days. Here I left them, and returned by myself, as I did not chuse a long absence from business.

There was but one post-chaise between Aberystwith and Welch-pool, the whole breadth of Wales; and that post-chaise was twenty miles off. I could not, without waiting, be accommodated at Aberystwith. I resolved therefore to walk to Shrewsbury, with my great coat in my hand, and to go in a stage coach from thence. This took me two days and a half. The weather was extremely hot, and the roads dusty, which overcame me to that degree, that I was indisposed for a month, though able to attend to my concerns.

I went again to Aberystwith, to bring back my wife and my daughter.

Returning by Shrewsbury, we were treated with great civility by Major Grant, who took us to the Castle, a place of strength when strength was wanted, and shewed us the House of Industry, and the field where Hotspur fell.

1788.

My tenant at Hollymoor having run away, as before stated, and left the farm in so ill a plight that I had no choice of tenants, I was obliged to let it to a third man, little better than the others. As I could not get the rent, I sold the place. Thus what I thought one of my best bargains, turned out bad. Instead of getting £.800 clear, I did not get £.400.

We determined to change our watering-place, and this year made a visit to Blackpool, in Lancashire, found much company, much pride, much vulgarity, accompanied with much good-nature. I was struck with the place, wrote its history, which was my fourth publication, price one shilling. The landlords met, agreed to take the whole edition, 750 copies, and I agreed to sell them at prime cost, six-pence each. Hudson and Bailey stood joint pay-masters. These worthy gentlemen, stationed at a distance, which often tries a man's honesty, obliged me to stay four years for the money. Bailey, in the interim, broke. Hudson would only pay his own share of the nine pounds. The other I lost.

We staid here near three months. In my return I was very particular in my examination of the size of Manchester. I thought the town about one third less than Birmingham; the streets worse, but the buildings better; perhaps the inhabitants richer.

We stopped at Buxton, but, as it was far in October, the company was thin.

A horse which I had purchased to carry double, while grazing in the field a few days after our return, was set fast in the watering-pit; and though a strong animal, the ignorant people, in getting him out, broke his back. This deprived us of a horse exactly suitable, and which we were never able to replace.

This year I published the History of the Hundred Court, being a supplement to the Court of Requests, price one shilling: also, The Battle of Bosworth Field, five shillings.

1789.

Writing a History from memory is a difficult task, especially when memory presents hardly any incident to the mind.

I purchased another horse at near twice the money, but he no way answered my expectation. Dealing in horses is as precarious as dealing in marriage.

Since the death of my wife's mother, our journeys to Aston were given up; we resolved therefore upon one to Halsted, in Leicestershire, to visit her brother, which we found agreeable in every respect but the weather.

1790.

The cruel asthma made slow but certain inroads upon my dear love. She was now unable to sit upon a horse. I resolved to indulge her with a chariot. But how to accomplish it was to be considered. I had no coach-house, nor ground to erect one, for I had no land but the garden in which my house stood. Several of my neighbours could have accommodated me, but none would. There is a pleasure in seeing a man who cannot help himself; and a pride in being able to assist, and in refusing assistance.

I applied to a lady, "Madam, your land "which joins me is appropriated to no particu- "lar use, I shall be obliged to you for a few "yards, fix upon it what price you please, and "I will give it." "No."

I applied to another in the same humiliating strain. "Will you give me fifty pounds "for the small field that joins you, about one "third of an acre?" "I will." This sum was then refused because more might probably be got. A hundred was demanded, and I paid ninety! Thus the necessity of one man becomes a temptation to another. Pride may induce the Philosopher and the Divine to expatiate upon the dignity and the excellency of man, but we take advantage of each other.

The coach-house, carriage, horses, &c. cost about 635 guineas.

1791.

The canal frenzy in Birmingham was at its height; a scheme that may benefit the next generation and ruin this. The Worcester canal was set on foot, which met with great opposition during two Sessions of Parliament. I was solicited to go as an evidence; made five journeys; was examined by both houses, and honourably paid.

In one of these journeys I treated my wife and daughter. But we had not been many hours in London before the former was almost deprived of breath. We were alarmed, took apartments in an airy part of Princes-street, Hanover-square. She was no better. We then removed to Hampstead. Our distress was inconceivable. We expected every hour to lose her. The people of the house were frightened, and wished us gone. With difficulty we carried her into a post chaise. The pure air seemed to revive her, and she was better for the journey.

This year began prosperously, as many had done before it. Trade was extended and successful. I had for twelve years desisted from buying land, and kept my money in business, so that I had been able to draw out a considerable sum to improve my houses, and to buy furniture, a carriage, &c. without feeling it. My family loved me; were in harmony. I enjoyed the amusements of the pen, the court, and had no pressure upon the mind, but the declining state of health of her I loved. But a calamity awaited me I little suspected: the Riots in 1791, which hurt my fortune, destroyed my peace, nearly overwhelmed me and my family, and not only deprived us of every means of restoring to health the best of women, but shortened her days.

I wrote a History of that most savage event at the time, with a view of publication, but my family would not suffer it to see the light. I shall now transcribe with exactness the manuscript copy.

A NARRATIVE

OF THE

RIOTS IN BIRMINGHAM,

JULY 14, 1791,

PARTICULARLY AS THEY AFFECTED THE AUTHOR.

DEDICATION

TO THE

LOVERS OF RIOT.

None can have a claim to these sheets prior to yourselves, who are in reality the Authors.

I congratulate you upon your refined taste for pleasure. You not only enjoy your own mental resources, if such exist, but those of your neighbours. Happiness and misery are like baubles in your hands. You, cannibal like, devour others to feed yourselves; or, like the destroying angel, scatter destruction without the controul of human laws.

It is among the dark-coloured savages of the earth that a breach of law appears first, and punishment follows; but you have the art of reversing this rule of nature, and punishing prior to the crime. Why should we wonder that you kindled a number of fires in Birmingham, for she, salamander-like, has subsisted for ages by fire. By you she has risen in the annals of fame higher even than ancient Rome, for Rome had but one hero to rejoice over her flaming buildings, while Birmingham had ten thousand. You have discovered a conciser way of acquiring property than by the antiquated mode of industry. Yours is the right to take what property you please, destroy the rest, and laugh at the sufferer.

PREFACE.

This Narrative was, perhaps, the first ever written upon the subject, and will be the last published. It was fabricated within three weeks of the event, when the heart was deeply impressed with the sad and unmerited consequences. I must have been a peaceable citizen. No lawyer ever became rich by my quarrels; and many men must have been gainers by my labour. Yet the severe treatment I met with from the vulgar, was enough to make me question whether I myself was not the offender who had burnt the houses, and destroyed the property of others.

While I exercised a power over a numerous class of people in the Court of Requests, I endeavoured to use that power with mildness. In matters of *right* all men are equal. No elevation can warrant one man to domineer over another. I have, in the History of that Court, told the public, that I considered the suitors as my children; and when any of this vast family looked up to me for peace and justice, I have distributed both with pleasure. But how unequal are the returns of favour for service! The man in office, with half the attention I paid, generally acquires a fortune, while my reward was destruction! In that tribunal where I treated others with kindness, and met with the reverse in return, my heart acquits me of every fault, except errors of judgment. These are incidental to every man, and may originate from misinformation. No Judge can try one hundred causes without a defect: how then can he try a hundred thousand? For this were my houses destroyed, my person insulted, and my life threatened.

NARRATIVE, &c.

This is my eighth appearance before the world as an Author, but with this difference from the former seven: they were subjects of choice, this of necessity; then I wrote from the *head*, now from the *heart*. They were pleasing subjects, but this is most melancholy. In those I was only a looker on, but in this an innocent sufferer.

I thought I had been acquainted with man. But after fifty years' study, new scenes opened which I had not beheld. It is easy to account for that temper which prompts to plunder, when the plunderer is a gainer; but that man should be a wholesale dealer in destruction, without benefit to himself, is diabolical. He can have no claim to the word *human* but his shape. His savage fangs tore me to pieces, and ploughed up that even path of contentment which time cannot again make smooth.

Birmingham, though nearly without a government, had continued in harmony during the forty years of my residence. Religious and political disputes were expiring, when, like a smothered fire, they burst forth with amazing fury. I have, in the history of this place, celebrated the mild and peaceable demeanour of the inhabitants, their industry, and hospitality; but I am extremely concerned that I am obliged to soil the fair page with the black cinders of their burnt buildings. A stranger would be tempted to inquire, whether a few *Bonners* were not risen from the dead to establish religion by the faggot? or, whether the church was composed of the dregs of the universe, formed into a crusade? or, whether the friends of the king were the destroyers of men? In the dark ages papist went against protestant, but in this enlightened one it is protestant against protestant. But why should I degrade the word religion? He who either prompts or acts such horrid scenes, can have no religion of his own.

The delightful harmony of this populous place seems to have been disturbed by five occurrences.

A public library having been instituted upon an extensive plan, some of the members attempted to vote in Dr. Priestley's polemical

Works, to which the Clergy were averse. This produced two parties, and its natural consequence, animosity in both. Whether the gentlemen of the black gown acted with policy is doubtful, for truth never suffers by investigation.

The next was an attempt to procure a repeal of the *Test Act*, in which the Dissenters took an active but a modest part. Ever well-wishers to their country, the Dissenters were foremost in the quarrel with Charles the First, but they only meant a reform of abuses. Matters, however, were soon carried beyond their intention, and they lost their power. They who brought him into trouble, tried to bring him out. They were afterwards the first to place his son Charles the Second upon the throne, who requited them evil for good. After suffering various insults from the house of Stuart, the Dissenters were materially instrumental in promoting the Revolution, and upon this depended the introduction of the Hanoverian line, which, to a man, they favoured. In a thousand mobs, in 1714, to oppose the new government, could have been found no more Presbyterians than in the Birmingham Jury who tried the rioters. Nor was there one Presbyterian in the rebellion the following year, nor in that of 1745. In both periods they armed in favour of the house of Brunswick. Their loyalty has continued unshaken to the present day, without their ever having been disturbers of their country. They concluded, therefore, that they had a right to the privileges of other subjects. They meant no more. Those who charge them with designs either against Church or State, do not know them. No accusation ought to be admitted without proof. Can that people be charged with Republicanism, who have, in the course of one hundred and thirty-two years, placed five Sovereigns on the British Throne? As I was a member of that committee, I was well acquainted with the proceedings, and will repeat two expressions uttered at the board. Mr. *William Hunt* remarked, " That he should " be as strenuous in supporting the Church of " England as his own." The whole company, about twenty in number, acquiesced in the sentiment. This gentleman verifies his assertion, by subscribing to more than one Church. I myself remarked, " That what we requested " was our right, as well as that of every subject; " we ought to recover it, but rather than involve " our country in dispute, we would resign it." This also was echoed by the whole body. These were all the Presbyterian plots either against Church or King, I ever knew. Hence it appears, the Presbyterians are as true friends to both as any set of men whatever, except those who hold church lands or court favours.

Controversy was a third cause. Some uncharitable expressions falling from the Episcopal pulpits, involved Dr. Priestley in a dispute with the Clergy. When acrimony is used by two sides, the weakest only is blameable. To dispute with the Doctor was deemed the road to preferment. He had already made two Bishops, and there were still several heads which wanted mitres, and others who cast a more humble eye upon tithes and glebe lands. The Doctor on his part used some warm expressions, which his friends wished had been omitted. These were placed in horrid lights; and here again the stronger side ever reserves to itself the privilege of putting what construction it pleases upon the words of the weaker. However, if the peace of society is broken, we cannot but regret it, whatever be the cause.

The fourth occurrence was an inflammatory hand-bill, which operated upon the mind, like a pestilence upon the body. Wherever it touched, it poisoned. Nothing could be more unjust than charging this bill upon the Dissenters, and, in consequence, dooming them to destruction. It appears from its very contents that it could not proceed from a *body*. If it *was* fabricated by a Dissenter, is it right to punish the whole body with fire and plunder? This is visiting the sins of one man upon another. An established maxim is, a man shall only be accountable for his *own*. It might be written by an incendiary of another profession, to kindle a flame. Perhaps the unthinking fell upon the Dissenters, because they were vexed they could not find the author. I have been tempted to question whether he meant any more than a squib to attract public attention; but it proved a dreadful one, which burnt our houses *.

The fifth was a public dinner at the hotel, to commemorate the anniversary of the French revolution. This, abstractedly considered, was an inoffensive meeting. It only became an error by being ill-timed. As the minds of men were ruffled, it ought to have been omitted. Though a man is justified in doing what is right, it may not always be prudent. We may rejoice with any society of men who were bound and are set free; but the French revolution is

* It appeared afterwards that it was fabricated in London, brought to Birmingham, and that a few copies were privately scattered under the table at an Inn.

more their concern than ours. I do not approve all its maxims, neither do I think it firmly fixed. One of its measures however I admire, that of establishing itself without the axe and the halter, a practice scarcely known in revolutions. Should a Prince and his people differ, the chief passion it would excite in me, would be a desire to make peace between them. To our everlasting dishonour, more mischief was done in the Birmingham riots, than in overturning the whole French government *.

Perhaps a preconcerted plan was formed to disturb the dinner. Many hints were dropped which seem to confirm it.

* With all these occurrences, I believe the riots would not have taken place, had it not been for two men of desperate fortunes, who probably expected a place or a pension; a hungry Attorney, and a leading Justice. The first succeeded, and was appointed Barrack Master. To patch up a shattered fortune he drew accommodation bills. He became a bankrupt, ruined many persons, died about the year 1794 many thousand pounds in debt, and his corpse, if I remember right, was arrested. I have been informed that his effects paid eighteen-pence in the pound.

The Justice had succeeded to an estate of about £.600 a year. He soon became poor, and was often arrested. He died a year or two after the Attorney, and in March 1810, his effects, in a first and final dividend, paid TWO-PENCE in the pound.

It is surprising that men of a liberal education should persevere in the antient mode of quarrelling for religion. She no where authorizes it. The Christian religion teaches meekness. Every thing which differs from this rule is unchristian. A man possessed of the least reflection well knows it is impossible to bring the human race into one mind, neither is it worth the trial. Disputes, instead of converting the man to my sentiments, tend to confirm him in his own. They may widen a breach, but never close one. Besides, it has never yet been determined what true religion is. It has varied in all ages. What was right to-day, was wrong to-morrow. Synods and Councils have been doing and undoing from the edicts of Constantine down to the convocations of the clergy.

As the true religion has its foundation in no fixed ideas, it follows that true religion is that which a man chooses himself, and not that which another chooses for him. Conscience can bear no controul. Can law hold dominion over the mind? To force a religion upon a man is an unjust exertion of power. What man has a right to direct his fellow men in their worship? What imperious mortal shall say to his Creator, "You shall have no incense

"but what passes through my hands. I will
"hold the keys of Heaven, and admit or repel
"what offerings I please!"

Were I to give a confession of faith, I should readily pronounce, that every religion upon earth is right, and yet none are perfect, for perfection is not with us. Infinite wisdom has appointed many ways to happiness. The road a man takes is of less consequence than his conduct in that road. The different modes of conducting worship are only ceremonials, which are, in themselves, indifferent. Every species of religion tends to improve the man, otherwise it is not religion. Should a Jew cheat me, I have no right to charge it to his religion, but to his *want* of religion: he must have fallen short of its principles. If a Presbyterian is accused of lying, he falls short of his profession. If a Churchman is accused of swearing, he will find it difficult to justify himself by the liturgy. Hence it follows, that I cannot blame either the King or the Church, though my houses were destroyed in those names, for it was done by people who would have sold their King for a jug of ale, and demolished the Church for a bottle of gin. The few among them who were instigators, better understood thirty-nine bottles of wine than the thirty-nine articles. These are the weeds of the Church, the tares among wheat. The real members of the Church of England disdain every idea of wanton cruelty. If one religion merits a preference to another, that preference ought to arise from an extension of benevolence. This character, I am told, belongs to the disciples of the celebrated Emanuel Swedenborg, for they, with open arms, enfold the *whole* human race, and treat them as brethren. Upon this principle a doubt arises, whether our national establishment is a true Church, for she has been unfriendly to the Dissenters in England, and the slaves in America. She has now been supported by ten thousand " d——n your bloods," armed with bludgeons and lighted faggots; she therefore seems under the necessity of justifying what these members have done, or disowning them as brethren. Should they be found to be " *fellow churchmen,*" the Church stands in need of purging, for her constitution is foul.

I am, however, a firm friend to our present establishment, notwithstanding her blemishes. When I attend its worship, for I occasionally do, I can sincerely join in the petitions for her prosperity, and that of the king; and in convivial moments have no objection to drink both; but not that church which was bellowed out of ten thousand filthy mouths, and chalked in disgrace upon as many houses on the 14th of July. This must be proved a church, before I can either pray for, or drink to, its success.

I never attempted to make a convert, nor ever will for this reason: I consider every person as possessed of the powers of free agency, and an absolute right to his own faith. If he asks my sentiments, I have a right to give them, but in no case to force his own; neither am I a slave to other men's creeds, forms, or articles of faith, for though they may be drawn from the sacred fountain, that fountain is open to me, and I can draw for myself.

It appears from the above confession of faith, that I am not only a Presbyterian, but a Churchman, a Quaker, a Baptist, a Roman Catholic, a Muggletonian, nay all the religions in the alphabet: in other words, I would have all perfectly free, because, as I wish to be supported in my own worship, I am bound to support every man in his. I never despised another because he differed from me; it was part of his birth-right, and I think it an honour that I have friends of every persuasion. The late worthy Mr. Newling, Rector of St. Philip's, courted my friendship, had it, has taken my arm and sheltered it under his own, with this affecting remark, "Though we pursue different "roads, we may meet at last."

It would be happy if a man could enjoy his own opinions, and let another alone in his. "The ardent desire of making proselytes," as I have observed in the History of Derby, "has "been the bane of the Christian world." However just might have been Dr. Priestley's sentiments, yet, had he not promulgated them on one side, and party violence opposed them on the other, perhaps the peace of my life had never been wrecked in the dreadful tempest of ninety-one, but I had continued upon an equal footing with my fellow-townsmen. If the Doctor chooses to furnish the world with candles, it reflects a lustre upon himself, but there is no necessity to oblige every man to carry one. It is the privilege of an Englishman to walk in darkness if he chuses.

The fatal 14th of July was now arrived, a day that will mark Birmingham with disgrace for ages to come. The laws had lost their protection, every security of the inhabitants was given up, the black friends of hell were whistled together, and let loose for unmerited destruction. She has reason to keep *that* anniversary in sackcloth and ashes. About eighty persons of various denominations dined together at the Hotel. During dinner, which was short, perhaps from three to five o'clock, the infant mob collected under the auspices of a few in elevated life, began with hooting, crying *Church and King,* and broke the Hotel windows.

All the endeavours to stop this violence were, "Do not break Dudley's windows, he is a "Churchman." The inference is plain, *You may break Presbyterian windows.* A few of our leading people have been reproached for their behaviour, and I must confess in all their vindications there is a fallacy. Their conduct divides itself into two parts, that *while the mob were assembling,* and that *when assembled.*

Only the *latter* of these is touched upon. There is too much reason to believe the superiors wished to raise the mob, and fatally succeeded, and I believe they afterwards wished to lay it but could not.

Tumultuous crowds seldom *rise of themselves,* except to redress a supposed grievance of their own, as a scarcity of work, oppressive taxes, a want of provisions, to prevent an inclosure, or raise the price of labour. If therefore they do not *rise,* nothing is plainer than that they must have been *raised. The Church and King* must have been put into their mouths, for they know but little of either. The fine arts of raising a mob are well understood. A smile, a glance, a word, nay even the presence of a superior not in professed opposition will do the work. Those trifles which are so far from criminating that they can scarcely be reduced to words, are well understood by a willing mob, and will accomplish the end. When a body of insurgents rose at Nottingham to demolish the mills because bread was scarce, one who commanded the mischievous tribe, said with a significant side-glance, " Do not meddle with Mr. " Wyre's mill." The true meaning was well understood, the mill was instantly destroyed, and the abettor safe. Had a mob asked the late John Wyrley, " If he would allow them " to knock the powder out of Dr. Priestley's " wig?" would he have *smiled* assent? When a rabble, assembled for mischief, look up to their superiors, is it prudent to say, " We will " always be friends to the Birmingham lads."* This is a laudable expression taken in a literal sense; but its meaning was fraught with destruction. If a Reverend Divine should influence half Birmingham, and should be told, " The mob are now destroying Dr. Priestley's " house," would it be prudent to say, " that's

---

* This was said by the Magistrate mentioned in Note, page 163.

" right?" These two small words are sufficient to prove his private sentiments, and half this is sufficient to fire a street. Perhaps this gentleman has a taste for antiquity; and as burning was the voice of the pulpit ages back, he may not wish to alter it.

As Mr. Chillingworth walked by the Hotel early in the afternoon of the 14th, twenty or thirty people were assembled, all quiet; he heard one of the town-beadles say to another: " This will be such a day as we never saw." " Why so?" says Chillingworth. After repeated inquiries, one of them replied, " The Gentle-" men will not suffer this treatment from the " Presbyterians, they will be pissed on no lon-" ger." The beadles could not make this remark without having heard hostile expressions fall from the Gentlemen, which proves a preconcerted plan.

Every political mob has an owner. That in the reign of Richard the Second had Wat Tyler. That under Henry the Sixth, Jack Cade. Those in the reign of Queen Anne were commanded by Dr. Sacheverel and his subalterns. Those under George the First by the Jacobites. That in 1780, by Lord George Gordon; and this, I am sorry to say, by some of our *principal* inhabitants.

It was now between eight and nine, the numbers of the mob were increased, their spirits were inflamed. Dr. Priestley was sought for, but he had not dined at the Hotel. The magistrates who had dined at the Swan, a neighbouring tavern, by way of counterbalance huzzaed *Church and King*, waving their hats, which inspired fresh vigour into the mob, so that they verily thought and often declared, they acted with the *approbation* at least of the higher powers, and that what they did was right. The windows of the hotel being broken, a gentleman said*, " You have done mischief " enough *here*, go to the meetings." A simple remark, and almost without a precise meaning, but it involved a dreadful combination of ideas. There was no need to say, " Go and burn the " Meetings." The mob marched down Bull-street under the smiles of magistrates. It has been said that these were compelled to echo the cry of the multitude, but it is not wholly true. While the insurgents were intoxicated with liquor and power, and carried vengeance where they pleased, it was necessary to say as they said; and many persons damned the Presbyterians who were their real friends; but

* This gentleman was the Attorney mentioned in Note, page 163.

till the New Meeting was condemned, this was far from being the case; every smile, word, or huzza encouraged them. Had the same wish existed to *repress*, as did to *raise* them, no mischief had ensued.

An enraged mob is one of the greatest calamities under heaven. One would think Lord George Gordon had taught a lesson that would have lasted for ages! This many-headed monster was designed to be let loose upon us as a gentle scourge only; but what man would play with a candle amidst gun-powder, because he thinks he is master of the blaze? If destruction is the consequence, does it palliate the evil to say, " he never meant it?" Nor is his striving to extinguish the flame, when the conflagration is beyond his power, an extenuation of his folly.

The New Meeting was broken open without ceremony, the pews, cushions, books, and pulpit were dashed to pieces, and in half an hour the whole was in a blaze, while the savage multitude rejoiced at the view.

I am now come to the second part of my narrative, and entirely agree with the magistrates, that it was not in their power, by *persuasions*, to quell the mob. But let me ask, when the spirit of a vile banditti is raised into fury, were they ever known to listen to persuasion? Every one can tell that nothing short of fire-arms can effect the purpose. This was the moment to arm the willing inhabitants, and send express for a military force.

The Old Meeting was the next mark of the mob. This underwent the fate of the New; and here again a system seems to have been adopted, for the engines were suffered to play upon the adjoining houses to prevent their taking fire, but not upon the Meeting-house, which was levelled with the ground.

The mob then undertook a march of more than a mile, to the house of Dr. Priestley, which was plundered and burnt without mercy, the doctor and his family barely escaping. Exclusive of the furniture, a very large and valuable library was destroyed, the collection of a long and assiduous life.

But the greatest loss that Dr. Priestley sustained, was in the destruction of his philosophical apparatus, and his remarks. These can never be replaced. I am inclined to think he would not have destroyed his apparatus and manuscripts for any sum of money that could have been offered him. His love to man was great, his usefulness greater. I have been informed by the faculty that his experimental discoveries on air, applied to medical purposes, have preserved the lives of thousands; and, in return, he can scarcely preserve his own.

A clergyman attended this outrage, and was charged with examining and even *pocketing* the manuscripts. I think he paid the Doctor a compliment, by shewing a regard for his works. I will farther do him the justice to believe he never meant to keep them, to invade the Doctor's profession by turning philosopher, or to sell them, though valuable; but only to exchange them with the minister for preferment. There may be fortitude in dying for treason, but there is more profit in getting *a living* by it.

Breaking the windows of the hotel, burning the two Meeting-houses, and Dr. Priestley's, finished the dreadful work of Thursday night. To all this I was a perfect stranger, for I had left the town early in the evening, and slept in the country.

When I arose the next morning, July 15, my servant told me what had happened. I was inclined to believe it only a report; but coming to the town, I found it a melancholy truth, and matters wore an unfavourable aspect, for one mob cannot continue long unactive, and there were two or three floating up and down, seeking whom they might devour, though I was not under the least apprehension of danger to myself. The affrighted inhabitants came in bodies to ask my opinion. As the danger admitted of no delay, I gave this short answer, " Apply to the magistrates, and request four " things: to swear in as many constables as " are willing, and arm them. To apply to the " commanding officer of the recruiting parties " for his assistance. To apply to Lord Beau- " champ to call out the militia in the neighbour- " hood; and to write to the Secretary at War " for a military force." What became of my four hints is uncertain, but the result proved they were lost.

Towards noon a body of near a thousand attacked the mansion of my friend John Ryland, Esq. at Easy hill. He was not at the dinner. Every room was entered with eagerness; but the cellar, in which were wines to the amount of £.300, with ferocity. Here they regaled till the roof fell in with the flames, and six or seven lost their lives. I was surprised at this rude attack, for I considered Mr. Ryland as a friend to the whole human race. He had done more public business than any other within my knowledge, and not only without a reward, but without a fault. I thought an obelisk ought rather to have been raised to his own honour, than his house burnt down to the disgrace of others.

About this time a person approached me in tears, and told me " my house was condemned " to fall." As I had never, with design, offended any man, nor heard any allegations against my conduct, I could not credit the information. Being no man's enemy, I could not believe I had an enemy myself. I thought the people, who had known me forty years, esteemed me too much to injure me. But I drew from fair premises false conclusions. My fellow sufferers had been guilty of *one* fault, but I of *two*. I was not only a Dissenter, but an active Commissioner in the Court of Requests. With regard to the first my sentiments were never rigid. There seems to me as much reason to allow for a difference of opinion, as of face. Nature never designed to make two things alike. Whoever will take the trouble to read my works, will neither find a persecuting, disloyal, or republican thought. In the office of Commissioner I studied the good of others, not my own. Three points I ever kept in view: to keep order, do justice tempered with lenity, and compose differences. Armed with power, I have put a period to thousands of quarrels, have softened the rugged tempers of devouring antagonists, and, without expence to themselves, sent them away friends. But the fatal rock upon which I split was, *I never could find a way to let both parties win.* If ninety-nine were content, and *one* was not, that one would be more solicitous to injure me, than the ninety-nine to serve me.

It never appeared when the military force was sent for, but I believe about noon this day. The express, however, did not arrive in London till the next, at two in the afternoon. What could occasion this insufferable neglect, or why the Riot Act was omitted to be read sooner, I leave to the magistrates. Many solicitations were made to the magistrates for assistance to quell the mob, but the answer was, "*Pacific measures are adopted.*" Capt. Archibald, and Lieutenants Smith and Maxwell, of recruiting parties, offered their service; still the same answer. A gentleman asked, if he might arm his dependants? "The hazard will be yours." Again, whether he might carry a brace of pistols in his own defence? "If you kill a man you must be responsible."

Thus sentenced and tied, we were to suffer destruction without remedy. Had the inhabitants been suffered to arm, there were people enough willing to oppose the rioters; but every degree of courage was extinguished, and an universal damp prevailed. The same timid spirit operated as was found in the ancient Britons, when they called in the Saxons.

About noon also some of my friends advised me " to take care of my goods, for my house " must come down." I treated the advice as ridiculous, and replied, " *That* was their duty, " and the duty of every inhabitant, for my case " was theirs. I had only the power of an indi-" vidual. Besides, fifty waggons could not carry " off my stock in trade, exclusive of the fur-" niture of my house; and if they could, where " must I deposit it?" I sent, however, a small quantity of paper to a neighbour, who returned it, and the whole afterwards fell a prey to rapine.

All business was now at a stand. The shops were shut. The town prison, and that of the Court of Requests, were thrown open, and their strength was added to that of their deliverers. Some gentlemen advised the insurgents assembled in New Street to disperse; when one, whom I well knew, said, " Do not disperse, " they want to sell us. If you will pull down " Hutton's house, I will give you two guineas " to drink, for it was owing to him I lost a "cause in the Court." The bargain was instantly struck, and my building fell.

About three o'clock they approached me. I expostulated with them. "They would have "money." I gave them all I had, even to a single half-penny, which one of them had the meanness to take. They wanted more, "nor "would they submit to this treatment," and began to break the windows, and attempted the goods. I then borrowed all I instantly could, which I gave them, and shook a hundred hard and black hands. "We will have "some drink." "You shall have what you "please if you will not injure me." I was then seized by the collar on both sides, and hauled a prisoner to a neighbouring public house, where, in half an hour, I found an ale-score against me of 329 gallons.

The affrighted magistrates were now sitting at the Swan in Bull-street, swearing constables, whom they ordered to rendezvous in St. Philip's Church-yard, "where they would "meet them." Here the new-created officers, armed with small sticks, waited with impatience, but no magistrates came. They then bent their course, without a leader, to New Street, attacked the mob, which had been with me, most furiously, and in a minute dispersed it. As my house was in the utmost danger, they ought to have staid to protect it, instead of which, they went to guard Mr. Ryland's, nearly burnt down. Here the mob came upon them with double force, took their weapons, totally routed them, maimed several, and killed Mr. Thomas Ashwin.

My son wishing to secure our premises, purchased the favour of *Rice*, one of the leaders, who promised to preserve his person and property, and assured him that his men would implicitly obey him. Hearing Mr. Taylor's house was in danger, they marched to Bordsley, one mile, to save it, but found another mob had begun to rob and burn it. I could assign no more reason why they attempted Mr. Taylor's property than Mr. Ryland's. No man could cultivate peace and social harmony more. His is the art of doing good by stealth. Offence was never charged against him; but, alas, he was a Dissenter. The sons of plunder, and their abettors, forgot that the prosperity of Birmingham was owing to a Dissenter, father to the man whose property they were destroying. He not only supplied thousands of that class who were burning his son's house, with the means of bread, but taught their directors the roads to invention, industry, commerce, and affluence; roads which no man trod before him. Nay, when the Meeting-houses were fallen, and the Church was falling, even this violent outrage itself was quelled by the vigilance of a Dissenter, Captain Polhill.

Rice and my son, being too late to render any essential service to Mr. Taylor's premises, returned to save our own. But meeting in Digbeth some of our furniture, *Rice* declared it was too late; that he could have *kept* off the mob, but could not *bring* them off. Perhaps the instant view of plunder had changed his sentiments. Meeting a rogue near the Swan, with a bundle of paper worth five pounds, *Rice* damned him, and ordered him to lay it down. The rogue instantly obeyed. *Rice* sat upon it, while my son requested a neighbour to take it in, who refused. He then applied to a second, but received the same answer, and was obliged to leave *Rice* and the paper to secure his own person.

Rice then joined the depredators in destroying my house and its contents, and the next morning was one of the leaders in burning my house at Bennett's Hill. These facts were proved against him on his trial by the clearest evidence, and yet an alibi was admitted from one who swore he was then drinking a pot of ale with a soldier at a public house; but, had he sworn he was drinking with the man in the moon, the oath would have been freely admitted.

In this man we behold a curious picture of the human mind. He could not keep out of action, though that action was mischief. Left to himself he would quickly destroy property without the least animosity to the owner, and, for a few shillings, would save it without the least love. Had he been time enough to prevent the mob, I have no doubt of his fidelity; but as he was not, he could not refrain from becoming a plunderer.

About five this evening, Friday, I had retreated to my house at Bennett's Hill, where, about three hours before, I had left my afflicted wife and daughter, and had seen a mob at Mr. Tukes's house in my road. I found that my people had applied to a neighbour to secure some of our furniture, who refused: to a second, who consented; but another shrewdly remarking that he would run a hazard of having his own house burnt, a denial was the consequence. A third request was made, but cut short with a *no*. The fourth man consented, and we emptied the house into his house and barn. Before night, however, he caught the terror of the neighbourhood, and ordered the principal part of the furniture back, and we were obliged to obey.

At midnight I could see from my house the flames of Bordsley Hall rise with dreadful aspect. I learned that after I quitted Birmingham the mob attacked my house there three times. My son bought them off repeatedly; but in the fourth, which began about nine at night, they laboured till eight the next morning, when they had so completely ravaged my dwelling, that I write this Narrative in a house without furniture, without roof, door, chimney-piece, window, or window-frame. During this interval of eleven hours, a lighted candle was brought four times, with intent to fire the house, but, by some humane foot, was kicked out. At my return I found a large heap of shavings, chips, and faggots, covered with about three hundred weight of coal, in an under kitchen, ready for lighting.

The different pieces of furniture were hoisted to the upper windows to complete their destruction; and those pieces which survived the fall, were dashed to atoms by three bludgeoners stationed below for that service. Flushed with this triumphant exercise of lawless power, the words, " Down with the Court of Conscience!"

"No more ale scores to be paid," were repeated. A gentleman remarked to the grand slaughterers of my goods, "You'll be hanged as the "rioters were in 1780." "O damn him," was the reply, "He made me pay fifteen shillings "in the Court of Conscience." This remark was probably true, for that diabolical character which could employ itself in such base work, was very likely to cheat another of fifteen shillings, and I just as likely to prevent him.

Burning Mr. Ryland's house at Easy Hill, Mr. Taylor's at Bordesly, and the destruction of mine at Birmingham, were the work of Friday the 15th.

Saturday the 16th was ushered in with fresh calamities to myself. The triumphant mob, at four in the morning, attacked my premises at Bennett's Hill, and threw out the furniture I had tried to save. It was consumed in three fires, the marks of which remain, and the house expired in one vast blaze. The women were as alert as the men. One female, who had stolen some of the property, carried it home while the house was in flames; but returning, saw the coach-house and stables unhurt, and exclaimed with the decisive tone of an Amazon, "Damn the coach-house, is not that down "yet! We will not do our work by halves!"

She instantly brought a lighted faggot from the building, set fire to the coach-house, and reduced the whole to ashes.

The beautiful and costly mansion of George Humphrys, Esq. was the next victim. He had prepared for a vigorous defence, and would most certainly have been victorious, for he had none but rank cowards to contend with, but female fears overbalanced manly courage. One pistol, charged with powder, sent them away; and though they returned in greater numbers, one blunderbuss would have banished them for ever. His house was sacked, and the internal parts destroyed.

The next sacrifice was the house of William Russell, Esq. at Showell Green. He had prepared men, arms, ammunition, and a determined resolution for defence; but, finding his auxiliaries rotten, he gave up his house and its contents to the flames.

The house of Thomas Russell, Esq., and that of Mr. Hawkes at Moseley-Wake Green, were the next attacked. They were plundered and greatly injured, but not burnt. To be a Dissenter was a crime not to be forgiven, but a rich Dissenter merited the extreme of vengeance.

Moseley Hall, the property of John Taylor, Esq. and inhabited by Lady Carhampton, mother to the Duchess of Cumberland, was not to be missed. Neither the years of this lady, being blind with age, nor her alliance to the Crown, were able to protect it. She was ordered by the mob to remove her furniture, and told, if she wanted help, they would assist her; but that the mansion must not stand. She was therefore, like Lot, hastened away before the flames arose, but not by angels.

As riches could not save a man, neither could poverty. The mob next fell upon a poor but sensible Presbyterian parson, the Rev. John Hobson, of Balsall Heath, and burnt his all.

From the house of Mr. Hobson, the intoxicated crew proceeded to that of William Piddick at King's Heath, inhabited by an inoffensive blind man, John Harwood, a Baptist; and this ended their work on Saturday the 16th, in which were destroyed *eight* houses, exclusive of Mr. Coates's, which was plundered and damaged.

Some of the Nobility, Justices, and Gentlemen arrived this day, sat in council, drank their wine, harangued the mobs, wished them to desist, told them what mischief they had done, which they already knew; and that they had done enough, which they did not believe; but not one word of fire-arms, a fatal proof that *pacific measures* were adopted. To tell a mob " They have done enough," supposes that something *ought* to have been done. A clear ratification of *part* at least of their proceedings.

On this day some curious advertisements appeared. I shall insert one or two for the dastardly spirit they exhibit; another for its singular composition.

" *Friends* and fellow Countrymen.

It is earnestly requested that every true friend to the Church of England, and to the laws of his country, will reflect how much a continuance of the present proceedings must injure that Church and that King they are intended to support, and how highly unlawful it is to destroy the rights and property of any of our neighbours. And all true friends to the town and trade of Birmingham, in particular, are intreated to forbear immediately from all riotous and violent proceedings, dispersing and returning peaceably to their callings, as the only way to do credit to themselves and *their cause*, and to promote the peace, happiness, and prosperity of this great and flourishing town."

"Important information to the Friends of Church and King.

Friends and Brother Churchmen.

Being conscious you are unacquainted that the great losses which are sustained by your burning and destroying of the houses of so many individuals, will eventually fall upon the County at large, and not upon the persons to whom they belonged, we feel it our duty to inform you, that the damage already done, upon the best calculation that can be made, will amount to upwards of *one hundred thousand pounds!* the whole of which enormous sum will be charged upon the respective parishes, and paid out of the rates. We therefore, as your *friends*, conjure you immediately to desist from the destruction of any more houses, otherwise the very proceedings of your zeal for shewing your attachment to your *Church and King*, will eventually be the means of most seriously injuring innumerable families, who are hearty supporters of government, and bring on an addition of taxes, which *yourselves and the rest of the friends of the Church* will feel a very grievous burthen. This we assure you was the case in London, when there were so many houses and public buildings burnt and destroyed in the year 1780, and you may rely upon it will be the case on the present occasion. And we must observe to you, that any farther violent proceedings will more offend your King and Country, than serve the cause of him and the Church.

Fellow Churchmen, as you love your King, regard his laws, and restore peace.

GOD SAVE THE KING."

This humiliating address, signed by sixteen gentlemen, disgraces the pages which record it. It was no more likely to soften the breast of the savages, than reflect honour upon the Authors. What should we think of the folly of that farmer who, while swarms of vermin were destroying his property, should call them *friends and brothers*, tell them sedately what mischief they had done, and humbly petition them to desist! I know not the authors, nor shall I ever inquire; but as I am well assured that many of the names crept in without the consent of the owners, I will not subject them to the public eye.

" Whereas some detestable villains, from the most wicked motives to injure Mr. William Windsor, a tenant of Mr. Brooke's at Ashsted, have circulated a report, that Mr. Windsor's buildings at Ashsted belong to the Corporation at Coventry. As such report is evidently intended to *incense the friends of Church and King* to destroy the property of the said W. Windsor, Mr. Brooke, whose *most hearty* attachment is well known to the real friends of Church and King, begs leave to address them with the most solemn assurance, upon the word and honour of a Church and King's man, that the Corporation of Coventry, nor any Presbyterian, have any concern or interest whatever in the buildings and property of the said W. Windsor, at Ashsted, nor any of the buildings of Mr. Brooke, or any other person at Ashsted. But that upon all occasions for the City of Coventry, where the said W. Windsor lived before he came to Ashsted, he uniformly voted against the Corporation and Presbyterian interest, and always *supported the real true blue,* which is the Church and King party. Mr. Brooke therefore is convinced that this address will be attended to by the *gentlemen of the Church and King party*, and offers a reward of ten guineas for the detection of the *rascals* who gave rise to so false a report.

CHURCH AND KING FOR EVER."

Some have suspected that this address, which deems every man a detestable villain who is uncertain whether W. Windsor or the Corporation are interested at Ashsted, and which tells us the friends of the Church are the destroyers of property, issued from a Spit-fire club. I shall convey this specimen of modern rhetoric to the next generation. The figures being in *real true blue*, cannot fade. I should suspect that William Windsor was a Presbyterian, from the great pains taken to shelter his buildings under the Church, and convince the world he is a *Church-and-King's man, and a real True Blue.* I have read of blue hospitals, blue boys, and blue devils, but never of a blue church, or a blue king. As, therefore, the Church of England is not of that colour, he cannot, by his own confession, be one of her sons. The man who supports the real True Blue, can only be he who wears a blue coat; consequently, as the Dissenters are, at this moment, the most depressed people in the whole Island, and as they wear blue indiscriminately with other denominations of Christians, he undoubtedly meant to elevate them to the rank of their fellow citizens: as such, he deserves a *Vote of Plate* equally with " The Gentlemen " of the Church and King party."

Dissentions died away, under the apprehension of common danger. Half the watch-word of the mob, *the Church*, was afraid; for many of the establishment had been plundered, and horror was painted in every face. They might say with Moses in the Mount, " I exceedingly " fear and quake." Nay, it appears from the above advertisements, that those who professed the most " attachment to Church and King" trembled.

Inquiries were made every moment, " When " will the military arrive to defend us?" but not one thought occurred of defending ourselves. Such is the infatuation of the mind, and such the consequence when mobs are masters.

With regard to myself, I felt more resentment than fear; and would most willingly have made one, even of a small number, to arm and face them. My family, however, would not suffer me to stay in Birmingham, and I was, on Saturday morning the 16th, obliged to run away like a thief, and hide myself from the world. I had injured no man, and yet durst not face man. I had spent a life in distributing justice to others, and now wanted it myself. However fond of home, and whatever were my comforts there, I was obliged, with my family, to throw myself upon the world without money in my pocket.

We stopped at Sutton Coldfield, and as we had no abode, took apartments for the summer. Here I fell into company with a clergyman, a lawyer, a country 'squire, and two other persons, who all lamented the proceedings at Birmingham, perhaps through fear, they being in its vicinity, and blamed Dr. Priestley as the cause. I asked what he had done? "He has "written such letters! Besides, what shame-"ful healths were drunk at the Hotel." As I was not at the dinner, I could not speak of the healths; but I replied, "If the Doctor, or any "one else, had broken the laws of his country, "those laws were open to punish him, but the "present mode of revenge was detested even "by savages." We left our argument, as arguments are usually left by disputants, where we found it.

Things passed on till the evening, when the mistress of the house was seized with the fashionable apprehensions of the day, and requested us to depart, lest her house should be burnt. We were obliged to pack up, which was done in one minute, for we had only the clothes which covered us, and roll on to Tamworth.

I asked the people at the Castle Inn whether they knew me? They answered in the negative. I had now a most painful task to undergo. "Though I have entered your house," said I, "as a common guest, I am a desolate wanderer, "without money to pay, or property to pledge." The man who had paid his bills during sixty-eight years, must have been sensibly touched to make this declaration. If he has feelings, it will call them forth. Their countenance fell on hearing it. I farther told them I was known to Mr. Robert Bage, a gentleman in the neighbourhood, whom I would request to pay my bill. My credit rose in proportion to the value of the name mentioned. Myself, my wife, son, and daughter, passed the night at the Castle at Tamworth.

We now enter upon Sunday the 17th. I rose early, not from sleep, but from bed. The lively sky, and bright sun, seemed to rejoice the whole creation, and dispel every gloom but mine. I could see through the eye of every face, that serenity of mind which I had lost.

As the storm in Birmingham was too violent to last, it seemed prudent to be near the place, that I might embrace the first opportunity of protecting the wreck of a shattered fortune. We moved to Castle Bromwich.

Ranting, roaring, drinking, burning, is a life of too much rapidity for the human frame to support. Our black sovereigns had now held it nearly three days and nights, when nature called for rest; and the bright morning displayed the fields, roads, and hedges, lined with *friends and brother Church-men*, dead drunk. There were, however, enough awake to kindle new fires. On Sunday the 17th they bent their course to Wharstock, a single house, inhabited by Mr. Cox, and licensed for public worship, which, after emptying the cellar, they burnt.

Penetrating one mile farther, they arrived at Kingswood Meeting-house, which they laid in ashes. This solitary place had fallen by the hand of violence in the beginning of George the First, for which a person of the name of *Dollax* was executed, and from him it acquired the name of *St. Dollax*, which it still bears. He was the first person who suffered after passing the Riot Act.

Three hundred yards beyond, they arrived at the parsonage house, which underwent the same fate.

Perhaps they found the parish of King's Norton too barren to support a mob in affluence; for they returned towards Birmingham, which, though dreadfully sacked, yet was better furnished with money, strong liquors, and various other property. King's Norton is an extensive manor belonging to the King, whose name they were advancing upon the walls, whose honour they were augmenting by burning three places of worship in his manor, and by destroying nine houses, the property of his peaceable tenants.

The Wednesbury colliers now assembled in a body, and marched into Birmingham, to join their brethren under *Church and King*: but finding no mob in the town, they durst not venture upon an attack, but retreated in disappointment. As they could not, however, return with a safe conscience without mischief, they attacked Mr. Male's house, at Belle Vue, six miles from the town; but he, with that spirit which ought to have animated us, beat them off.

While I was hidden at Castle Bromwich, a gentleman sent up his compliments and requested admission. We appeared personal strangers. He expressed a sorrow for my misfortunes, and observed in the course of our conversation, " That as I was obliged to leave " home abruptly, and had uncertainty before " me, perhaps I was not supplied with a suffi- " ciency of cash; that he was returning from "a journey, and had not much left, but that "what he and his servant had was at my ser- "vice, and to-morrow he would send him with "whatever sum I should name." Surprized at so singular a kindness, which I could neither merit nor expect, I requested the name of the person to whom I was indebted for so benevolent an act. He replied, "*John Finch*, banker "of Dudley." Those generous traits of character fictitiously ascribed to heroes of romance, were realized in this gentleman. With sorrow I read in the public papers, in December following, the death of this worthy man, whom I never saw before or after. I could not refrain from going to take a view of my house at Bennett's Hill, above three miles distant from Castle Bromwich. Upon Washwood Heath I met four waggons, loaded with Lady Carhampton's furniture, attended by a body of rioters, with their usual arms, as protectors. I passed through the midst of them, was known, and insulted, but kept a sullen silence. The stupid dunces vociferated, "No popery! Down with "the Pope!": forgetting that Presbyterians were never remarkable for favouring the religion of that potentate. In this instance, however, they were ignorantly right; for I consider myself a true friend to the Roman Catholics, and to every *peaceable* profession, but not to the spiritual power of any; for this, instead of humanizing the mind, and drawing the affections of one man towards another, has bound the world in fetters, and set at variance those who were friends.

I saw the ruins yet burning of that once happy spot, which had, for many years, been my calm retreat; the scene of contemplation, of domestic felicity; the source of health and contentment. Here I had consulted the dead, and attempted to amuse the living. Here I had exchanged THE WORLD for my little family.

Perhaps fifty people were enjoying themselves upon those ruins where I had possessed an exclusive right, but I was now viewed as an intruder. The prejudiced vulgar, who never inquire into causes and effects, or the true state of things, fix the idea of criminality upon the man who is borne down by the crowd, and every foot is elevated to kick him. My premises, laid open by ferocious authority, were free to every trespasser, and I was the only person who did not rejoice in the ruins. It was not possible to retreat from that favourite place without a gloom upon the mind, which was the result of ill-treatment, by power without right. This excited a contempt of the world.

Returning to Castle Bromwich, the same rioters were at the door of the Inn, and I durst not enter. Thus the man, who, for misconduct, merited the halter, could face the world; and I who had not offended, was obliged to skulk behind hedges. Night came on. The inhabitants of the village surrounded me, and seemed alarmed. They told me it was dangerous to stay among them, and advised me *for my own safety* to retreat to Stonnal. Thus I found it as difficult to procure an asylum for myself, as, two days before, I had done for my goods. I was avoided as a pestilence; the waves of sorrow rolled over me, and beat me down with multiplied force; every one came heavier than the last. My children were distressed. My wife, through long affliction, ready to quit my own arms for those of death; and I myself reduced to the sad necessity of humbly begging a draught of water at a cottage! What a reverse of situation! How thin the barriers between affluence and poverty! By the smiles of the inhabitants of Birmingham I acquired a fortune; by an astonishing defect in our police I lost it. In the morning of the 15th I was a rich man; in the evening I was ruined. At ten at night on the 17th, I might have been found leaning on a mile-stone upon Sutton

Coldfield, without food, without a home, without money, and, what is the last resort of the wretched, without hope. What had I done to merit this severe calamity? Why did not I stay at home, oppose the villains at my own door, and sell my life at the dearest rate! I could have destroyed several before I had fallen myself. This may be counted rash, but unmerited distress like mine could operate but two ways; a man must either sink under it, or become desperate.

While surrounded by the gloom of night, and the still greater gloom which oppressed the mind, a person seemed to hover about me who had evidently some design. Whether an honest man or a knave gave me no concern; for I had nothing to lose but life, which I esteemed of little value. He approached nearer with seeming diffidence. "Sir, is not your "name Hutton?" "Yes." "I have good "news. The light-horse, some time ago, passed "through Sutton, in their way to Birmingham." As I had been treated with nine falsehoods for one truth, I asked his authority. He replied, "I saw them." This arrival I knew would put a period to plunder. The inhabitants of Birmingham received them with open arms, with illuminations, and viewed them as their deliverers.

We left the mob towards evening on Sunday the 17th returning from King's Norton. They cast a glance upon the well-stored cellar, and valuable plunder, of Edgbaston Hall, the residence of Dr. Withering, who perhaps never heard a Presbyterian sermon, and yet is as amiable a character as he who has. Before their work was completed, the words *light-horse* sounded in their ears; when this formidable banditti mouldered away, no soul knew how, and not a shadow of it could be found.

Exclusive of the devastations above-mentioned, the rabble did numberless mischiefs. The lower class among us, long inured to *fire*, had now treated themselves with a full regale of their favourite element. If their teachers are faithful to their trust, they will present to their idea another powerful flame in reversion.

The reader will pardon me if I draw a parallel between the great Lord Mansfield and myself. He fell by a lawless mob in 1780, and I in 1791. He said in the House of Lords what I, with sorrow, say out: " I speak and " write from memory, for, alas! my books are " destroyed, never to be replaced."

The self-created law-givers, however, (the mob) conferred upon me a dreadful kindness; they did not crucify me among thieves, for my fellow-sufferers are men of the most respectable characters.

As the prosperity of Birmingham depends upon its commerce, and the security of the inhabitants, every obstacle raised against these acts with multiplied force. It is therefore sound policy to give encouragement to one, and stability to the other. The ten persons, who claim redress for their sufferings, are masters of nearly a million sterling, all arising from the manufactures of the place. This property could not have been acquired without an honour and improvement to the town, and a benefit to every inhabitant. Three of the sufferers, who are merchants, employ more than ten thousand people. The punishment inflicted on individuals becomes a public detriment, by injuring the place, and a private one by cutting off the bread of the laborious class.

Next morning, Monday the 18th, I returned to Birmingham, to be treated with the sad spectacle of another house in ruins. Every part of the mutilated building declared that the hand of violence had been there.

My friends received me with joy; and though they had not fought for me, they had been assiduous in securing some of my property, which, I was told, " had paved half the streets in Birmingham."

Seventeen of my friends offered me their own houses; sixteen of them were of the established church, which indicates that I never was a party man. Our cabinets being rifled, papers against government were eagerly sought after; but the invidious seeker forgot that such papers are not in use among the Dissenters. Instead, however, of finding treasonable papers in mine, they found one of my teeth wrapped in writing paper, and inscribed, "This tooth "was destroyed by a tough crust July 12, 1775, "after a faithful service of more than fifty- "years. I have only thirty-one left." The prize was proclaimed the property of a King, and was conducted into the London papers, in which the world was told, "that the Anti- "quaries had sustained an irreparable injury; "for one of the sufferers in the late riots had "lost a tooth of Richard the Third, found in "Bosworth Field, and valued at £.300."

Some of the rioters absconded. A thousand might have been taken, if taking had been the fashion, but the taker had every obstacle to encounter. As their crimes glared in the strong light of the sun, or rather the fire, the actors were generally known, and the proofs full. Fifteen were committed. Their trials were a mere farce, a joke upon justice, and truly laughable. It is a common remark, that "a "man will catch at a *twig* to save his life;" but here the culprit had no need to seek for a twig, he might be saved by a straw, a thread, or even by the string of a spider. Every assistance was thrown out, and every one was able to bring a rioter out of danger.

The Solicitor of the Treasury was sent from London to conduct the trials of the rioters. He treated me with civility, and said, "If Mr. "Ryland and I would go to his lodgings at "Warwick next Sunday morning at ten, he "would shew us a list of the Jury, and we "should select twelve names to our satisfac- "tion." I thanked him, and took the journey accordingly. Upon perusing the list, I was surprized to find they had but ONE sentiment. I returned the paper with an air of disappoint- ment. "They are all of a sort," said I, "you "may take which *you* please." At that mo- ment John Brooke, the true blue Church and King's man, and the attorney employed against the sufferers, entered, and as silently as if he had listened behind the door. He had, no doubt, fabricated the list. We instantly re- treated.

Rice's case has been mentioned. Another was saved, *because he went to serve the sufferer.*

Whenever the offender procured a character, and one may be picked up in every street, he was sure to be safe. The common Crier rang his bell while Mr. Ryland's house was in flames, to call *on* the mob; but at the trial, " he did " it to call them *off*." Another was charged with " *Pulling down and destroying*," but as the house was afterwards burnt, it was wisely inferred, " he could neither pull down nor de- " stroy that which was burnt."

It was proved against *Hands*, " That he " tore up Mr. Ryland's floor and burnt it;" but he got clear by another attesting that there was no floor. *Careless* stole the pigs, which every one believed, but he was acquitted by his sister swearing that, " he drove them out to " save them." *Watkins* escaped, because the evidence could not tell the number of the rioters. *Four* witnesses, perfectly clear and consistent, accused *Whitehead*, but he was acquitted by the evidence of *one* only, James Mould, who denied all they had said, and observed, " That Whitehead did all he could to " save my property." The real fact was, I hired Mould, with nine others, to guard my house at Bennett's Hill, on Friday night. When the riots were over, he was the man who informed against Whitehead as a ringleader, described his person, name, trade, and place of abode; consequently was the sole cause of his being taken. If, however, he swore him into danger, he was allowed to swear him out. How the Court *looked*, and how the Jury *felt* when facts were set aside, and oaths and characters took their place, I leave to those who were present to decide*.

To acquit the guilty, is declaring him innocent in the face of the world, and is injurious to society. If the law takes its course, and there be found room for mercy, let it flow from its proper fountain, the Crown. By the false lenity of the court, villainy became triumphant. Some of the sufferers' witnesses were injured in their property, others personally abused, and others threatened with death. Nay even the sufferers themselves were daily insulted in the streets. Nor did the behaviour of the insurgents end here; every master who offended his *servant*, in reality offended his *master*, and endangered his house.

Thus *order* is inverted, we are making large strides towards anarchy, and are perfectly ripe for another tumult. As the fishes cannot live

* A gentleman, soon after this, hunting with Mr. Corbett's fox-hounds, was so sure of killing the fox, that he cried, " Nothing but a Birmingham Jury can save him!"

out of their element, so no class of men can act with propriety out of their sphere.

Three criminals were executed; *Cook* for destroying the house of Mr. Russell; *Field* for that of Mr. Taylor; and *Green* for Dr. Priestley's. Mr. Russell would have solicited a pardon for Cook, but found his character so notoriously bad, that there was no ground for his plea. Those of Field and Green are better known to others than myself; they were represented as infernals let loose among men. The world will be apt to draw this conclusion, *None were executed for the Riots*.

The laws of England carry the same level hand to every description of men, a local agreement subsists between the whole body of laws, and every individual: they demand *obedience*, and he *protection*. This agreement cannot be broken without some mismanagement. As by the late convulsions in Birmingham, every man was put in fear, many were plundered, some burnt, some ruined, others obliged to fly, two lost their lives, and all this without one breach of the law; this question naturally arises, *is our Police upon a respectable footing?*

Although the public are in possession of the *toasts* drunk at the Hotel, I shall subjoin them,

that the people both *in* and *out* of Sutton may judge how far they were *shameful*. The company, out of respect to monarchy, had procured from an ingenious artist three figures, which were placed upon the table. One, a fine medallion of the king, encircled with glory, on his right an emblematical figure, representing British Liberty; on the left, another representing Gallic Slavery breaking its chains. These innocent and loyal devices were ruinous; for a spy, whom *I well know*, was sent into the room, and assured the people without, "That the Re-
"volutionists had cut off the King's head, and
" placed it on the table." Thus a man, with a keen belief, like one with a keen appetite, is able to swallow the grossest absurdities.

1. The King and Constitution.

2. The National Assembly, and Patriots of France, whose virtue and wisdom have raised twenty-six millions from the meanest condition of despotism, to the dignity and happiness of freemen.

3. The Majesty of the People.

4. May the Constitution of France be rendered perfect and perpetual.

5. May Great Britain, France, and Ireland, unite in perpetual friendship; and may their

only rivalship be, the extension of peace and liberty, wisdom and virtue.

6. The rights of man. May all nations have the wisdom to understand, and courage to assert and defend them.

7. The true friends of the Constitution of this country, who wish to preserve its spirit by correcting its abuses.

8. May the people of England never cease to remonstrate till their parliament becomes a true national representation.

9. The Prince of Wales.

10. The United States of America; may they for ever enjoy the liberty which they so honourably acquired.

11. May the revolution in Poland prove the harbinger of a more perfect system of liberty extending to that great kingdom.

12. May the nations of Europe become so enlightened as never more to be deluded into savage wars by the ambition of their rulers.

13. May the sword never be unsheathed but for the defence and liberty of our country; and then, may every one cast away the scabbard till the people are safe and free.

14. To the glorious memory of Hampden, Sidney, and other heroes of all ages and nations, who have fought and bled for liberty.

15. To the memory of Dr. Price, and all those illustrious sages who have enlightened mankind in the true principles of civil society.

16. Peace and good will to all mankind.

17. Prosperity to the town of Birmingham.

18. A happy meeting to the friends of liberty on the 14th of July 1792.

The sum total of the above toasts amounts to this, a solicitude for the perfect freedom of man, arising from a love to the species. If I were required to explain the words *Freedom* and *Liberty* in their full extent, I should answer in these simple words, *that each individual think and act as he please, provided no other is injured.*

The military and security arriving, the run-away sufferers returning, and every man in this land of liberty having the free use of his tongue and judgment, it was curious to observe the difference of sentiment. The Dissenters, perhaps to a man, were deeply affected with the melancholy event, as breaking that harmony which had never been disturbed since the fiery days of Sacheverell. The members of the Establishment were divided into three classes: the first, lamented the treatment offered to their neighbours, assisted them in distress, wished a reparation of their loss, and a re-establishment of harmony. These are the mild, the peaceable, and the real members of the Church of England. I am willing to hope they are the most numerous, although the most silent. The next class looked on with indifference, while our houses were in flames, were rather pleased with the novelty, and laughed at us when the scene was over. The third, at the head of whom stood the bigoted part of the clergy, thought our sufferings too mild, called them in the pulpit, " wholesome correction," and wished the same tragedy acted again. These have but two fears; one, lest church preferment should not fall into their hands, and the other, the fear of death; for then the words of our Saviour may be fulfilled: " With whatever measure ye mete, it " shall be measured to you again."

If I were asked the difference between a bigoted and a moderate clergyman, I should explain both in two instances. The Sunday subsequent to the riots, a sermon was preached in one of our Churches from the words of St. Paul, " Let " every soul be obedient to the higher powers." Here those absurd doctrines of the Stuarts, passive obedience, and non-resistance, flamed as warmly as our buildings had done a few days before. Scarcely having a coat to my back, it could not be expected I should attend this sermon. But a constant hearer declared, "That "he went to church with a happy disposition "to improve by social worship; but, had he "followed the dictates of the preacher, he must "have come back a ruffian."

In the evening, another clergyman took the pulpit, and harangued from the words of the same Apostle, "Let your moderation be known "unto all men." And now the fatal doctrines of the morning were hoisted over-board, and in their stead was placed that mild and Christian temper which ought to adorn every hearer, and be cultivated in every pulpit.

The Application to two Sermons.

Thus the good priest, to make men wise,
    Employs his talents and his hours;
While sycophants, who wish to rise,
    Fawn, spaniel-like, on higher powers.

We have now taken a concise view of the rise and progress of a species of punishment inflicted on innocence, which would have been insufferable for the greatest enormities; and with a tear I record the sorrowful thought, that there appeared afterwards no more repentance on one side, than there had been faults on the other.

End of the Narrative of the Riots of July 1791.
    Written in August that year.

THE HISTORY

OF THE LIFE OF

WILLIAM HUTTON.

1791 CONTINUED.

Having now no place of abode, I attempted to hire a house at Ashsted, which lies between my two former habitations; but Brooke, who was the proprietor, refused to let it to me: whether from the fear lest he should not be able to protect his own house from the violence of his own party, if occupied by a Dissenter, I know not; but I believe it. After several other fruitless applications, Richards, the master of Vauxhall tavern and bowling-green, consented to lodge and board my family at the hazard of his own property. We stayed there till Christmas, and found the utmost civility.

The cruel treatment I had met with totally altered my sentiments of man. I had considered him as designed to assist and comfort his species; to reduce the rough propensities of his nature, and to endeavour after perfection, though he could not reach it. But the return I met with for having sacrificed nearly two days a week of my time, and no small portion of my talents, to the gratuitous service of the public, during nineteen years, convinced me that the nature of the human species, like that of the brute creation, is to destroy each other.

These considerations determined me to withdraw from all public business, to spend the small remainder of existence with my little family, and amuse myself with the book and the pen.

It is curious to consider to what a vast extent popular prejudice will run. Very few men were more liberal in their religious and political sentiments than myself, but now the slightest actions of my life tended " to sap Government, " and pull down the Church." As a deer, selected from the herd to be run down, I was forbidden the society of man. Three or four friends met me once a week to sup at Vauxhall. We were charged with scheming against Government. We were threatened with an attack, and the house with being burnt. We were obliged to desist. Even so lately as April 1798, as I passed at three in the morning through Woodcock-lane, in my way to Mamble, to consult with a tenant about the repairs of a house, I was accosted in the dark by three men, whom

I did not know, but took for night strollers. They asked whither I was going? Not accustomed to such a salutation, I replied, "Not "far." I understood afterwards they were the patrol. They knew me, and reported "That "I was going to some Jacobin Club which "was plotting against Government, and they "had a good mind to have followed me." If they had, I should have led them a dance of twenty miles to breakfast at Kidderminster.

The fatal 14th of July, 1791, was by far the most important era of my life. The tide of existence was turned into another and a bitter channel. A black cloud was raised over my head, which the sun of prosperity can never disperse. I entered Birmingham July 14, 1741, as a runaway 'prentice, a forlorn traveller, without money, friend, or home. And that day 50 years began those outrages, which, when a wealthy inhabitant, drove me from it, and left me in a more deplorable state of mind than at the former period.

These events occasioned the disorder of Mrs. Hutton to make rapid strides. We were alarmed, and determined to take her to the Hot Wells near Bristol. My daughter accompanied her in the carriage, and this was the first journey in which my attendance was omitted, owing to the confused state of my affairs.

During this interval, I purchased for £.300 the little cottage which is near me at Bennett's-hill, to hide our heads, while we rebuilt our own house. We repaired and entered the cottage, Dec. 18, quitting Vauxhall with gratitude for the kind treatment we had met with there.

Two months prior to the riots, I had published the History of Derby, price seven shillings.

1792.

The sufferers at the riots were numerous, and their situations various. The attack was so sudden, and the case so uncommon, that they were as little acquainted with the mode of proceeding, to obtain restitution, as with the Act of Parliament by which they were to be guided. Every sufferer had endeavoured to save all the property he was able, but this proved the worst method he could have pursued. We supposed the reimbursement was to equal the loss; but the act, originally intended to cover all, might be restricted to what was destroyed within the building, and what the rioters took out. Large quantities of property removed by the owners, and afterwards found and destroyed by the mob, were lost. A poor reward for activity and expence! Some of the sufferers understanding this, declined a suit; and others declined it from the cost of suing.

There is a latitude in the determination of a Jury, to take in the whole damage, or narrow it to a part. In the riots of 1780, the country being favourable to the sufferers, the Jury repaired the whole of their losses.

It is inconceivable what trouble and anxiety we underwent in preparing for the trials to recover our lost property. Every obstacle of human invention was thrown in our way. I was induced to wish I had given up my claim, and lost all.

At the trials every insult was offered to the sufferers that the malice of an enemy could contrive. The two judges, Baron Thompson and the Lord Chief Baron Eyre, were shocked at the foul treatment; and the latter remarked that, " He had never, in his whole life, seen " so much rancour and ill-blood."

I shall give the claim of every sufferer, and the amount of the verdict.

My son's claim, being trifling, was allowed without any deduction; which was so contrary to the feelings of the Jury, that one of them was heard to say to the foreman, after they had returned into Court, "We must go out again; "you have made a mistake; you have given "the whole of the claim!"

Name.	Claim.			Allowed.		
	£.	s.	d.	£.	s.	d.
John Taylor, Esq.	12,670	9	2	9902	2	0
Thomas Russel, Esq.	285	11	7	160	0	0
William Piddock	556	15	7	300	0	0
John Harwood	143	12	6	60	0	0
Thomas Hawkes	304	3	8	90	15	8
——— Cox	336	13	7	254	0	0
Parsonage House	267	14	11	200	0	0
H. Dollax	198	8	9	139	17	6
William Russel, Esq.	1971	8	6	1600	0	0
John Ryland, Esq.	3240	8	4	2495	11	6
Old Meeting	1983	19	3	1390	7	5
Geo. Humphreys, Esq.	2152	13	1	1855	11	0
Dr. Priestley	3628	8	9	2502	18	0
Thos. Hutton (my son)	619	2	2	619	2	2
Wm. Hutton (myself)	6736	3	8	5390	17	0
	£.35,095	13	6	26,961	2	3

The loss of some of the sufferers, particularly of Mr. Taylor, Dr. Priestley, and myself, was considerably more than the claim. The real loss of Mr. Taylor amounted to upwards of £.22,600; that of Dr. Priestley to upwards of £.4,500; and my own to £.8,243. 3s. 2d.

exclusive of the loss I sustained by the interruption of my business, owing to my stock in trade being chiefly demolished. The verdict of some of the sufferers did not cover the expence of the suit. My part of the expences of my own trial amounted to £.884. 15s. 9d.

The sum allowed was paid with as much reluctance as if the sufferers had destroyed their own property. It was two years before we received it; and I am of opinion that we never should have had it at all, but for the vigilance of Lord Aylesford, and some of the county gentlemen, who seemed determined that the Hundred of Hemlingford should not lie under the stigma of so vile a fraud.

As the beams of the sun create a number of irksome flies, so my former success had raised up a worthless fellow to pursue the same trade. Being now depressed, this man tried every method to ruin me, or to drive me. Among others he hired a paltry engraver, who had cheated me of ten pounds, and was consequently my enemy, to exhibit me in a caricature, to excite the ridicule of the populace.

Another misfortune, but a far less, attended me. One of my coach-horses was stolen, and the other fell lame.

1793.

My dear wife grew worse, owing to the prevalence of the disorder, and the frowns of the world.

In September the money was paid by the Hundred. A part of this I was resolved should never enter the trade again, but be laid out in land. And it soon appeared, through the decline of trade, it would have been ill-employed.

Sept. 5, my son married; and as I ever thought it the duty of a father to bring forward and aid his son, at Christmas I gave him the trade, reserving the estates for my own use.

As I had spent a long life in activity, and had observed many, who, having declined business, seemed half lost, and had pined away with inaction, I chose to assist my son gratuitously, which he as gladly accepted as I offered.

This year I amused myself with writing verses, and produced twenty-six poems, several of which have been published.

1794.

My dear wife was in extreme pain; choaked up; she could not breathe; she wished to be released. There is a degree of anguish to which death is preferable. She felt that degree. We thought her under the operations of death, and the physician told us, March 8, that he believed she could not continue above forty-eight hours. He might be right in his conjecture, though the event did not take place, for at the expiration of that time she appeared to be in the convulsions of death, and was every moment expected to breathe her last, when the door of her chamber was forced open by the wind. The noise rouzed her, and she gradually recovered, so that she lived nearly two years after, though in a state of great suffering, being unable to bear her own weight, or lift up her hand; and what was much worse, unable to lie down.

April 24. The day was fine. We carried her over to the new house. She seemed to be entertained, and " wished she might not return " to the cottage." We took the hint, instantly set about a removal, and accomplished it that afternoon to her wish.

The poetical productions this year were eighteen.

1795.

If the body is unemployed it becomes the nursery of disease. If the mind is unemployed a languor commences, and the man becomes a burthen to himself. Both were designed for action. As I had done with public concerns, which had engrossed much of my time and thoughts, I was reduced to a circumscribed circle; something therefore must supply the place. Walking and assisting my son, employed the body; studying and writing, the mind.

Oct. 1, I went into Herefordshire, in consequence of an estate being advertised for sale, which was likely to suit me. I rose early and walked to Tenbury, thirty-eight miles. This my friends considered as too large a step, but *I* considered, that as Providence had favoured me with limbs, it was but gratitude to use them. These are human tools, which, like files, may be worn out by hard labour; or, like them, may lie by till they become useless with rust.

Here within five miles of the estate, I might probably learn some particulars concerning the land; for though common fame is the greatest liar we know, yet, when uninterested, she will often tell truth.

I conversed with the tenant, I applied to the vendor, and I purchased the estate.

During this year Mrs. Hutton was extremely ill. Not a moment's comfort through the whole. All the time I could spare was devoted to her assistance, and all, we both thought, too little. It was now she uttered that endearing expression mentioned in 1755, which I can scarcely think upon without tears.

The amusements of a restless pen this year were eleven poems.

1796.

My practice had long been to rise about five, relieve the nurse of the night, by holding the head of my dear love in my hand, with the elbow resting on the knee. At eight I walked to business at Birmingham, where I stayed till four, when I returned. I nursed her till eight, amused myself with literary pursuits till ten, and then went to rest.

Jan. 23, I had left her as usual with the waker and my daughter, and had slept two hours. The sitter-up called me gently. I awoke in surprize. "Don't be frightened." "Is she gone?" "Yes." She had departed at half an hour past eleven.

I arose. My dear treasure, whom they were preparing to undress, was laid upon the carpet. Grief stops the pen. The scene is affecting. I am undergoing a second death. I can stop the pen, but not the tear.

There were but three women in the world who loved me. My sister, wife, and daughter. I have lost two. How rarely do we find a pure affection which springs from the heart, and not only flows pure, but increases with time.

My daughter, whose affection and sorrow were equal to mine, lost her health. Her mother and she had been close and intimate friends. This alarmed me. For her recovery we took a journey in July to Barmouth in Wales, which in some measure answered the purpose. The excursion was but melancholy: we had lost a dear companion, who had always been of the party.

Favoured with a memory beyond most men, I procured a book in quarto, divided, by ruling, into 365 columns, according to the days of the year, with the month and day to each; and endeavoured to recollect an anecdote, as insignificant and remote as I was able, for every day, rejecting all under ten years old. I began March 9, 1796. When eight months were elapsed, Nov. 9, I had covered all, except 21 days. I then gave up the pursuit, leaving the rest to chance. I afterwards recollected eleven more, and there now remain ten columns open.

Unhappy if my time was not filled up, and as unwilling to do mischief, the year brought forth nineteen poems.

1797.

My daughter lost her health when she lost her mother. This, added to a cold caught by keeping on wet clothes, brought her into an alarming state. She had been six weeks under the care of a physician, and had been daily growing worse, which gave rise to another journey into Wales, contrary to the advice of every friend. But if she stayed at home death seemed inevitable; and if she went out, it could not be worse. A bold venture might save her life.

We fixed upon Caernarvon, and set out Aug. 5, as we had done the year before, on horse-back, the servant riding before her, and I single. She could barely sit upon the horse. We slept at Wolverhampton. The next day we dined at Shiffnal, where she was obliged to repose three hours upon the bed.

She arrived at the Inn at Haggate, at the foot of the Wrekin, eight miles farther, quite exhausted. It was impossible to pursue our journey. We called in Mr. Cartwright, an apothecary of eminence at Wellington, who seemed to understand her case, and told her, what she already knew, that she had been roughly treated by her physician.

The people at the Inn shewed us great civility. Here we concluded to stay, and see what time and change of air would bring forth. I left her a fortnight. On the 19th I returned; and we pursued our march with some pleasure, going one stage a day.

In October I went to conduct her back; she was amazingly recovered.

This year I purchased an estate in Herefordshire, adjoining that bought in 1795: and this year the Muse brought forth thirteen poems.

1798.

Suppose an animal, a jackass for instance, should eat, move, and sleep, during a whole day, and every day the same, what author durst write his life? His shaking, braying, and browzing, would scarcely produce anecdote sufficient for history.

This is exactly my case. If my actions were observed round the day, the observer would see nothing. And yet he would see as much, should he watch me round the week. He might as well write the progress of a clock.

I have now, July 24, passed through nine months of my seventy-fifth year, without one incident of moment.

As I cannot state what is to come, I must stop here, after mentioning my poetical productions of the present year, which are eight in number; and giving my religious and political sentiments.

What pleasure the effusions of my fancy will give the world is not tried, but I have had my full share in their fabrication. They have a moral tendency.

Religion and Politics are the two grand hinges upon which human life turns. I can assure the reader, that my sentiments on these two points differ from most men's, perhaps from his own.

All denominations of religion, I apprehend, ought to be free. Give freedom, and they will never plot. A national church is generally in partnership with a state. They serve as crutches to each other. This will be found an unnatural alliance, for they are very distinct things. One is to set matters right in the next world, the other to guide and protect in this. Religion is a meek and humble thing, it never seeks after trappings, nor are they ever encouraged in the New Testament, which we accept as the foundation of religious practice. Lands appropriated to the Church are unnecessary: they encourage idleness. Every congregation ought to choose, and support its own pastor.

The whole of religion is comprized in two words: a man's duty to the Supreme Being, and to man. Both are laid down in the Scriptures. If it is thought presumption to interfere between one man and another, what power ought to controul the intercourse between a man and his Maker?

It has long been disputed, but never determined, whether monarchy, aristocracy, democracy, or a mixture, is the best mode of government? Perhaps that is best which is the best executed, because most happiness will be the result. All have been tried, and all have been dismissed.

If we look into the history of the World, we shall find that a new institution is tolerably pure; but, as time corrupts all things, it becomes burthensome by its degeneracy, and the people try a change. This may set matters right for awhile, time will derange that, and then we fly to another.

Thus I have written the history of nearly seventy-five years of my life; and, what I have not seen in any other writer, have kept every year distinct. Whether I shall continue to make any further progress, or another shall lay the cap-stone upon the building I have erected, must be left to time.

Perhaps not one in a thousand of the human race has been favoured with so long an existence; nor one in that number enjoyed the health I have been favoured with; nor one in ten thousand enjoyed equally the benefits of Providence, notwithstanding I felt most severely the loss of my dearest friends, and fell under the calamities of 1791.

I have lived to see one person an infant, and his son an old man! Have observed about three generations pass by, and five times the number of the present human race sink into the grave! Perhaps not one in twenty of the now living remember the transactions of seventy-three years, accompanied with precise dates.

When I consider that within my memory the surface of the earth is totally altered, that the old buildings upon that surface have disappeared, and the new become old, that the former inhabitants have given way to the present, whose opinions and manners are different, I may say with Dr. Young, "This is not the "world in which I was born."

July 24, 1798 *.

1798 CONTINUED.

Since I concluded the history of myself some time has elapsed; and I thought life would probably roll on in silence to its ultimate period, which cannot be far distant. I lost the

---

* My father began to write the foregoing History of his family on the 8th of May, 1798; and he finished his own History at the above date, July the 24th, in the same year. After this period he continued his remarks annually. Ed.

pen * with which I wrote the whole Volume, without suspecting that I should take up another. But incidents arise which a man cannot foresee, though none, except an hermit, can be a more perfect recluse than myself. Walking, business, reading, and writing, generally fill the day.

On the 17th September I walked forty-six miles, ten the next day, and forty-two the third. About two or three days afterwards I fell lame in the internal part of the left heel, having injured the tendon Achilles.

Thus I limped out of this year, and limped into the next.

1799.

I tried a variety of applications for my heel, without any apparent benefit. Not being able to walk, I purchased a little horse, but instead of curing the foot, he fell down and lamed a hand. I tried Buxton, which amused at least; and I do not know whether Time was not the most skilful surgeon.

* This pen was afterwards found, and is kept as a relic.

Being advised to try sea-bathing, I took a journey to Caernarvon, but found no relish for the sea, except so far as it pleased the eye.

During a stay of six weeks I traversed the country daily, and saw a variety of curiosities. I attended to men, manners, and occurrences; was highly delighted, and arranged my remarks, which I intend as a present to some bookseller, should he judge them worthy of notice.

The pleasure of such a tour does not terminate with the tour itself; for the mind, during a long season, returns with avidity to the repast. Nor is this all: the end of one journey opens the prospect of another. Having tasted delicious fruit, we long to taste it again. Besides, go where we will, something is left unseen, or not seen enough. The delight of the last journey gave rise to another the following year.

1800.

May the 1st I lost my brother, aged seventy-eight. We had resided peaceably together sixty-nine years, as I have recorded in the history of the family.

However secure a man may think he treads, yet he may fall by unforeseen events, against which prudence itself cannot guard.

While sitting in the shop with my son on Friday, June 27, two men entered, followed by about twelve others, all strangers, and asked to "see the warehouses."

"Certainly."

"Your secret warehouses."

"We have no secret warehouses," answered my son, with all the confidence of innocence. One of the people was stationed at each door, and each avenue; while the remainder entered every warehouse, thirteen in number, and every room, closet, and recess in the house. They seized and carried off all the boards for carding buttons that they could find, damaged the goods as much as they pleased, and seemed to wanton in power.

They sent away eighteen cart-loads, to the value of about five hundred pounds; and were so intent upon the work, that they would not allow me time to take an account of the plundered property. I could not forbear remarking "That this was a second edition of rioting;" in which they, with much composure, acquiesced.

"They gave us to understand that they were
"officers of Excise; that they had an order
"from the Board to procure a warrant from the
"Justices, to seize all the button-boards, and
"paste-boards, they could find in Birming-
"ham; that they had applied to my son first
"as the principal dealer; that though the but-
"ton-boards were exempt from duty by the act,
"yet that the Excise officers who surveyed the
"Lancashire mills, which had furnished the
"Birmingham market, would not suffer button-
"boards to be made, without charging them
"with the same duty as paste-board; and this
"having totally destroyed their trade, the ma-
"kers had complained to the Board of Excise,
"which had ordered this seizure to institute an
"inquiry."

Thus, without the least fault committed by us, our characters were traduced, and we were branded for rascals.

Two days after I received a hint "that ano-
"ther visit was intended us." We instantly procured assistance, and removed all the boards the officers had refused to take, to the amount of six hundred pounds, into a neighbour's house.

When two days more had elapsed, we saw, with the utmost astonishment, the same officers surround the neighbour's house, and seize this large deposit! Nothing but sorrow stared us in the face. We had not acted amiss, yet must be the victims of tyranny. We had now more than eleven hundred pounds worth of property fraudulently taken from us, and our only prospect was, a loss of trade, and a destructive suit with the Crown.

We were given to understand, that a false friend had lodged an information, in hopes of a prize. I stated the case, and the clauses of the Act, in a letter to the Commissioners of Excise. They were struck with astonishment, and observed that, " It was improper to meddle " with us, who were not makers."

Men in power have as much right to trifle, as to act in an arbitrary manner. After a lapse of three months, we were informed that we might have all our property again, paying the expences of seizure, which amounted to upwards of forty pounds. This was complied with.

We durst not apply to justice for redress, having too mighty a power to contend with.

Struck with the beauties of Caernarvon and its environs, my daughter and I, attended by the servant and horses, in the style of last year, made a tour of six weeks. The journey was delightful. I made remarks additional to my last year's tour, which lies ready for somebody.

1801.

April the 14th, my brother Samuel died, and, like my father and sister, at the age of sixty-seven. I am now the only survivor of a generation consisting of nine.

My year runs round like a boy who beats his hoop round a circle, and with nearly the same effect, that of a little exercise. I rise at six in Summer, and seven in Winter; march to Birmingham, two miles and a quarter, where my son receives me with open arms. I return at five, in one, and four in the other, when my daughter receives me with a smile. I then amuse myself with reading, conversation, or study, without any pressure upon the mind, except the melancholy remembrance of her I loved; for although six years are nearly passed since I lost her, yet her dear image adheres too closely ever to be forgotten, even for one day. How different my case from his who rejoices at nothing so much as the loss of a wife, except the liberty of procuring another.

I am now in my 79th year. I have only two incidents to record; a journey, and the loss of a friend.

In June 1800, some friends paid us a visit, and agreed with my daughter to make a tour to the Lakes in Cumberland, the following June. They wished me to be of the party. My consent was quickly obtained, for, having many years had a strong inclination to see the famous *Roman Wall*, which crosses the Island of Britain from the German ocean to the Irish sea, I embraced the plan; because, while they were engaged at the Lakes, I could take a trip to my favourite object. The year winged away in feasting upon a pleasure to come.

June arrived, when our friends declined the tour, but we would not be disappointed. My daughter was to mount behind her servant, upon one of the horses, and I to walk on foot, a mode of travelling, which, of all others, I prefer. Many arguments were spent upon me to ride, but in vain. I comforted myself that, being upon a stage coach road, I could be taken up if unable to perform. We agreed not to impede each other on the way, but to meet at certain inns for refreshment and rest.

July 4, we set out, and continued together till we came to Penrith in Cumberland, when my daughter turned to the left for the remainder of the Lakes, and I proceeded to Carlisle, where the Wall runs. I went down to the Irish sea, returned through Carlisle to Newcastle, marched to the *Wall's End*, and back again, through Newcastle to Carlisle, having crossed the kingdom twice in one week and six hours, melted with a July sun, and without a drop of rain.

I then returned to *Hest Bank*, three miles North of Lancaster, the place of rendezvous, where I found my dear girl. From thence, by easy marches, we arrived at Birmingham Aug. 7, after a loss on my part of perhaps one stone of animal weight by perspiration, a lapse of thirty-five days, and a walk of 601 miles. My remarks upon this journey are now printing by John Nichols, Esq.

As so long and singular a journey on foot was, perhaps, never wantonly performed by a man of 78, it excites the wonder of the town, and causes me frequently to be stopped in the street, to ascertain the fact.

The second occurrence was the loss of my worthy friend Robert Bage, whom I had known 66 years, and with whom I had lived upon the most intimate terms of friendship during 51; a person of the most extraordinary parts, and who has not left behind him a man of more honour or generosity. I have lost my oldest friend. He died September 1. Mr. Bage was the Author of *Mount Heneth, Barham Downs, James Wallace, The Fair Syrian, Man as he is,* and *Man as he is not;* all much favoured by the world. I wrote, by public desire, the memoirs of his life, which were published in the Monthly Magazine for December 1801.

1802.

In June, the History of the Roman Wall was published in octavo, price seven shillings; and in October, I saw an extract of my life appear in *Phillips's Annual Public Characters**. Twenty-two pages are employed to flatter my vanity. My worthy friend Mr. Pratt, the celebrated Gleaner, had a prior idea of writing my life, and had procured materials. He requested my daughter to furnish him with any minute incidents which occurred in our journey to the *Lakes* and the *Wall.* I shall transcribe her answer.

* Sir Richard Phillips's account of my father was extracted from the History of his Life, and is given frequently in his own words. My father lent the manuscript to a person employed by Sir Richard. ED.

To Samuel Jackson Pratt, Esq.

Dear Sir,

Our Summer excursion in 1801, was ardently wished for by both. My father's object was to see the *Roman Wall*; mine, the Lakes of Cumberland and Westmoreland. We talked it over by our fire-side every evening the preceding winter. He always insisted upon setting out on foot, and performing as much of the journey as he should be able in the same manner. I made little objection to his plan, reserving myself for a grand attack at last.

When the time drew near, I represented to my father that it was impossible he should walk the whole way, though I agreed with him that he could walk a considerable part; the only difference between us was, whether he should ride to prevent mischief, or *after* mischief was done. I besought him with tears to go as far as Liverpool in a carriage, and walk afterwards, as he might find it expedient; but he was inflexible. All I could obtain was a promise that he would take care of himself.

I rode on a pillion behind the servant, and our mode of travelling was this: my father informed himself at a night how he could get out of the house the next morning, before the servants were stirring. He rose at four o'clock, walked to the end of the next stage, breakfasted, and waited for me. I set out at seven, and when I arrived at the same inn, breakfasted also. When my father had rested two hours, he set off again. When my horse had fed properly, I followed, passed my father on the road, arrived before him at the next inn, and bespoke dinner and beds.

My father was so careful not to be put out of his regular pace, that he would not allow me to walk by his side, either on foot, or on horseback, not even through a town. The only time I ever did walk with him, was through the streets of Warrington, and then, of my own accord, I kept a little behind, that I might not influence his step. He chose that pace which was the least exertion to him, and never varied it. It looked like a saunter, but it was steady, and got over the ground at the rate of full two miles and a half in an hour.

When the horse, on which I rode, saw my father before him, he neighed, though at the distance of a quarter of a mile, and the servant had some trouble to hold him in. He once laid the reins upon his neck, and he trotted directly up to my father, then stopped, and laid his head on his shoulder.

My father delivered all his money to me before we left home, reserving only a few pieces of loose coin, in case he should want on the road. I paid all bills, and he had nothing to do but walk out of an inn when he found himself sufficiently refreshed.

My father was such an enthusiast with regard to the *Wall*, that he turned neither to the right nor the left, except to gratify me with a sight of Liverpool. Winander Mere he saw, and Ullswater he saw, because they lay under his feet, but nothing could detain him from his grand object.

When we had reached Penrith, we took a melancholy breakfast and parted, with a tear half suppressed on my father's side, and tears, not to be suppressed, on mine. He continued his way to Carlisle, I turned Westward for *Keswick*. After a few days' stay there, I went back to *Hest Bank*, a small sea-bathing place near Lancaster, where we had appointed to meet.

While I remained at Hest Bank, I received two scraps of paper, torn from my father's pocket-book; the first, dated from Carlisle July 20, in which he told me he was sound in body, shoe, and stocking, and had just risen from a lodging among fleas. The second, from

Newcastle, July 23, when he informed me he had been at the Wall's end; that the weather was so hot he was obliged to repose under hedges, and that the country was infested with thieves. But lest I should be under any apprehensions for his personal safety, he added, they were only such as demolished his idol, *The Wall*, by stealing the stones of which it was composed.

On the fifth morning after my arrival at Hest Bank, before I was up, I heard my father hem! on the stairs. I answered by calling out Father! which directed him to my room, and a most joyful meeting ensued. He continued here four days, wondered at, and respected by the company. We set out on our return home in the same manner as before, and reached it in safety.

During the whole journey, I watched my father with a jealous eye. The first symptom of fatigue I observed was at Budworth in Cheshire, after he had lost his way, and been six hours upon his legs, first in deep sands, and then on pavement road. At Liverpool his spirits were good, but I thought his voice rather weaker. At Preston he first said he was tired; but having walked eleven miles farther to Garstang, he found himself recovered, and never after, to the best of my remembrance, uttered the least complaint. He usually came into an inn in high spirits, ate a hearty meal, grew sleepy after it, and in two hours was rested. His appetite never forsook him. He regarded strong liquors with abhorrence. Porter he drank when he could get it: ale and spirits never. He mixed his wine with water, but considered water alone as the most refreshing beverage.

On our return, walking through Ashton, a village in Lancashire, a dog flew at my father and bit his leg, making a wound about the size of a sixpence. I found him sitting in the inn at Newton, where we had appointed to breakfast, deploring the accident, and dreading its consequences. They were to be dreaded. The leg had yet a hundred miles to walk in extreme hot weather. I comforted my father. "Now," said I, " you will reap the fruit of your tem- " perance. You have put no strong liquors or " high sauces into your leg; you eat but when " you are hungry, and drink but when you are " thirsty, and this will enable your leg to carry " you home." The event shewed I was right. The wound was sore, and the leg round it was inflamed, as every leg under such circumstances must be, but it never was very troublesome, nor ever indulged with a plaster.

From the time we parted at Penrith, till we reached home, the weather was intensely hot. My father frequently walked with his waistcoat unbuttoned, and the perspiration was so excessive, that I have even felt his coat damp on the outside from the moisture within; his bulk visibly diminished every day. When we arrived at Wolsley bridge, on our return, I was terribly alarmed at this, and thanked God he had but one day more to walk. When we had got within four days of our journey, I could no longer restrain my father. We made forced marches, and if we had had a little farther to go, the foot would fairly have knocked up the horse! The pace he went did not even fatigue his shoes. He walked the whole six hundred miles in one pair, and scarcely made a hole in his stockings.

I am, Dear Sir,
Your very sincere friend and
obedient servant,
CATHERINE HUTTON.

Thus, while I give a faithful history of our journey, my daughter gives as faithful a one of myself.

Poets have often drawn a happy life in their *wishes*, and painters in the delineation of their *pictures;* but, by the complaints of individuals, we should be apt to conclude that happiness is *only* to be found in the *pen* and the *pencil!* The truth is, we groan under the cloud, and forget the bright day. Happiness is more in our own power than we apprehend. Like a shy nymph, she must be courted, may be won, is soon offended, and then disappears.

What is a happy life?

Suppose a man endeavours after health, and his endeavours are blessed with such success that, by a proper use of his animal powers, he can, at fourscore, walk thirty miles a day. Suppose him, by assiduity and temperance, to have obtained a complete independence, that he can reside in a house to his wish, with a garden for use and amusement, is blessed with a son and a daughter of the most affectionate kind, who attentively watch his little wants with a view to supply them: add as an appendage to this little family a pair of old and faithful horses, who are strangers to the lash, and whose value increases with their years. Still add to a taste for reading, the benefits arising from a library of choice Authors. Would you pronounce this a *happy man?* That man is myself. Though my morning was lowering, my evening is sunshine.

A DAY.

To Dr. Withering, *who inquired*
How I spent my Time.

So much one day is like another,
It might be taken for its brother.

At six o'clock I raise my head,
Toss the warm covering off my bed,
Dress, and, if thoughts sprang in the night,
Distinguish them in black and white;
Survey the skies with half a scowl,
And prophecy if fair or foul.
Then to my Girl I softly creep,
To steal a kiss whilst fast asleep;
For when the foot but lightly moves,
We stand a chance to win the gloves.

My hat put on, I quit my door,
Set out to walk two miles or more;
Animal pow'rs now set a-going,
The mental powers sets a-flowing.
They orderly begin to chime,
Ending in measure tipp'd with rhyme.

At Birmingham I meet my Boy,
And never met him without joy;
For life to melancholy tends,
If 'tis not cheer'd by valued friends.
Nay, if to solitude we give,
We scarcely can be said to live.

Thoughts of the pen I now lay by,
On paper only cast an eye.

My glasses, newspapers, and I, late,
Enter the parlour to be private.
" Let's see what statesmen are contriving,
" How the politic nags they're driving."
But how can I men's actions view,
Who know so little what they do?

My joyous breakfast come at last in,
I relish like a ploughman fasting ;
Chat with all comers on each head,
But after all there's nothing said.
The servant finishes debates,
Opens with, " Sir, the dinner waits."
Who would not enter with all his heart,
To taste plumb-pudding, tart, dessert?
Let me with these sweet dishes join,
And you, my friend, may take sirloin.

Nought now remains (the floor well trod),
But warm my shins or take a nod;
Till gloves are on, hat o'er the eye,
" 'Tis striking five, and so good bye."

The bulky town recedes from view,
I meet with bows, and " How d' ye do?"
The rain and I each other chase,
We're often found in close embrace.
Though fair without and pure within,
I like her not to touch my skin.
When Aston steeple strikes my eye,
It steals for her I lov'd a sigh.

An intercourse, now lost, I mourn,
How to forget I ne'er can learn.

One mile walk'd o'er, the traveller sees
My little cot peep through the trees.
Dear cot! in which I ever find,
That best of blessings, peace of mind;
Which ne'er gave anxious thought or sigh,
Until the fourteenth of July;
When laid in ashes by ill men,
But, phœnix like, thou rose again.

Hid from the world, from care, from din,
I cast a pleasing look within.
There I, with truth it may be said,
Write for the living, wake the dead;
Converse with those who liv'd of yore,
And feed on what they fed before.
Transactions at command appear,
Bringing to view each distant year.

Now, in heroic verse, I'll state,
How, as I enter through my gate,
Old Cerberus bounces from his bed,
Not grac'd with three, but with one, head;
Bullies, in thund'ring strains, about,
Resolv'd to keep invaders out:
But the discov'ring who I am,
Converts the monster to the lamb.
He greets me with that mouth and eye,
Rais'd, the past moment, to destroy;
Makes his tremendous jaws expand,
And gently leads me by the hand.

Severity might give him blows,
Humanity the pat bestows.

The birds my little grove retain,
Welcome me with their pleasing strain.
In gratitude they sing their best,
Because they hold a peaceful nest;
For neither nest nor bird has been
Disturb'd, since first my grove was seen:
A place, perhaps, by right divine,
As much their freehold as 'tis mine;
And, as we both are now possessors,
Both may bequeath it our successors.
Nor shall it in the frost be said,
I e'er withheld a crumb of bread.

My pair of greys the Muse engage,
They, in my service, see old age.
They hear my voice, they make no stand,
But take the bread from master's hand;
Perceiving an exhausted store,
They follow me in quest of more.
I turn, which their slow footstep checks,
"So, my poor lads!" and pat their necks.
They never knew a treatment harsh,
Strangers to want, as to the lash.

I meet my servants growing old,
But never meet them with a scold.
My equals in an eye divine,
Why not my equals then in mine?

Puss cocks her tail, begins to crawl,
And rubs her side against the wall.

She ne'er in all her life has spoke,
Or she would say, "Give me a stroak."

But what that pleasure can surpass,
When my Girl sees me through the glass,
Rises to meet me, while her joy
Takes full possession of her eye?
Whatever comfort age can find,
Lies in the storehouse of her mind.

Now garden, converse, book, or pen,
Tea, supper, music, please till ten;
When the bell rings, to " bring a light,"
I rise and burrow for the night.

Of blessings can I wish for more?
They amply satisfy fourscore:
And I enjoy, others partaking,
A little heav'n of my own making*.

Nov. 20, 1802.

Last year I treated the reader, or rather myself, with an unfashionable journey on foot, while my carriage slept in the coach-house, and my horses grazed in the field. From walking being so disgraceful, we should conclude that feet were not made for conveyance; that there was a pride in being *unable* to walk, and *that* pride was hurt if caught in the act.

* These verses have been published in the Volume of Poems, but, at my Father's particular request, they are inserted here. ED.

I now consented, however, to take our annual excursion in the usual mode, in a visit to Derby, Matlock, Leicester, and Fotheringay. We commenced our tour June 19, stopped at Derby to view the scenes of my childish adventures, and ruminate on transactions, none of which bore a shorter date than sixty-seven years. Here memory had her full scope in examining ten different places of my residence, and those of my ancestors for a hundred and fifty years. I was a stranger at home. I knew no soul; not a soul knew me. The generation to which I was once united was gone.

After two days stay we drove to Keddleston, were admitted on sending in my name into that scene of wonder, *the Hall.* Every thing was grand and expensive, and every thing new except the books and the plate. The Park is most beautiful, and the oaks of a magnitude seldom seen. Lord Scarsdale, I was told, had been offered one hundred pounds each, for nine trees, and seventy pounds each for thirty. Perhaps some of the trees are as old as the family, which came over with William the Conqueror. I perfectly remember the old hospitable hall in my infancy, and the owner in his.

We arrived at Matlock, which, though I had before visited, I had not seen. The man of taste will be delighted with the variegated walks and scenes. Mr. Arkwright's improvement of the rocks is most charming, and is only equalled by his kindness in exhibiting them to the public eye.

On the side of a Hill called the Heights of Abraham, is a favourite serpentine walk of about half a mile, where the prospect varies at every turn, and is always pleasing. A spacious alcove accommodates the wanderer, in which I paid the following tribute:

> The fools write *on*, the fools blot out,
> Some with a pencil, some a clout.
> Scribblers, refrain your idle talk,
> And thank the owner for this walk;
> For should the want of health appear,
> Who seeks that gem may find it here.

Some amusement may be drawn from the various characters assembled at a public table. In one man we could observe a silent hearer, though not wanting in intellect. In another, a harmless head upon the shoulders of a lawyer. Another had acquired the gout, and a thousand a year, by the sale of tobacco; yet had not forgotten the important value of a shilling. A fourth, an officer just returned from killing the French, now attempted to kill the ladies, but perhaps succeeded in neither. In one lady we saw nothing charming but the *outside* of her face. In another, the inestimable treasures of good sense, prudence, and temper, within. In a third, a Venus of Medicis tipsy. The Clergy are sometimes charged with an unsocial behaviour, with keeping at a distance, preserving the rust of the College, and not suffering us to approach so near as to rub it off. During a fortnight's stay at Matlock, we were favoured with the company of six Sons of the Church who reversed this charge, for they were all open and friendly. In one might be observed the extreme of modesty. In another, good judgment, with now and then an oath. A third was a jolly soul, contented with his glass and his poverty. A fourth united riches, civility, and dignity. Another never uttered a sentence of his own, but followed his leader; yet possessed one of the best hearts that ever filled a human breast. The sixth was a buck of the first magnitude, whether in person, song, glass, or joke; but all were good-natured. One evil attends a watering-place, we contract friendships which are shipwrecked in a day.

An inhabitant of Matlock has, by the labour of seventeen years, added another wonder to the place, by penetrating a rock in the hill called Proud Masson, which, opening from cave to cave, leads the traveller three or four hundred yards, with the sparry lustres shining by his candle. He has named it Cumberland-cave. Admittance one shilling.

But the greatest wonder I saw was Phebe Brown. She is five feet six inches in height, is about thirty, well-proportioned, round-faced and ruddy, has a dark penetrating eye, which, the moment it fixes upon your face, sees your character, and that with precision. Her step (pardon the Irishism) is more manly than a man's, and can cover forty miles a day. Her common dress is a man's hat, coat, with a spencer over it, and men's shoes. As she is *un*-married, I believe she is a stranger to breeches.

She can lift one hundred weight in each hand, and carry fourteen score; can sew, knit, cook, and spin, but hates them all; and every accompaniment to the female character, that of modesty excepted. A gentleman at the new bath had recently treated her rudely, " She had a good mind to have knocked him " down." She assured me, " she never knew " what fear was." She gives no affront, but offers to fight any man who gives her one. If she never has fought, perhaps it is owing to the insulter having been a coward, for the man of courage would disdain to offer an insult to a female.

Phebe has strong sense, an excellent judgment, says smart things, and supports an easy freedom in all companies. Her voice is more than masculine, it is deep-toned. With the wind in her favour she can send it a mile. She has neither beard nor prominence of breast. She undertakes any kind of manual labour, as holding the plough, driving a team, thatching the barn, using the flail, &c.; but her chief avocation is breaking horses, for which she charges a guinea a week each. She always rides without a saddle, is thought to be the best judge of a horse or cow in the country, and is frequently employed to purchase for others at the neighbouring fairs.

She is fond of Milton, Pope, and Shakespeare, also of music, is self-taught, and performs on several instruments, as the flute, violin, harpsichord, and supports the bass-viol in Matlock church. She is a marks-*woman*, and carries the gun on her shoulder. She eats no beef or pork, and but little mutton. Her chief food is milk, which is also her drink, discarding wine, ale, and spirits.

Curious to see the burying-place of the greatest subject that ever lived in England, *Cardinal Wolsey*, nay, he who even governed the most absolute king, Henry the VIIIth, we drove to Leicester. Great part of the front of the Abbey is standing, and discovers the vestiges of former grandeur; but I sought in vain for the Chapel. Could I have found that, I could have found the Chancel, which, no doubt, was the place of Wolsey's interment. Tradition pointed out the spot, but on this I could not rely.

I had, during many years, an ardent desire to see Fotheringay; a place celebrated in all our histories, as the depository of two Princes, the birth-place of a King, and the scene of the murder of a Queen.

Visiting a friend in this tour, twelve miles north of Leicester, and being only twenty-eight from the favourite spot, I determined to walk thither, though every person I consulted, assured me there was nothing to be seen. Approaching the place, I thought the steeple one of the handsomest I had remarked. In the Chancel, at the Communion-table, are the monuments of the two Princes opposite each other, exactly alike, of stone of a fine texture, painted white. Both were erected by Queen Elizabeth in 1573. On the right is that of the second

Edward, Duke of York, grandson to Edward the Third, and great uncle to Henry the Fifth. He resided at this Castle, was killed at the battle of Agincourt, and interred in a religious house here, founded by his father, and endowed by himself. Here he rested till Henry the Eighth destroyed the house; when his remains lay neglected forty years, till deposited under his monument at the above date.

On our left, and facing the other monument, is that of Richard, Duke of York, and Cicely his wife. He was nephew to the above Duke, and father of Edward the Fourth; was killed at the battle of Wakefield in 1460, in fighting for a crown which he ought to have enjoyed without fighting. This is a lesson to kings, never to violate the rules of justice; for the quarrel between the Roses totally destroyed the family of Henry the Fourth, who was the aggressor. It is also a lesson to subjects, to let contending kings fight their own battles; for this cruel contest ruined one hundred thousand families!

An old inhabitant of Fotheringay assured me, that he had seen a written agreement between the Duke of York and an Architect, in which the latter was to erect a church for three hundred pounds, the Duke finding materials; but he was killed before the work was completed.

In the pulpit are the royal arms carved in wood, which my guide told me were those of Richard the Third, who perhaps put a finishing hand to the church. The pulpit is as old as the building, and on each side of the supporters was a boar, Richard's crest: one of these is still perfect. He was born in the Castle in 1452. His character I have delineated in the Battle of Bosworth Field.

I saw the place where the Castle had stood, adjoining the village. It is about eight acres, upon a flat, of an oblong form, and remarkably strong, but there is not one stone left upon another, and yet I had all the satisfaction I wished. The trenches are wide, deep, and nearly perfect. The river *Nen* washes one side, and fills the other three. The whol area is in grass, a farm-house and a few nettles excepted. With the soil thrown out to form the trenches is composed a conical hill, whose round base perhaps covers an acre. This rises twenty yards, and terminates in a flat, thirty yards in diameter. On this flat, in the centre, has stood a tower, circular as the hill, which covered a diameter of fifteen yards; and this tower was surrounded by about eighteen turrets, which stood upon the verge of the mound. Fifteen of their foundations I counted.

At the foot of this artificial hill stood the Castle. The people of the country have stocked up the stones to the very foundation for building and the roads; and left the trenches so complete, that the various rooms may be discovered. Exclusive of many apartments for private use, I could particularize three state rooms; in one of these, no doubt, Richard the Third was born.

The Great-Hall, in which the unfortunate Mary, Queen of Scots, was beheaded in 1587, appeared very conspicuous. It is thirty yards by twenty-four, and had two entrances. I sought for the benches on which sat her thirty-six insulting Judges; and the scaffold, raised two feet high, at the upper end of the Hall, where she suffered, but could find no traces of either.

What will unprejudiced posterity say of Elizabeth, when they are told that Mary in distress fled to her for protection, upon a promise of safety ; but, instead of finding an hospitable reception, was, through a mean jealousy, kept a prisoner eighteen years, and then destroyed? Every sham plot laid to her charge ended in a vapour, except that of plotting for her own liberty, of which none had a right to deprive her. Perhaps no scheme was ever carried on with more deceit than that of her destruction. If her son, James the First, was not an actor in this base tragedy, he was pleased with the piece and the performers, though he endeavoured to establish a contrary opinion. He pulled down the harmless castle of Fotheringay, out of revenge for his mother's death, but took the murderers into favour! Perhaps he was as jealous of his mother as Elizabeth. He loved a crown as well as she, to which his mother had a prior right. The two sovereigns well understood each other, while the scape-goat was being destroyed.

Deeply impressed with former transactions, while standing upon the very spot on which Mary suffered, I left the place with regret and with a sigh.

1803.

Having arrived at fourscore, allow me to state some of the feelings attendant upon that advanced age.

I am strongly attached to old habits and old fashions, even though absurd. Instead of longing for a new coat, I part with an old one as with an old friend.

I forget some lessons, and cannot learn others. One lesson however I must learn, to eat without teeth.

The farther we advance in years, the more we are affected with both heat and cold. In early life our feelings are but little influenced by either.

I can better remember the transactions of seventy years, than of yesterday; pour liquor into a full vessel, and the top will run off first. Perhaps I can recollect being in a thousand companies, every person which composed them is now departed except myself. Upon whatever family I cast a distant eye, I remark in that family a generation has sprung into life, passed through the bloom of the day, and sunk into the night. My old friends have slipped off the stage, and I am as unfit to unite with new, as new cloth with old. Thus I am become a stranger to the world which I have long known.

As age *in*creases, sleep *de*creases; when a child in health enters upon life, it can sleep twenty-two out of the twenty-four hours. Its sleep will diminish about three hours upon the average every year during the next three, when activity will enable it to nurse itself. That reduction will afterwards be nearly one hour every ten years, till he arrives at eighty, when four or five will be his hours of sleep.

It is curious to contemplate the fluctuation of property. I have seen the man of opulence look with disdain upon a pauper in rags. I have seen that pauper mount the wheel of fortune, and the other sink to the bottom. I have seen a miserable cooper not worth the shavings he made, place his son to a baker, and *his* son become a rich *banker*, a *member of parliament*, and a *baronet*.

The indisposition of my daughter induced us to try the effect of air, water, and sea-bathing, at Scarborough. During the first four weeks of our residence there, she found no improvement of health, but afterwards she gradually mended for the seven weeks following, the time of her abode. This improvement continued about five months. The success prognosticates another tour.

As I made remarks upon this most agreeable journey, which I communicated to John Nichols, Esq. who is now printing them in octavo, I shall here decline the subject.

1804.

This year opened, as the nine preceding years had done, with melancholy reflections upon the loss of an excellent woman, who had acted a principal part in the drama of my life, which produced the following poem *.

To the memory of a dear Girl, once named SARAH COCK, *who died Jan.* 23, 1796.

> Sarah, when thou first came over,
> Though no smile upon me came,
>   I assum'd the faithful lover,
> Two hearts united in one flame.
>
> During forty years possessing,
> Whene'er thou approach'd my sight,
>   My heart, as conscious of the blessing,
> Felt a ray of pure delight.
>
> Pity was to love united,
> When came seventeen years of pain,
>   Thy drooping head my hand invited,
> Which my dear could not sustain.
>
> When ill-natured time bereav'd me
> Of thyself, the source of joy,
>   Two dear treasures thou bequeath'd me,
> Dear as sight is to my eye.

---

* These verses have also been published in the volume of Poems.

O! I mourn the day I lost thee,
As the year winds round its way,
Many a sigh and tear thou cost me,
Sorrow never sleeps a day.

Gentle spirit, can I find thee,
When the lamp of life shall cease,
To my anxious bosom bind thee,
Where thou long possess'd a place?

Jan. 23, 1804.

My tour to Scarborough was published in June, and arrived there a few days before us, in our second journey. This visit of twelve weeks gave as much delight as the last, and more health to my dear girl, which foretels a third in 1805.

In this second tour to Scarborough, I made a more minute inquiry into the particulars of the dreadful battle of *Towton field*. The whole country, as observed, was uninclosed. That spot which sustained the heat of the conflict, is now an inclosure of about twenty acres, rather hollow, but upon elevated ground, and is called *Towton Slade*. The land adjoining the Slade, on the North, descends to the place where some springs rise that form the rivulet which was tinged with blood, not that blood shed in the battle, but in the pursuit, in which, to the disgrace of the age, no quarter was given.

I was shewn two tumuli where the slain were deposited. In Saxon church-yard, half a mile from the Slade, I saw the tomb of Lord Dacre, who fell on that fatal day. His epitaph is in the old English character.

In November my volume of Poems was published, " not by the advice of friends," but the contrary, for the advice was, " To keep the " piece to myself." Whether this offspring of the brain can support itself, or, whether I have produced a cripple which cannot make its way through the world, must be left to the judgment of others.

There is an inconsistency in the character of man. In youth he sets but a small value upon his property, and is much inclined to spend it, while, having life before him, there is the utmost reason to save it for future use; but in old age, when he cannot from the shortness of his day use it, he is anxious to accumulate and keep it. I am strongly tinctured with this unphilosophical bias; for though in early life I did not spend money because I had none, yet I am as willing to acquire as if my date was that of Methusalem.

From early infancy *land* was my favourite object, and though a thousand pounds in the stocks may be as productive as a thousand in land, yet I should despise the one and grasp at the other. My desire, like a bottomless pit, cannot be filled. This year closed with purchasing the manor of *Woonton*, joining my own in Herefordshire.

It is curious to observe the rapid rise of land. I gave for the land on one side of the hedge in 1795, eleven pounds per acre, and on the other in 1804, twenty-four pounds!

December the 24th, died an ingenious Artist, Moses Haughton, whose productions as a painter will live longer than he lived himself, sixty-six years. He painted nineteen portraits of my family, five of which were of myself. Eleven of these portraits embellish the grand manuscript copy of my own History, and that of my family, in my son's library. His son has erected a beautiful monument to his memory in St. Philip's Church, in which is exhibited a medallion of statuary marble, with an excellent likeness of the father, in basso relievo.

1805.

Nothing occurred this year except another journey to Scarborough. I believe it will be my last. I found greater difficulty in performing the walking part of it from Sheffield to Scarborough than before.

1806.

The efforts of memory are surprising. I can remember my mother dandling me on the knee, feeding me with the infant spoon, and nursing me in the arms. I also remember the form and colour of my dress. But although eighty-two years have passed by, yet that space of time seems amazingly short; the reason is obvious, memory only brings the two points of *then* and *now* into view, and skips over every incident between the two. But when we look forward, if but for *one* year, the time appears long, because we foresee an infinite number of incidents between the two points.

In February I ate a dinner which proved too rich for the stomach to digest. It produced a slight surfeit; the first indisposition during twenty-three years. A few weeks after, I was attacked with a violent fit of the ague. These gave a shock to the constitution, which it perhaps will never recover. Twice in the winter, in reading by candle-light, I set fire to the book by holding it too near the blaze, my sight failing.

April 4, I walked from Bilsdon in Leicestershire to Atherstone, thirty-two miles, which I accomplished with tolerable ease, but believe it will be my last material walk.

I was never more than twice in London on my own concerns. The first was April 8, 1749, to make a purchase of materials for trade, to the amount of *Three Pounds!* The last, April 14, 1806, fifty-seven years after, to ratify the purchase of an estate which cost £.11,590. *One* laid a foundation for the other, and both answered expectation.

1807.

Of all the afflictions attendant upon the human frame, the cancer stands in the first class. It is generally terminated by death or the knife. About the year 1777, a small exuberance appeared on the top of my thigh, which, after ten years growth was not bigger than a large pin's head, and of no consequence. During the next ten years it grew to the size of a pea, looked angry, and exuded a small degree of moisture. But not being painful, or impeding action, it was disregarded. As time advanced, it proceeded with greater rapidity till about 1804, when it had reached the size of a shilling, and discharged copiously a watery fluid. I consulted an eminent surgeon, who said, "I do "not like its appearance. Perhaps it may not "shorten your life, but you had better let me "take it out." Upon consulting a Physician, he replied, "there is no immediate danger, but "there is a chance of its becoming a cancer." Two years elapsed, when I shewed it again, now as large as a half crown, to the surgeon, my worthy friend John Blount. It appeared with horrid aspect. In surprise he pronounced it a cancer. "You must," said he, "submit "to the knife or the coffin. You may live one "year, or you may live one month, but the "whole of your existence will be miserable." I considered that which *must* be done, had better *soon* be done. February 1, two surgeons laid me on a table, in about twenty minutes finished the cutting, and in ten more sewed up, dressed the wound, and carried me to bed. This I kept about six days. In seven days more I was able to walk abroad, and in twelve more the cure was completed.

I paid a visit in July to Bosworth Field, but found so great an alteration since I saw it in 1788, that I was totally lost.

August 4, I lost my poor horse Cobler, at the age of 22. I considered him as one of my family, had sung his praise in verse, had fed him with pleasure, and he had served me fifteen years with fidelity.

If we carry a cheerful face into company, it naturally excites cheerfulness in that company; we see them pleased, and feel happy returns in our own bosom. We made a visit to Matlock of about a fortnight, in which we found much delight, and contracted so many friendships that we were unwilling on all sides to part.

In the History of my ancestors, I mention that a person came from Northallerton to Derby, in about 1701, to bring my Grandfather back to the former place, to take possession of an estate, to which he was become heir at law. My Grandfather entertained, and then conducted the messenger one mile on his return, and dismissed him with this remark, " Let them " take the estate who will, I would not go so " far for a better." My daughter wishing to spend a month at Coatham, in the North of Yorkshire, and Northallerton being nearly in the road, I requested her to make inquiry after the Hutton family. It was extinct in that place; but four miles distant, she found a gentleman resident upon his own estate, who seemed to be a relation. It is probable, from circumstances, that his may be the identical land my Grandfather refused, but I have neither the means nor the wish to attempt to recover it.

At the very moment of writing this, time is completing my 84th year: four times the space which forms the man. When I compare the two extremities of this long period, it exhibits a total change of life and manners. In the morning of my days, I ate when Fortune chose to suffer me, for she fed me with a sparing hand; I could at any time have gladly attacked a second dinner, immediately after a first: but now plenty awaits me.—In that early period I had an utter aversion to letters, which wholly precluded improvement: but now one of the greatest pleasures of my life is reading, and I have the gratification of a library to my wish. —In former times *dress* was eagerly coveted, and not easily attained: but now, having dress fully in my power, I have totally lost the relish.— Money! that darling of every one, which buys all things except *health* and *content*, was hidden from my eyes. I once saved every farthing I could procure, which, at the end of two years amounted only to fourpence halfpenny! This occurred between the age of four and six. But now I command more than I can use.—Punishment was an unwelcome attendant. My father, though he loved me, was too much attached to the whip; he forgot that a gentle word properly applied, was a better excitement. But now I am under no chastisement, no not even that of the *pen*.

The Authors of the Monthly Review, criticizing my tour through North Wales, bestow upon the work some encomiums, after which they remark, " We believe that this veteran " traveller has at length taken a longer jour- " ney, the important details of which he will " not transmit to us poor wanderers below." This occasioned the following:

To the Authors of the Monthly Review.

My Dear Friends,

I learnt from your Review for the last month that I was dead. I cannot say I was very sorry, though I had a great respect for the man. Your kind expressions will not be charged with insincerity, for praise is lost upon the defunct. You may as well, by these presents, bring me to life in your next, for till then I cannot attain my former rank among the living. Your fiat musters my friends about me, some in tears, but all terminate with a smile. Others, as I walk the street, cast at me a significant glance, as if surprised to see me above ground, and uncertain whether the ghost or the body moves; but a moment determines that the ghost holds its proper place. Three verses addressed to you, inoffensive as your own remark, will probably be found in the Gentleman's Magazine.

I am, with sincere respect,
Yours, till a second death,
W. HUTTON.

From my Shades, at Bennet's Hill,
  near Birmingham, Aug. 13, 1807.

IN THE GENTLEMAN'S MAGAZINE.
To the Authors of the Monthly Review.

No wonder a man, when his courtship is o'er,
Should enter his name as a *wed*-man;
The wonder consists, when a man is no more,
He should still write his name though a *dead*-man.

Your work for July tells the world that I'm dead,
And have ceas'd to become an inditer,
But, by praising my book it will rather be said,
That you keep me alive as a writer.

Shall I drop the pen who am but eighty-four,
And smother a tale if worth telling?
I have long'd and still long to take one journey
   more,
And foot it to *Johnny Groat's* dwelling.

Aug. 12, 1807.

In the next number the Reviewers published my letter with the following remark. "We

"insert the above with much pleasure; and as
"we have now a contradiction of the report to
"which we alluded, under our venerable friend's
"own hand, we will engage, if he requires it,
"never again to state an event which we hope
"is yet distant, till we have, in like manner,
"*his own certificate of it.*"

This year my son gave me my birth-day dinner, and with the dessert, my daughter presented to me the following lines, which, I must own, are more remarkable for affection than elegance.

DEAR FATHER,
 Allow me to congratulate you and myself on your birth-day,
 The interest we feel for your life and health will make it a mirth-day,
 Eighty-five times have you seen the eleventh of October,
 You have risen from poverty, and liv'd in plenty, with a mind always sober,
 You have lov'd your children, indulg'd your household, and never treated us with rigour,
 You have kept your health and good humour, and still retain your vigour.
 May God, of his infinite mercy, long spare these blessings,
 And I promise you, my dear Father, you shall not want for caressings,

>I should have acquitted myself better had it been my lot to make your plumb-pudding,
>For writing verses is a thing I never could do any good in.
>If they are not poetry, they are truth, so I don't care a button,
>And am, your most affectionate daughter,
>>CATHERINE HUTTON.

1808.

Time is equivalent to money. I remarked, in the History of the Riots, in 1791, that I had lost more than one day in a week during nineteen years, in serving the public. It follows, that I have lost a fortune by acting for the benefit of others.

Perhaps there is not one in ten thousand who lives to the age of *eighty-five;* but where is there one, who, at that age, *begins* to write a book? I launched into Authorship at the late period of fifty-six, a season in which most writers land on the shore of retirement; but as I began late, suffer me to retire late. Had I, instead of being bred in the cold damps of penury, been trained to letters, more than fourteen books would have issued from my pen. I never wrote for profit, and yet the world has amply rewarded me; nay, the pen itself has rewarded its own labour, for the pleasure of writing is inconceivable.

August 7, this year my daughter and I set out for *Coatham*, a watering-place upon the Northern coast of Yorkshire, distant 184 miles. We were absent six weeks; and I am now writing the memoirs of that excursion, which will make the fourteenth book I shall have published in the period of thirty years.

As this is the last I shall exhibit to the world, I will particularize each, with the name and date: some of them, I believe, are out of print.

The History of Birmingham	1781
Journey to London	1784
The Court of Requests	1787
The Hundred Court	1788
History of Blackpool	1788
Battle of Bosworth Field	1789
History of Derby	1790
The Barbers, a Poem	1793
Edgar and Elfrida, a Poem	1793
The Roman Wall	1801
Remarks upon North Wales	1801
Tour to Scarborough	1803
Poems, chiefly Tales	1804
Trip to Coatham	1808

Some of them have since risen to double their original price.

1809.

The infirmities of age inform me that I am drawing towards a conclusion. Much has been said, but little is known, of futurity. The subject is too deep to be fathomed, but none can escape the trial.

When a man is ushered into the world, he possesses talents fitted for that world: he knows many, he converses with many, and is a man among men; but when he draws towards eighty or ninety, his talents become blunted, his vivacity is lost, his powers are fled, his former acquaintance are swept off the stage, he cannot associate with new, and he is no longer a man among men.

I have lived to bury two generations, and among them many friends whom I loved. I do not *know*, nor am *known* by any soul living prior to my twenty-seventh year. But although I barely live myself, I may have taught others to live. I was the first who opened a *Circulating Library* in Birmingham, in 1751, since which time many have started in the race. I was the first who opened a regular *Paper Warehouse* in 1756: there are now a great number. I was also the first who introduced the *barrow with two wheels:* there are now more than one hundred. I may, in another view, have been beneficial to man, by a life of temperance and exercise, which are the grand promoters of health and longevity. Some whom I know have been induced to follow my example, and have done it with success.

The entertainment we met with at Coatham last year, induced us this year to make another visit to the same place. We began our journey with a design of being absent six weeks, as before, which was effected. Some circumstances of this second visit will be found in the Trip to Coatham, now in the press.

While travelling between Derby and Burton, I remarked to my daughter, "That we were at "that moment passing over the identical spot "of ground, on the same month of the year, "the same day of the month, the same day of "the week, and hour of the morning, on which "I had travelled over it sixty-eight years be- "fore; but with this difference, I then walked "in the bloom of eighteen, but now moved in "the withering age of eighty-six. Then, I "appeared as a run-away apprentice, but now "as a gentleman. Then I travelled with "blistered feet, but now at ease in my own "carriage."

1810.

A faithful friend is a real treasure. His sensations are mine. If he is wounded, I am hurt. By his cares mine are reduced. His happiness augments mine. Friendship is a partnership of sentiment, and one that is sure to profit, for by *giving* we are gainers.

May 15th, I lost my valuable and worthy friend William Ryland, after an intimate connection which continued, without the least interruption, more than 59 years. While batchelors, we daily sought each other out. While passing through the married state, which continued in each about 40 years, the same friendly intercourse continued; and while widowers, the affection suffered no abatement, the secrets of one were the secrets of both. His life was a continued series of vivacity, good humour, and rectitude. I have reason to believe he never did a bad act knowingly, or uttered a bad word.

A man may have many friends, but seldom has, at the same time, more than one bosom friend; the cabinet is generally fitted for one jewel only. In taking a retrospective view of a protracted life, I find six of these cabinet counsellors, from whom nothing was hidden;

five were separated by removal of place, and one by death.

We took, this year, a third journey of six weeks, into the North of Yorkshire; but the Hotel at Coatham being shut up, we took up our residence at the Red Lion, Redcar, and were completely accommodated. My Trip to Coatham had made its appearance about a month, and attracted some notice, and I respectfully accepted as much praise as the company chose to give. Mr. Christopher, Bookseller at Stockton, told me he had purchased 100 copies, and did not doubt the sale.

The ladies were intent upon scrutinizing the characters mentioned, page 128 of that work, and thought they had succeeded in making every cap fit the proper head, except the widow with £.700 a year, which set them fast.

Passing through Derby, Aug. 23, I saw workmen taking down an old house, between the Town Hall and the Corn market, which brought to remembrance, that eighty-five years before, when I was two years old, I went to school in that house with my brother, one year older, both in petticoats, John Jackson master. I saw the very room, a chamber, laid open. I recollected that the servant-maid took, and brought us back. On Market-days she brought our dinner to school, and I well remember we had buttered oat-cakes. This little anecdote, which shews the extent of memory, should have appeared in 1725, but was not recollected. Perhaps I am the only man who had seen this house eighty-five years before, and who saw its end.

The workmen found a bottle of Red-port, of a remarkably fine flavour, under some rubbish.

I was present at a dispute, whether this spirited bottle had slept in silent security fifty or one hundred years? But the important question could not be determined.

1811.

At the age of eighty-two I considered myself a young man. I could, without much fatigue, walk forty miles a day. But, during the last six years, I have felt a sensible decay; and, like a stone rolling down the hill, its velocity increases with the progress. The strings of the instrument are, one after another, giving way, never to be brought into tune.

My father died of the gravel and stone at the age of sixty-seven: his brother of the same disorder, at fifty-one. I first perceived the gravel at twenty-seven, but it was for many years of little consequence. In 1804 I went to Worcester, to the sale of an estate; which being ended, I spent the evening with five or six gentlemen, all strangers to me. The conversation turning upon the above complaint, I remarked that, during the last twenty or thirty years I had been afflicted with the gravel, and had had three or four fits every year, which continued, with excruciating pain, from one to four or five days. " I will," said one of the gentlemen, " tell you a certain cure. Abstain " from spirits, wine, and malt liquor; drink " cyder, perry, or milk; and, although it will " not totally eradicate the gravel, you will " never have another fit." I replied that I never drank spirituous liquors, and seldom wine, but daily used the produce of malt; that though I had four cyder farms, I could not conveniently be accommodated with cyder or perry, but was fond of milk.

Though I had but little expectation from this tavern prescription, I have followed it during the last seven years; in which time I have not drank a quart of malt liquor, or had a fit of the gravel. The only evil attending this change of beverage is that, when I call for milk upon a journey, it is apt to cover my landlady's face with a cloud, but her countenance brightens up when I pay the price of wine.

Lines written to a gentleman who requested my worthy friend Mr. Blount, to procure for him a specimen of the hand-writing of Dr. Priestley, Matthew Boulton, Esq. and William Hutton.

> Priestley and Boulton, learn'd and sage,
> Rank with the foremost of the age;
> And to such company invite
> The man who ne'er was taught to write,
> Is like to him, of whom 'tis told,
> He dirty farthings mix'd with gold.
>   Whether my lines are bent or straight,
> Excuse the hand of eighty-eight.
> No praise can ever be their due;
> But my best thanks belong to you.

November 17, I walked twelve miles with ease.

1812.

In 1742 I attended divine service at Castle Gate Meeting, in Nottingham. The Minister, in elucidating his subject, made this impressive remark: that it was very probable, in sixty years, every one of that crowded assembly would have descended into the grave. Seventy years have elapsed, and there is more reason to conclude that I am the only person left.

This day, October 11th, is my birth-day. I enter upon my ninetieth year, and have walked ten miles.

CONCLUSION

BY CATHERINE, DAUGHTER OF

WILLIAM HUTTON.

Mine is the melancholy task of " laying the " cap-stone on the building." I undertake it with tears to the memory of my father and friend.

Minute as the foregoing Narrative is, I hope a few additional particulars of its author and subject will not be unacceptable. These may be the more readily pardoned; as I look upon my father's history to be the most complete picture of human life, from its springing into existence, to its wearing out, by the natural exhaustion of the vital principles, that ever was drawn by man; and the few touches that are added, will be chiefly such as mark the progress of decay, and put the finishing stroke to the whole.

In the year 1791 my Father carefully inspected the remains of the City of Verulam, and had begun a history of that place, which was undertaken with the same ardour and spirit of research, as his History of the Roman Wall. This he intended for his friend Mr. Nichols; but his remarks were destroyed at the riots, and he could never resume the subject.

In 1796, after we had lost my beloved mother, my Father's affection and mine being less divided, centered more upon each other. On our journey to Barmouth, it was so evident, that we were sometimes taken for lovers, and sometimes for husband and wife. One person went so far as to say to my father, " You may " say what you will, but I am sure that lady ". is your wife."

At Matlock at the age of seventy-nine, my father was a prodigy. He was the first acquaintance and guide of new comers, and the oracle of such as were established in the house. Easy and gay, he had an arm for one, a hand for another, and a smile for all. When he was silent, he was greatly admired for his placid and benign countenance.

At table my father spoke little; but one night after supper he asked me for a glass of wine. I felt some surprize at the unusual demand, but I poured it out. He drank it, and pushing his glass to me again, said, " Give me " another." " I dare not, Father," said I, " I

" am afraid it will make you ill." " I tell thee " give me another," said he smiling, " It will " do me no harm." I gave it him in silence, and with fear.

The effect of two glasses of wine upon my father's temperate habit was extraordinary. He spoke of his former life, he became animated, his eyes sparkled, his voice was elevated, every other sound gradually died away. The company looked at him with astonishment. The near heard him with attention, the distant bent forward with anxiety; of twenty-three persons at table every one appeared a profound and eager listener; and, in the pauses of my father's voice, a pin might have been heard to fall to the ground.

After my father had published his Tour to Scarborough, the principal inhabitants of that place courted his acquaintance. Several of them visited him, and invited him to their houses. He was pleased with their attention, but declined their invitations. One of them said to me, " We do not know how to shew " our respect for your father. He will not " dine with us, he will not drink with us. " Will you tell me what we can do for him?" I replied, that the esteem they had already manifested for my father was all he could desire.

In his eighty-third year my father walked to visit his new purchase in Leicestershire. On one day, as he has mentioned in his Narrative, he walked thirty-two miles. On the next he walked eighteen, which brought him home. I met him as he entered the house, pale, exhausted, and scarcely able to mount the stairs. He said it would be the last long walk he should take; and his prediction was verified.

Nine days after, my father set out for London, in a mail coach, and travelled all night. As soon as he had breakfasted in town, he walked from Duke Street, Manchester Square, to King Street in the Borough, to deliver a letter that had been committed to his charge, and then walked back to Duke Street.

We remained in London a week, and my father was walking the greater part of every day. I endeavoured to convince him that his strength was less than it had been, and his need of rest was greater; but he could not be made to comprehend me, though he exhibited evident marks of fatigue. The effects of what he called his surfeit still remained, and made him loathe his food. On his return home he was sick for four-score miles, and tasted nothing the whole way. The confinement of the coach during so many hours, occasioned his legs to swell.

A walking journey was now impracticable. My father expressed no desire to go another way, and I thought rest was better for him than going from home in any way; I therefore went to Scarborough without him, to the extreme regret of us both.

On my return I found my father in possession of more strength, more bulk, more appetite, and more cheerfulness, than when I went.

At the age of eighty-four my father was in high spirits at Matlock. He walked and talked with every body, was caressed and admired by every body, was the principal charm of the society, and the bond that held us together. To be beloved and reverenced by a man's own family is not always the lot of eighty-four years; but to be idolized by strangers is a thing scarcely before heard of.

From Matlock I proceeded to Coatham, and my father returned home. My account of that place pleased him so much, that the next year he determined to see it himself. We went together in the carriage. After examining Sandall Castle he had a bilious attack; and, I believe, never would have reached Coatham without my nursing and purveying.

Arrived at Coatham my father was well. He conversed, played his part with the chickens, and two parts with the puddings. He was still determined upon long walks, and I was anxious to circumvent him. I heard him inquiring the way to Wilton Castle. I took no notice; but I begged him to go an airing with me, and I set him down at its foot, leaving him to walk back at his leisure, and thus cheating him of one half of the way. He would then walk to Skelton Castle, seven miles distant; but he was aware of my contrivances, and gave me no other notice of his intention than by saying, "I shall not ride with thee to-morrow." I suspected the secret, extorted it from him, and met him six miles of the way with the carriage. It was well I did, for he joined me, heated and worn down with fatigue.

My father never having been called upon, during more than four-score years, to submit to weakness or inability, pursued a track he was no longer able to tread, and smiled at my remonstrances. His answer to them was, "I will endeavour to take care of myself."

On our second journey to Coatham at the age of eighty-six, my father always staggered at first getting out of the carriage, and would probably have fallen if he had not been stopped.

I got out first, and directed the assistants how to proceed; for he could only bear to receive help in conjunction with his own strength, and not to have his own strength replaced by that of another. His health, spirits, and appetite, were good. I dreaded his walking over Marston Moor, thinking it might prove no less fatal to him than it had done to Prince Rupert; but he came off with flying colours, and highly delighted with the discoveries he had made.

At Coatham my father measured himself against what he was at Coatham last year, and we both grieved to find how much he had lost.

His sight, his hearing, his strength, both internal and external, his powers of motion and of conversation, were impaired. He was still, however, the admiration of a respectable company. The elderly sought him, and the young, both men and women, pressed forward to serve him.

The following winter was the first that my father sat whole evenings by his fire-side unemployed, because he could not see to read or write. He did both at times by the help of a very glaring lamp, but it was painful to him. He walked daily to and from Birmingham, and walked about the streets when there; but he could scarcely rise from his chair without assistance, and could not bend his arm back, to put on or pull off his coat and waistcoat.

At Redcar, the ensuing summer, my father was generally silent, except when land was the topic. He sat much in his own room, in company with a volume of old magazines, but he was content. He still walked to Marsk, a distance of five miles, out and in, before breakfast.

In the winter I perceived my father's joints grow stiffer, his limbs grow weaker. He did not sleep so much or so soundly as formerly, and his spirits were not low, but gone. Cheerfulness had given place to silence. On the other hand his appetite was excellent, and, if he had a bad night, there remained no traces of it on the following day. He suffered a fortnight's confinement with a broken shin without injury to his health, and, in the mean time, the shin got well.

During the winter neither my father nor myself dared to mention a future journey, a subject that had formerly enlivened our fireside. In March he said, "Would you venture on "another journey in summer, if we should be "no worse than we are now?" My reply was, "I should like it." My father said, "So should "I." I had many fears that the journey would be too much for him, but I was determined not to express them, if he chose to make the trial.

In June my father's faculties remained unimpaired, except the faculty of comprehending what was said. If there are nerves which convey ideas to the mind, these nerves were blunted by time. His body began to bend, his step was shortened, his sight was confined to one object at a time, and frequently to a part even of that.

In July, when we went to Redcar, my father did not know his weakness, till he tried his strength. I do not believe it would have been possible for him to have got through the journey, if the coachman's box-coat had not been folded in the form of a cushion, and laid at his back, which kept him in a reclining posture; yet he walked a mile and a half on the sands as soon as he got there.

My father's slowness of speech and apprehension threw him much out of society at Redcar. In a large company few would have the patience to wait for his observations, or to make him a partaker of their own. The man who, two years before, had been the principal object of attention, was now seldom addressed by any body, and, if he spoke, was not heard. We are no longer estimable in society, than while we are capable of contributing either to its profit or amusement.

There were some strangers, however, who took the trouble to understand, and who duly appreciated my father. And there were two sensible interesting young women, Miss Greatheads of Darlington, who had met us one summer by accident, and two by appointment, who retained all their veneration for my father, with a mixture of pain for the neglect of some of the others.

The last evening of our stay at Redcar, the party happened to be small, and was composed of such as, if this meet their eye, will not be displeased at my calling them our friends. My Father was again the first person of the company. He desired me to sing the wife's part of Burns's song of *My spouse, Nancy*, and, at the age of eighty-eight, he sung that of the husband. He went from home no more.

In November my father still rose from his bed without help; and bending, and almost tottering, under the weight of four-score and eight years, he walked to Birmingham. When there, he seldom went out, as his sight was so imperfect that he hardly knew where he was, in streets that he was not accustomed to.

About four o'clock I saw him approaching his house with a short step; generally a little fatigued, sometimes a great deal. After emptying his pockets of newspapers, and of money, if he had any, if there were a little sunshine left, he read; but that was now become a great difficulty, even by a good light, and, by an indifferent one, or by candle-light, it was impossible. When he could not see to read, he dropped into a quiet sleep, which lasted about half an hour, and greatly refreshed him.

Though my father could not rise from his chair without assistance if he had sat any time, yet, on the 27th of October, Sunday, on which day of the week he had ceased to go to Birmingham, his walks round the drive before his door amounted to ten miles, and on the 18th of November to twelve, taking three walks each day. He had neither sickness nor pain. He was fat, looked well, ate well, slept tolerably, and was never out of humour.

At the age of eighty-nine my father was well in health, and what was extraordinary at that age, increased in size, but his infirmities increased also. He still walked to and from Birmingham, and I believed that his walks and his life would finish nearly together.

Fear and uncertainty had kept us both silent through the winter respecting another journey; but in April my father owned that he should like to go to Redcar if he were no worse. I believed the journey would be of service to him, as it had been before, if he were able to undertake it; and though I dared not take the responsibility of an adviser, I was most willing to encounter the fatigue of a nurse. Silence again prevailed.

When a month only was wanting of our usual time of setting out, I broke the spell by saying, " Father, I must write to Miss Great-
" heads : what shall I say about our going to
" Redcar ?" The question shook his whole frame. It was not, " Shall I, or shall I not
" go to Redcar ?" It was, " Am I able to go
" again from home, or is my circle brought
" down for ever to two miles and a quarter from
" my own house ?"

After some conversation it was agreed that my father should take a week to consider of the matter. That expired, I meant to have asked for his determination, but he prevented me, by saying that he durst not venture to go.

As my own health required change of air, I went to Swansea, and though I could not leave my father without anxiety, I left him without terror.

In the manuscript life of my father the handwriting changes in 1808, and the lines cease to be straight. In 1809 and 1810 the hand becomes very unsteady, and the pen frequently touches the paper where it was not intended to do so. In 1811 and 1812 it was scarcely legible, and at the end of each of these years he made use of my pen to express his thoughts. The last letter he ever attempted to write was the following, addressed to me at Swansea; and it was the last time he ever attempted to write any thing but his name.

"*Bennett's Hill, Aug.* 25, 1812.

My dear Love,

I have taken up the pen, but know not how to use it. Things are much as when you left us, except that we are fifteen days older.

The servants are extremely attentive to me; they forestall my wishes.

If a worthy man, named William Spencer, should catch your eye, shake hands with him upon my account. I cannot proceed.

W. H."

My father had lived to see himself twice in fashion in Birmingham. Till the riots he was courted and respected. For some time after the riots he was insulted. He was now reverenced and admired. Two portrait-painters in Birmingham, requested him to sit to them, and one of them placed his picture in the public library of the town. Mr. Pratt, seeing it, wrote some very handsome lines underneath, which he desired might be inserted in the new edition of the History of Birmingham. As that work has met with some interruption, I shall insert the verses here.

EXTEMPORE LINES,

Written under the Portrait of WILLIAM HUTTON, *in the Library, Union Street, Birmingham.*

The well-known form, and venerable grace,
Here mark the sage Historian of the place.
Though ninety winters round his reverend head
Have roll'd their tempests, and their snows have
    shed;
And these with Time, imperious Time, combin'd
To waste at once the *body* and the *mind;*
This their confederated power defies,
And *that* the manly action still supplies:
While gently sloping to a soft decay,
We still behold the Nestor of the day!
The Ajax too! for still a native force
Keeps the fair tenor of his daily course.

His morn, his ev'ning walk, preserve their
    length,
While many a noon-tide feat of hardy strength
Remains, to shew *intemperate* Age and Youth,
This living moral of eternal Truth,
That, ere to half his honour'd years they come,
Indignant Death shall sweep them to the tomb.

With strangers my Father was never out of fashion. While he was able to walk to Birmingham, he was seated, during a great part of the day, on a bundle of paper, by the fire-side of my brother's warehouse, which was facing the street door. This Mr. Pratt called " Mr. " Hutton's Throne." No day passed in which strangers were not observed to pass and repass several times, looking in, so as to leave no doubt that their object was to obtain a sight of the Historian of Birmingham.

As my Father was to be seen near a door always open, so he was to be spoken with in a shop always ready to receive customers; and a multitude of persons, from different parts of the kingdom, have introduced themselves to him, as readers and admirers of his works. The late Duke of Norfolk, the late Mr. Gough, Dr. Priestley, Dr. Kippis, Mr. Pratt, Mr. Berrington, Dr. Mavor, and Mr. Kemble, were of the number. One gentleman presented his son, a child of four years old, to my Father, bidding the boy take especial notice of Mr. Hutton, that, when he grew old himself, he might remember he had seen him.

After the year 1812, my Father mentioned his Memoirs no more.

In his ninetieth year, my Father's strength and activity gradually diminished. He still walked to and from Birmingham, but he was a machine hard to set a-going, and, when going, not to be stopped. The end of his walk became a short run, in which he leaned forward in proportion to his velocity. In May he fell several times, but he was desirous to hide it from his family, because he feared that my brother and myself might endeavour to throw some obstacles in the way of his walking.

On Tuesday, the 5th of October, when my Father wanted six days of completing his ninetieth year, he set out on his accustomed walk to Birmingham. When he had reached half way, his strength began to fail. When he got into the streets, his helpless situation attracted the notice of numbers of people, who offered him their assistance. He was afraid he should have been overturned by their kindness, for a touch would have thrown him off his balance. He took the arm of one, and at length reached the Paper Warehouse, which now belonged to his grand nephew, Samuel Hutton. He had been two hours in walking two miles and a quarter. On his return, he was lifted into his carriage by three men, and out of it by two. In both cases he was perfectly sensible, silent, passive, and helpless.

I met my Father at his gate, and leaning upon me and a servant, he walked into the house. " Now," said he, bursting into tears, " I have done with Birmingham !" Too surely did I believe him, and most sincerely did I weep with him!

My Father had always a surprising facility in recovering fatigue. Rest was sure to succeed it immediately, and the happy consequences of rest were soon visible.

The three following days my Father accomplished several walks in his own ground, without difficulty; on the Saturday, therefore, he ventured to walk to the nearest part of the town, which is only a mile and a half from his house. He performed it with ease. He returned half way tolerably well, when he began to run backwards, and must have fallen, had not a woman servant, whom I had sent to watch him, and whom he would not have suffered to be so near him had he known it, caught hold of him. With great exertion on both sides she led him till they were within three hundred yards of his own house, when, finding it impossible to proceed any further, she supported him in the best manner she was able, and sent for a chair, in which he was carried home by two men. He was the model of Patience when he was set down.

This was the last walk my Father ever attempted out of his own ground, except to the cottage of my brother, whose ground and my Father's were only separated by the turnpike road.

My Father was totally free from pain and uneasiness. He moved round and round his gravel walk, being careful to accomplish his Birmingham distance, and his mind accommodated itself to a small circle, when a larger one was no longer in his power.

In January 1814, my Father was attacked with the cramp. He was frequently obliged to be got up, after having been one, two, or three hours in bed, and to pass the remainder of the night in a chair. As soon as he quitted the recumbent posture, the pain left him. He dozed through the day, and hung his head almost to his knees as he sat upon his chair. It was melancholy to contemplate the ruins of a strong man, and most melancholy when that man was my Father.

My Father's pain went with the frost. He was again in perfect health, slept quietly, ate manfully, and walked three miles a day in his kitchen, but his limbs performed their offices slowly, and with difficulty. His mental faculties had not suffered, and I would have taken his judgment, or trusted his memory, rather than my own.

Summer renewed my Father's life. It took him again into the air, and brought with it the enjoyment, though not the strength, of the preceding summer. On the 1st of August I left him, with a view of passing a month at Malvern Wells. I believed it would be the last time I should leave him.

On Thursday the 11th, I received a letter from my brother. I opened it with suspense, bordering upon terror, and was not able to fix my eye upon the beginning. The first that caught my sight was the end, " If you do not " come home, I shall write again in a post or " two." It was enough. I left the room, and when I was able to read my letter, I found it in substance as follows.

My Father had dined at the cottage on Sunday in good health. On Monday he had eaten but little, and had had no sleep during the night. On Tuesday he had fallen three times, and had persisted in walking, notwithstanding the intreaties of those about him, saying, "If "I once give up my walking, I shall never re- "cover it again." In the night of Tuesday, he had raved and talked incessantly, and twice got out of bed, though he was not able to stand. Three times he vomited. At five o'clock on Wednesday morning he was quite still, and the attendants believed him dying. At twelve o'clock on Wednesday, when the letter was written, my Father was got up, and was better, but my brother concluded his account by saying, "How can we expect a return to health at "ninety-one?"

I was in my gig before six o'clock the next morning, and at home before eight in the evening.

I passed the day in sad composure, prepared to undergo all the fatigue my nature could support on the road, and all the sorrow that might await me at home. I neither felt pain nor hunger. Food did not seem necessary to my existence.

As I passed through the village near our house, I expected, every moment, that some kind neighbour would stop me, to tell me of my Father's death; and, as soon as the house was in view, I looked for the same intelligence through an open window.

I found my Father dressed, and sitting on the sofa.

The scenes that had presented themselves to my Father's imagination during the tumult of Nature, made a more vivid and lasting impression on his mind than if they had been real. The day after I came home, he amused himself with relating them to me.

" I was in the Narrow Marsh, in Notting-
" ham," said my Father, " in a room where
" twelve men were drinking and smoking. I
" remember their faces well, and even their
" cloaths, though they were all strangers to me.
" The cause of our meeting was to fix the price
" of frame-work hose. When the business was
" discussed, they divided into parties of three
" or four, and I got into a boat, and sailed
" among them. At first the motion was de-
" lightful; but I was soon carried on with such
" rapidity, that I was in the utmost terror lest
" I should run foul of some of the men. By
" great good luck, however, my boat, though
" going with prodigious swiftness, crossed from
" one side of the room to the other, and I
" missed them all."

A thought instantly struck me, on mention of the boat. "Pray," said I to my brother, "what had my Father for dinner on Sunday?"

"Harico of mutton and gooseberry pudding; and he ate very heartily."

"Then," said I, "the whole is accounted "for. He has eaten a dinner he could not di- "gest, he has retained it with increasing mi- "sery; the motion of the boat was occasioned "by sickness; when the stomach was relieved "of its burden, my Father sunk into repose, "and was supposed to be dying, and he has "been recovering ever since."

The apothecary whom I sent for confirmed all I had said, and added that my Father would be as well as before, which was really the case.

This event altered my opinion of the probable duration of my Father's life. The preceding winter I had been under daily apprehensions of discovering some symptom that might indicate a speedy change; but now, having weathered such a storm, I concluded he had great internal strength left, and I was blind to danger when it actually stared me in the face.

My Father was now well, but so infirm that he could not sit down on his chair, or lie down on his bed, or rise from either, without assistance. He continued his walks in the kitchen, but they were performed with difficulty, and not without danger.

On the 11th, the 19th, and the 24th of December, my Father fell. By one fall he was not hurt, by another his hip was bruised, by another he received a severe contusion over the eye; but Nature still retained her happy propensity to make all well again. In these repeated falls my Father never uttered cry or groan. He lay immovable till he could be lifted up, and the calm character of his countenance was never disturbed. These warnings were too many to be slighted. Such a number of falls could only proceed from the utter inability of the frame to support itself. He walked no more alone, but leaned on the arm of a servant.

In the Winter my Father had frequent returns of the cramp. A frost never failed to bring it, and a thaw generally took it away. Not being able to pass the night in a chair, as he had done the last Winter, he lay in bed, groaning under excruciating and irremediable pain.

The temporary alienation of mind under which he had laboured in August, now attacked my Father at intervals, but only in the night. It was not delirium, it was not insanity, it was not childishness—it was a kind of illusion. Imaginary objects presented themselves before his eyes, and made a much stronger impression upon his mind than those he really saw. In the dead of night he saw candles burning in his room, though there was no light but the fire; and a number of persons conversing together, though there was no one but the servant who attended him.

My Father's belief in these appearances was firm, and he related them to me as facts, with a fluency of speech that he was not capable of on any other subject. Sometimes they were ludicrous. I shall give one in his own words as a specimen.

On the 14th of January, 1815, my father said, " I observed one thing this morning that " I never saw before. You know the fire draws " every thing into its vortex. I got into the " current, and it drew me towards itself, in " spite of all my resistance; and, when I got " near, it turned me half round, and seated " me on the fire!"

" You found it a warm seat, did not you?" said I.

" Yes," replied my Father, " I made an ef- " fort, and got off immediately. One does not " like to sit upon the fire, if it be only a few " embers."

"I suppose," said I, "you are now con-
"vinced that it was not really so?"

"I am as sure as I live," replied my Father, in a tone of reproach for my incredulity, "that "it was so."

I could have wept at this wavering of a noble mind, and I could have laughed at the oddity of the incident. I did neither; I proceeded seriously to shew my Father that he was mistaken. He listened, doubted, inquired, and was convinced he had been deceived. In consequence of my pursuing this method, his doubts arose before he communicated his visions to me; and he asked whether the circumstances he detailed were truth or fiction. Sometimes he would say, "I do not see how this "could have happened; yet every thing ap- "peared so perfect at the time, that I was as- "sured of its reality." He was always disturbed by these imaginations, and restored to serenity when I had convinced him that they were not truths.

In March the cramp and the illusions quitted my Father. After his morning walk he came up weary, grew sleepy, and was laid down on his bed, where he rested quietly. In the evening my brother passed two hours with us, and reading and conversation amused my Father.

He made judicious remarks on the one, and joined in the other occasionally, though not in a very articulate voice. At ten o'clock he was undressed, and lifted into bed, where he could not turn himself, however uneasy he might lie.

In May my Father's estates in Herefordshire were in a perplexing situation, and my brother was in London. One tenant paid no rent, and answered no letter that was sent to demand it; another had lately entered on his farm, and wanted a reduction of rent; and another wished to transfer his lease to a new tenant: repairs too were wanting. My Father was conscious of his own inability to manage these matters, and his mind was struck with the dread of misfortune, without being capable of ascertaining whence it might arise. He grew hot and restless, passed many nights wholly without sleep, and part of them in great confusion; became thinner, paler, and had not so good an appetite. His legs, which hitherto had preserved their shape and bulk, now shrunk. Notwithstanding all this, he still walked, and Summer had taken him from the kitchen into the open air.

I am inclined to think that a natural decay, and the untoward circumstances of the Herefordshire farms, operated upon each other;

that the vexation would not have produced such violent effects, if life had not been drawing near its close; and that life would not have ebbed away so rapidly, if it had not been for the anxiety.

I looked upon Winter as the season when my Father's dissolution would take place, because he had recovered a greater degree of health in the two preceding Springs, and I think that Nature made several efforts now to heal the wounds that had been made, but they were counteracted by fresh incidents.

In June my Father performed no action of his life without assistance, except carrying a spoon to his mouth. His walks were reduced to a quarter of a mile each, but he took four in the day. He passed the greatest part of the afternoon, as well as the morning, on his bed.

I now perceived a wheezing, a cough, and a shortness of breath, after getting up stairs. As soon as I heard these, I knew they were the ministers of death, the agents appointed to convey my Father to another world, though I could not guess at the time they would take in performing their office.

On the 26th of July I set out for Malvern Wells. I knew I should be within call; and believing my Father in no immediate danger, I consigned him to the care of persons I could trust: I thought my own health required change of air, and that it was necessary to arm me for the mournful scenes I might have to go through.

I returned home on the 24th of August, and found my father thinner, weaker, and more spiritless than I left him. How far he had felt my absence I know not. I rather think Nature was so far worn out, that it did not afford him matter of lasting regret. When I had been gone three weeks, he said to the person who attended him in my place, "Our folks" (meaning me and the servant) " will be at home to-" morrow." " No," replied she, " you know " they were to stay a month." My father said, " Is a month so long?"

From my return on the 24th of August, to the 13th of September, my father declined apace. He took a very small quantity of food, and did not relish even that. He was a shorter time out of his bed, and did not rest so well when in it. He had great difficulty in uttering the few sentences he spoke, and we had not less in understanding them. His cough was become extremely troublesome. He listened with attention to the anecdotes I related of Malvern; and when I told him that Lady Gresley had expressed a desire of being introduced to me because I was his daughter, he said, "It is a feather in my cap."

For some time past my father had found it extremely difficult to lower his foot, so as to touch the first stair; on Thursday the 14th of September, he found it impossible. He stood, holding by the bannisters, and could not move. The servant who was waiting at the bottom of the stairs came up, and, laying hold of the leg, endeavoured to make the foot descend; it was not to be done. I led my father back.

During the last week my father had several times expressed a wish to see his friend and apothecary Mr. Blount, particularly on account of his cough. As I was assured that my father's case was out of the reach of medicine, and no less certain that when he ceased to cough he must die, I delayed sending for Mr. Blount. Yesterday I had sent for him, and this evening he came.

My father's purpose was now evident, though his explanation of it was very inarticulate. It was to ascertain, positively, whether there were any hope of relief, or whether he were arrived at that stage of existence where hope is extinct. While Mr. Blount was feeling his pulse, my father said to him, "I suppose I am worn out?" Mr. Blount's answer was, "No, not yet,"

On Friday the 15th, my father performed his four accustomed walks round the circle of a quarter of a mile each, but with great exertion and fatigue. I had not the least apprehension of the melancholy catastrophe that was approaching. On Saturday the 16th, my father had had a very restless night. He took his first walk round the circle, and came in very much wearied, and out of breath, though not more so than I had seen him before. He was put into bed, and slept as usual. He was roused to his dinner, but did not attempt to go down stairs. He ate only two small apples made into sauce, which I gave him with a spoon. I offered him minced beef, cream cheese, and preserved fruit. At last he said rather hastily, " I have no appetite, and I 'll " eat nothing more!" an expression that was fatally verified.

I led my father to the top of the stairs on his way for his second walk, and with great hesitation and tardy movements he got to the bottom. I then placed myself at a window that overlooked his promenade. I watched him with silent anguish as he was gently hauled along by the servant. His countenance was pale, his chin rested on his bosom, his body was bent, and he was scarcely able to drag one leg after the other.

When my father was going his second round, the servant who had lived with him twenty years, who had been his faithful attendant in every journey he had taken during that period, and whom he had treated as a friend, looked up to me, and shook his head, saying in a voice understood by me, though not by my father, "Very bad!" I went down immediately, "Father," said I, "I am afraid you are tired, "you had better not go your six times round." "I am tired," replied he, "but I will go one "more, however." That one was his last. He was brought into the house quite exhausted. I placed a chair behind him, and he was let down upon it.

Having rested a few minutes, my father got up stairs—to go down no more. By the time he could be laid in bed, he was in such agony that he groaned aloud, and exclaimed, "Oh! "God, think on me!" He did not rest, being harassed by a perpetual cough. At the end of two hours, he was, at his own desire, taken out of bed. It was now the time of his third walk, and as I believed that his doors were for ever shut upon his walks, I asked if he would take a turn in the next room. He said, "I'll try."

A woman servant led my father by both hands, and I supported him on the back. His feet could not be gotten into any thing like a perpendicular line with his body. When we were returning, he cried, " I am got to my " last, I cannot walk another step!" By our taking almost all his weight, he reached his chair, but as it had a small foot-step, we were not able to place him in it. My brother, who then entered the room, tried to lift the foot so that it might stand upon the step—it was immovable. My father was then seated on his chair by my brother and myself taking him under each arm, and the servant lifting his knees. When he sat, his legs shot forward. The joints of his knees bent no more!

My father's breathing was so short and difficult, that we were not without apprehensions that every breath might be his last. Every breath was an agony, and attended with a cough, an unavailing effort to bring up the mucus that oppressed him. The struggle occasioned a fever.

My eyes were now completely open to the event that was approaching. A waistcoat was laid for my father to wear the next day. " No," said I, " take it away, he will never want a " waistcoat more." I knew he had nothing to do but to perform the last sad task of mortality —to die.

My father articulated nothing, but a very indistinct "Good night, my love," to me. His groaning and coughing continued all night, with very little intermission.

On Sunday the 17th, about nine o'clock, he was carried in his bed-cloaths to the sofa. He passed the day in coughing and groaning, and about three o'clock he cried out in agony, "Oh! God, relieve me!" He sucked half a peach with avidity, saying, " It will give " me cold." "Do you want cold?" said I. He answered, "Yes."

I think, after this day the bitterness of death was over. At seven o'clock in the evening my father was carried to bed, as he had been taken from it, in the bed-cloaths. He did not cry out, nor groan, during the whole night, and nothing seemed to disturb him.

On the morning of Monday, my brother read to my father for I believe two hours. When he was asked if he chose to have the reading continued, he answered, "Yes." But, whether he understood what was read, whether the voice soothed him, or whether it was a mechanical fondness for a book that still remained, I am not able to determine.

My father drank more than a quart of milk in the course of the day. He remained in bed till seven o'clock in the evening, when he was carried to the sofa, where he continued about an hour and a half. He lay awake till about two in the morning, with little coughing or groaning. It is believed he slept a little about three.—He slept no more.

I went to my father at seven o'clock in the morning of Tuesday the 19th, and found him in a bath, with excessive perspiration. He looked red, he felt hot, and he breathed very short and hard. He was supported by bolsters. As hitherto the best repose he had taken had been in the natural posture of lying down, I had the bolsters removed, and himself laid down gently. But no sooner had his head sunk on the pillow, than he cried, " I shall be " dead! I shall be dead!" He was instantly raised up, to lie down no more.

About ten o'clock my father spoke for a considerable time, as if he were uttering connected sentences, but my utmost efforts could not distinguish what he said. He discovered a great desire to make himself understood, and some disappointment when he found he could not.

I wept violently. " Father," said I, " you " are very ill; it grieves my heart to see you so." He said, " There is only one pinch more to " come." He then made me comprehend that he wished to be moved to the sofa.

From this time till half-past two o'clock he was placed against the end, the corner, and the back of the sofa, by turns, as he exhibited symptoms of restlessness. He could not articulate his words, and my brother and I, who attended him, had great difficulty in finding out his wants. He was perfectly sensible, but took little notice of what was passing in his room. He drank a little milk, and nothing else.

At three o'clock my father was shaved as he sat bolstered up on the sofa, and he stretched his under-lip while its beard was taken off.

From about half-past-two o'clock till ten at night, my Father neither moved head nor foot, and his looks seemed to say, " Do not move " me." His eyes were open during the whole time, and sometimes wandered round in a manner not usual to him. His breath was excessively hard, quick, and short, but his countenance was composed, and he neither coughed nor groaned. Once I asked him if he sat easy? His answer was, " O yes." He spoke no more.

Believing his end approaching, my brother and I determined not to remove our father if he remained at ease. But between ten and eleven, when I had placed his bolsters in a manner that I thought calculated to afford him more support, he began to discover symptoms of uneasiness. Shocked at the idea of his having a hard sofa for his place of repose through the night, I insisted upon his being put into bed. He suffered very little by the removal.

I looked at my father's pale countenance, and open unmeaning eyes, and wished him, what I knew he could not have, a good night. He seemed insensible of the vain wish.

Samuel Hutton, the grand-nephew of my father, and the present possessor of his house and business at Birmingham, a most deserving young man, who reverenced my father as a parent, and by whom he was beloved as a son, earnestly intreated permission to sit up with his uncle. After making every arrangement that I thought could contribute to the comfort of both, I left them.

My cousin did not perceive any alteration in my father during the night. He quitted the room at half-past five o'clock in the morning, and a woman servant, who had been accustomed to attend my father, took his place.

At half-past five in the morning of Wednesday the 20th of September, the servant observed a slight convulsion in my father's legs. This lasted about a minute, and returned twice afterwards. A little before six his breath was heard in his throat.

About a quarter before seven the servant frequently cast her eyes upon her master, and thought he breathed rather quicker and shorter. Soon after she observed him open his mouth, as if gaping a very little for breath. He did not do this more than six times. There was, at this time, such long intervals between each breath, that she tried to hold her own breath so long and could not. She then thought the breath had stopped, but was not certain: she put her ear to the face and could not hear it. She called the man servant, who ran up stairs instantly, and said his master was gone.

The tidings were soon brought to me. I rushed into my father's room half dressed and half frantic. He was sitting in bed exactly as I had left him. Not a thread that was near him had been disturbed. I remember his fixed eyes, and his pale serene countenance. I kissed his warm forehead, but I know not what I said.

Bitter sorrow has been my portion while I have been tracing the events of the last four days.

Perhaps I have been too circumstantial in my relation of my father's decease. To die is the lot of every man, and my father has done no more; but Mr. Blount said, that it seldom happened to a medical practitioner to witness such a case: a human being quitting the world from the natural and total wearing out of the structure, without any mixture of disease. If this, and the interest my Father may have excited in the course of his Narrative, do not make my apology, I have greatly erred.

Since I have lost my father, reflection has pointed out many things left undone that I ought to have done; but I do not recollect any that I did, and ought not to have done, or that I did not do to the best of my power. I have the satisfaction of his own testimony in my favour. He has said to me more than once, " It " is impossible to be better nursed than I am." He said once, " Thou dost all thou canst to " smooth the rugged way I have to go." And he said once, " I was thinking a few days ago " what faults thou hadst." " Pray, father," said I, " Do not think too much on that subject." Without noticing my interruption, he added in a solemn manner, " To my great satisfaction I " could find none."

I am not so infatuated as to believe I have no faults. I know them, and I feel them; but I am grateful to Almighty God that my parent's fondness could cover them.

I shall be censured for reciting my own praises. Be it so. They are the praises of my father, and I will not lose an atom of them.

My father recollected with gratitude to Providence the success that had crowned the exertions of his youth. " How thankful ought I " to be," he would say, " for the comforts that " surround me. Where should I have been " now if I had continued a stockinger? I must " have been in the workhouse. They all go " there when they cannot see to work. I have " all I can wish for. I think of these things " every day."

My father seldom spoke of his death; but I have reason to believe he constantly watched its approach, and was sensible of every advance he made towards it. Some expressions I have mentioned tend to prove this; and while I was at Malvern he said to his attendant, " I shall " not be long for this world."

My father has delineated his own character in the history he has written of his life. Little more remains to be said, and I hope that little will not be too much.

I think the predominant feature in my father's character was the *love of peace*. No quarrel ever happened within the sphere of his influence, in which he did not act the part of a mediator, and endeavour to conciliate both sides; and, I believe, no quarrel ever happened where he was concerned, in which he did not relinquish a part of his right. The first lessons he taught his children were, that *the giving up an argument was meritorious*, and, that *having the last word was a fault*.

My father's love of peace made him generally silent on those inexhaustible subjects of dispute and animosity, religion and politics. His sufferings at the riots drew his sentiments from him, and he gave them without reserve. They will be found too liberal for the present day. Public opinion, like the pendulum of a clock, cannot rest in the centre. From the time of the riots it has been verging towards bigotry and slavery. Having reached its limits, it will verge towards the opposite extremes, infidelity and anarchy. Truth is the centre; and, perhaps, my father's opinions may not have been wide of the mark.

The few lessons of good breeding that reached my father in early life were never forgotten by him. His friend Mr. Webb had said, " Billy, " never interrupt any person who is speaking." My father was a patient hearer. He waited till his turn came; and frequently, in the clamour of a public table, his turn did not come, and what he had to say was lost. I never knew him make one of two persons speaking together. He did not begin till another had ended, and he stopped if another began.

My father's conduct towards his children was admirable. He allowed us a greater degree of liberty than custom gives to a child; but, if he saw us transgressing the bounds of order, a single word, and that a mild one, was sufficient to bring us back. He strongly inculcated the confession of an error. A fault acknowledged was not merely amended: in his estimation it almost became a virtue.

My father was an uncommon instance of resolution and perseverance, and an example of what these can perform. Another, I might almost say, every other, would have sunk under supposed inability, when he was falling to the ground; and would, therefore, have been irrecoverably in bed, while he was still walking. My father was so tenacious of his activity and independence, that he performed every one of his accustomed actions, till it was not possible for him to do it once more. I have no doubt that he prolonged his powers and his life by these exertions. The ill consequences of exercise are precarious, those of sitting-still are certain.

My father was nearly five feet six inches in height, well made, strong, and active; a little inclined to corpulence, which did not diminish till within four or five months of his death. From this period he became gradually thin. His countenance was expressive of sense, resolution, and calmness; though when irritated or animated he had a very keen eye. Such was the happy disposition of his mind, and such the firm texture of his body, that ninety-two years had scarcely the power to alter his features, or make a wrinkle in his face.

THE

HISTORY

OF THE

FAMILY OF HUTTON,

FROM 1570 TO 1798,

BY

WILLIAM HUTTON, F. A. S. S.

PREFACE.

HE who writes the History of his Family brings himself into a premunire. He must either be unfaithful, or divulge the errors of his dearest friends. As all have defects, he must accuse *them*, by laying those defects open; or *himself*, by concealing them. True judgment lies in endeavouring to steer clear of both.

The memoirs of a private family bear but little weight in the scale of history. Few anecdotes offer. An Author ought to be blessed with a double portion of genius to be entertaining. He may be said to write upon nothing: like the Israelites, to make bricks without straw. And when his work is finished, like that of the brick-maker, it may be burnt.

The writer of a private history, like a man in a mist, sees but few objects, and the reader wanders over a dry desert without relief. Such a work is seldom read *out* of the family; nay, I am inclined to think it is seldom read *in* it. Hidden from the light, it sleeps in silence; often in the strong box, with the title-deeds of the family.

The principal transactions of the heroes of the Hutton race, may be comprised in a tombstone history. They were born, they lived, and they died. But though the characters were placed in still life, some of them were very singular.

THE HISTORY, &c.

When a man has written a book and lost it, I know nothing more difficult than to write it again. Dr. Priestley assured me he never could. The past efforts of the mind are almost as hard to be recalled as the past hour.

In 1779 I wrote the History of the Family of Hutton, which slept very quietly upon my shelf for twelve years. But in 1791, when the rioters chose to amuse themselves with the destruction of every kind of property, land excepted, which I had spent threescore years in collecting, the History of my Family fell in the general ruin. I was more affected at the loss of this history than it merited; and, for seven years, endeavoured to prevail upon myself to begin another, but was never able to succeed, though solicited by friends.

Sometimes the most important incidents in a man's life spring out of trifles. "Do you "court Miss Simpson?" said Mrs. Adams to her friend. "Not I: I shall never have any- "thing to say to her." "Nay, you may do "worse." From this simple word he began the lover, which ended in the husband. A week ago, May 1, 1798, a letter dated 1779, from one relation to another, accidentally fell into my hands, in which it was said, " That " Mr. Hutton had written the history of the " family, and that it was a good one." This trifling remark raised up that resolution which had lain dormant for seven years.

Authors tell us, " that all families are equally " ancient, as being descended from Adam." However, none can pass current without proof impressions in their favour; and, I am apprehensive, many counterfeits are offered in circulation.

If I cannot penetrate into the dark ages of antiquity, yet my family, like every other of long standing in England, no doubt carries the blood of the Britons, the Romans, Saxons, Danes, and Normans.

Most families have an attachment to a favourite name, which descends with the heirs of the house. Thus the family of Gresley retain that of Nigel, Ferrers that of Sewell, and Blount that of Walter; all prior to the Conquest. Ours never forsakes those of Thomas and Catherine. These names, though in a plain style, have existed for ages, and it would be deemed a family transgression to infringe upon them. There were, in 1786, but six males, and four of them were Thomas; three females, and two of them were Catherine; so that the present generation may always be said to represent the last.

If they have not had an estate entailed upon them, they have had a name.

Again, some families have had their propensities and dislikes to a profession, or an amusement. A family, I well know, has pleaded at the bar during four generations, without advancing or sinking a step. Another has filled a pulpit, and to as little purpose. In a third, the sporting-bag and the gun have been handed down from one generation to another.

Something like the reverse has been the case of my family. My grandfather's grandfather made hats, but none of his descendants ever touched one, except to wear it. His son, my great grandfather, was a shearman, and the last who handled the shears. He afterwards kept a public-house, but none of his descendants cared to sell ale. His son, my grandfather, was famous for dressing flax, catching fish, keeping pigs, and writing down sermons. He was the last of the family that had any of these propensities. My father was a woolcomber; but with him the family bid an eternal farewell to the fleece. He placed his three sons (two brothers and myself) to a stocking-maker; they forsook the trade, and perhaps are the last that will ever have occasion to forsake it.

The characteristics of the family were *honesty* and *supineness*. The last was fatally verified in my grandfather, who refused to travel from Derby to Northallerton to possess an estate, although his household was upon the verge of want.

My ancestors have been steady in religion, for they were Dissenters from the first establishment of that sect under Bishop Hooper. They have been as steady in their love of peace, and of pudding; remarkable for memory; not much given to receive, keep, or pay money; often sensible, always modest. The males inactive, the females distinguished for capacity. All these important points will be proved upon them as I relate their history. They are outlines of the few pictures I shall draw.

THE FIRST GENERATION,

FROM 1586 TO 1656.

That branch from which I am descended was resident at Northallerton, but at what time they settled there is uncertain, and whether originally of Yorkshire or Cumberland equally uncertain; but, I believe, they were all from one stock. The first of whom we have any certain knowledge was

THOMAS (perhaps),

A Hatter of eminence at Northallerton, who lived in repute, and employed many workmen. With him sunk the elevation of the family.

SECOND THOMAS,

FROM 1616 TO 1691.

The son of the first Thomas, and, I have reason to think, not the eldest, was my father's grandfather, born at Northallerton in 1616, and bred a shearman.

The civil wars breaking out in 1642, between Charles the First and his Parliament, he entered into the service of the latter under the

Earl of Manchester, as a private trooper, and served afterwards under Sir Thomas Fairfax and Oliver Cromwell. From these famous Generals he learned the art of Victory, was at several engagements, as Marston-moor, Naseby, Worcester, &c., and was one of the detachment sent in pursuit of the unfortunate Charles the Second, when secreted in the oak at Boscobel. I have heard my father say, the troops nearly guessed where the King was, but did not choose to search.

In 1647, the regiment in which Thomas served, marching over St. Mary's bridge at Derby, in their way to Nottingham, he observed a girl of fifteen a few yards below the bridge, lading water into her pail, while standing upon her batting-lag *(beating-log)*, upon which the dyer stands to beat his cloth. Some soldiery jokes ensued, when our trooper dismounted, and cast a large stone with design to splash her; but not being versed in directing a stone so well as a bullet, he missed the water, and broke her head.

Alarmed at this unexpected result of his rude attack, he hastened towards the front of the regiment to avoid the consequence. Thus the man who had boldly faced an enemy in the field, fled with fear from a harmless female.

Offered injuries disarm. She instantly, with cries and tears, left her pail and went home, for her residence was only at the bridge foot, where her mother was frightened to see a stream of blood.

The unknown consequences of this adventure hung upon the trooper's mind. He left the regiment in 1658, after a service of sixteen years, when, " the world being all before him " where to chuse," he fixed upon Derby, followed his occupation, courted a young woman, and in 1659 married her. In the course of their conversations he proved to be the very man who had cast the stone, and she the girl with the broken head. Her name was Catherine Smith*. She was sixteen years younger than her husband.

Their residence was about the middle of Bridge-gate, where they kept ale and harmony about thirty years. During that period they produced ten children. He died in 1691, at the age of seventy-five. A well-made man, about five feet nine.

Three pieces of antiquity belonging to this warrior fell into my possession, which I preserved as relics. A brass spoon of a singular

* This anecdote has been extracted from the present work, and published in my History of Derby.

construction, ill suited to the shape of the mouth, graced with the image of a Saint at the top. This he carried in his pocket for his own use during his military peregrinations.—His broad-sword, drawn for liberty, his companion and guard during sixteen years' service. These were both taken from me at the Riots.—The third was a fragment of a mug that had been daily used for fourscore years, which the Rioters did not think worth taking, because it was empty.

THE THIRD GENERATION,

Comprehending the time from the birth of the first to the death of the last, that is, from 1659 to 1734.

THOMAS,

My Grandfather, the eldest son of the second Thomas, born in 1659. He never resided out of St. Alkmund's parish, nor one hundred yards from the Church. Neither did he ever travel more than twelve miles from home, and that but once; or more than thirty yards to procure a wife.

While an infant in arms, a neighbour's female child, three or four years older than himself, was very fond of him, frequently nursed him, and taught him to walk. Their parents observing this tenderness between the two infants, said to each other, " Who knows but these two " may one day make a match?" which really happened twenty-two years after. Thus it may be fairly said, he was beloved by one female from the day of his birth to that of his death. Her name was Elinor Jennings. She was born in St. Alkmund's church-yard, where, seventy years after, she was interred. Her father was a baptist preacher one day in the week, and a shoemaker the other six. I knew her in 1726. She died in October the ensuing year.

Thomas, the present subject of my pen, was bred a flax-dresser, which occupation he followed through life. He was a man remarkably quiet, easy, and inoffensive, totally unfit for business, or the protection of his property, though very small; not adapted to combat the rough passions of man, but formed for a milder world, a kind of cypher in the creation.

He married about the age of twenty-four Elinor Jennings, as above related, and resided in one of those small houses in Bridge-gate, which front St. Alkmund's church on the North, and which you leave close on the left as you cross Bridge-gate from the Church-yard, entering the foot road to Darley. I think those dwellings each consist only of a room on the ground floor, and a chamber over it. Here was as much love as the house could contain, which was excellent furniture; and here my father was born.

With all Thomas's simplicity, he was fond of indulging in his little pleasures. The fishing-rod was his dear delight. Not a fish swam in the Derwent but he knew it; nor had it a recess or a hole but he knew where to find it.

Their various sorts of food were as familiar to him as his own, and he had rather want food *himself* than be unprovided with theirs. Three or four days a week he attended with his rod to the detriment of his family. Not satisfied with the time given by the Sun, he followed up his favourite amusement by the light of the Moon, and often found his way home with an empty stomach after midnight.

Fond of pigs, he could not bear to see the sty empty. I have heard my father say, that the frequent pressure of the pail upon his own head, in bringing food for the swine, damped his growth two inches.

The consequence of this bristly predilection was, sometimes a loss of money, and always of time.

Strongly biassed by religion, he made a practice of taking down the sermon in short hand. At his death he had accumulated a sack full, so that he might be said to have collected the religion of an age into a hempen focus.

In or about 1701, a person came to Derby to bring him to Northallerton, to take possession of an estate, then of £.40 a year, now, perhaps, worth £.200, to which he was become heir at law. He thanked the messenger for his kindness, entertained him, and told him, " He " would not travel so far for an estate of much " greater value; neither did he care who pos- " sessed it." I mentioned this anecdote to a friend some years back, and observed, I would have gone to America for an estate of that value. He replied, he would have gone to the devil.

When a man can take up a fortune at one grasp, it is something easier than sweating out a life to raise one. My Grandfather's neglect of the Yorkshire estate was not his sole oversight. A person of the name of Hutton, about a second cousin, had spent 40 years as coachman in the *Curzon* family, and saved about a thousand pounds. Thomas, though his nearest relation, and urged by his friends, who made no doubt of his having all, refused the acquaintance of this man. The consequence was—he had nothing.

This quiet being, this milk-and-water character, who was extremely respected as having never been concerned in a quarrel, done an ill thing, or said an ill-natured one, died of a decline three weeks before Christmas, in 1708, at the age of forty-nine. He was about five feet three inches.

ELIZABETH.

Of the remaining nine children, who were contemporary with the present Thomas (my Grandfather) and descended from the last, I can give but little account; some of them, I apprehend, died in infancy. The eldest was *Elizabeth*, afterwards married to one *Gilbert*, a blacksmith. She was said to have enjoyed the honour of supplying Derby with oat-cakes during threescore years. She survived the other nine. I personally knew her; a little old woman, as cross in her temper as ill-nature could make her. She died in 1734, at the age of seventy-three, without a mourner.

JAMES

was another, of whom I am obliged to be silent.

John,

another. This man purchased the house East of St. Mary's bridge, now the site of the China works, for £.35, but being master of only £.28, he mortgaged the premises to Mr. Crompton, a banker, for the other seven. Becoming old, poor, and inheriting the indolence of the Hutton family, he suffered the trifling interest to remain unpaid, till the mortgagee seized the premises. The freehold, in 1743, became the property of my father, who assigned over his interest to Mr. Crompton for a guinea. Thus it appears that my family were as little able to *keep* as to *acquire* property.

Catherine

was the youngest of the ten children. She married a Boltbee, whom I knew. He died in 1728. They left a daughter, who died in 1743 unmarried.

Thus we have wandered through the third generation, consisting of something like this, 0000000000, ten cyphers. No issue survives except from the eldest, my Grandfather, the third Thomas, so that we are again reduced to a single head.

THE FOURTH GENERATION.

FROM 1685 TO 1768.

The children of the third Thomas (my Grandfather) were six. The two first died in very early life, of whom nothing can be said, except that they slept before their time; nor is it of much consequence whether a man sleeps at one, or one hundred. When the candle is out, no matter how long it has burnt. The other children were, Thomas, William (my father), George, and Catherine, of whom in order.

THOMAS,

The eldest of the surviving children, was born in 1687. He was one of the finest characters I ever heard of; and, in point of temper, filial duty, amiable manners, prudent conduct, industry, and religion, he stands at the head of the Hutton family. His genius was singular, in executing whatever he undertook; his handwriting surpassed that of most masters, his mechanical knowledge was wonderful.

Arriving at man's estate, he paid his addresses to a girl of the name of Catherine Magson, but the affair terminated in addresses. Afterwards, the next brother William (my father) courted her, but *their* love ended as the last. These weighty concerns being finished, the flame of love kindled in the breast of George, the youngest brother, but it expired like the two former. I knew this woman twenty-five years after, in 1743, and was not surprized that they desisted, but that they ever made the attempt. I thought her one of the most large and masculine of her sex. I concluded she rather courted them than they her. I saw her handle a sword with the graces of a dragoon. How this could tally with domestic happiness is doubtful. What may we expect when a woman steps out of her sex? I thought this Amazonian female better adapted to kill with her hand than her eye.

Thomas, from the age of twenty, when he lost his father, supported a poor mother and a young sister by his hand labour. From the same source he paid all his father's debts.

He died of a mortification in the bowels, in 1717, at the age of twenty-nine. He was about five feet ten inches.

WILLIAM (my father,)

The second son of the third Thomas, born July 25, 1691. His name would have been

James, after his uncle, but party spirit running high at the revolution between the contending sovereigns, James and William, and his father being a partizan of William, he called him after that monarch, which introduced the name into the family.

During his minority, he swept the school for his education, and was farther employed in procuring food for his father's hogs, play for himself, and *apples* by every means he could devise. One of these was as follows. His father's landlord not having room to deposit his crop of apples from the adjoining orchard, requested the tenant to let them lie till wanted in his garret, which was guarded by a trap door. No cunning exceeds that of a child when interest prevails. William procured a long stick, which terminated in a hook, and, rising one stair higher than his own height, raised the door with his head, and drew as many apples every day as he chose to eat. He soon looked pale, lost his appetite, and *seemed* approaching a consumption, but the heap of apples was found in a *real* one. Many bushels were missing, and his father gave him the most severe of all his corrections.

He was bound apprentice to *Moses Orme*, a woolcomber, Jan. 1, 1709, three weeks after the death of his father, and at the age of seventeen and a half; consequently his servitude could not expire till he arrived at the mature age of twenty-four and a half, which further indicates the supineness of the Hutton temper.

During his servitude, he acquired thirty pounds over-work, which supported him in a creditable style of dress, and enabled him to purchase a watch, rare in those early days. In the interval between the expiration of his servitude and his marriage, which was two years, he dressed gaily, took care of his person, played at bowls, carried the finest head of hair in Derby, and at the same time carried within a considerable share of pride; and nothing is more laudable than pride, guided by reason: it keeps a man out of many a mischief. The girls thought him a handsome man.

Unfortunately, in this interval, a cold settling in his right eye, he was directed to one *Finney*, an eye-doctor, who undertook to cure him, *with the blessing of God*, and whenever he applied a nostrum, put up a prayer for its success. But auxiliary powers were needless; for, by his own applications, he drew the very eye-ball out of his head, and it hung upon the cheek by the two ligaments, like the egg of a bird upon a string. I heard him say, that through excruciating pain, he had not one hour's sleep during three weeks. The eye was again deposited in its socket, and moved with the other, but was for ever deprived of sight, and continued to increase in size during life.

Feb. 8, 1718, he married *Anne* the daughter of *Mathew Ward*, Grocer, of Mountsorrel, by whom he had nine children, who will compose our fifth generation. Whether my parents married from *love* or *custom* is uncertain, for I never saw any endearments pass between them. My mother was approaching the middle size, had very dark hair, was a brown beauty, with eyes perfectly black.

Soon after marriage, my father became a master in the little way, as every man must who begins with nothing. But his family rapidly increasing, and he having no economy or talents for trade, he failed in six years for a few trifling debts, amounting in the whole to about fifty pounds, most of which his effects discharged.

And now poverty stared him in the face. Employment, as well as prudence, was wanting, to which was added the dead weight of five small children. This happened in the year 1725.

Every future view of prosperity was now closed; and the mind, sinking under misfortunes, became incapable of exertion. His occupation taught him to drink, which he learned with willingness, while his family wanted bread. Memory could point out many a dreadful situation in which we were placed during the eight ensuing years. My poor mother more than once, one infant on her knee, and a few more hanging about her, have all fasted a whole day; and when food arrived, she has suffered them, with a tear, to take *her* share. Time produced nothing but tatters and children.

On Christmas-day 1728, a knife was wanted for dinner; and as my father was never in the habit of *buying*, except ale, he sent my sister from King's Street to the Morlege to borrow one. She did not succeed; but on her return she found one, which proved exactly the thing wanted; and I well remember there was great joy over a trifle. Success supplied the want of value.

My mother was an exceedingly prudent woman, but prudence itself can never make the marriage state happy, except practised by both parties. She was praised and respected by all who knew her. My father and she lived together fifteen years, when she died of her ninth child, March 9, 1733, at the age of 41.

And now the restraints of a wife ceasing, and the children being too young to influence, my father seemed to relinquish the cares of a parent. At her death he was left with five children, Catherine, aged fourteen years, residing with her aunts at Swithland, Thomas ten, William (myself) nine, Anne two, and Samuel, five weeks, which last was put out to a wet nurse.

My father was peculiarly circumstanced in a love affair. While a bachelor, about the year 1716, he had paid his addresses to a young woman who favoured his suit. It happened that she married another man, and he another woman, both less beloved. She buried her husband, and he his wife, and in 1735 they became lovers again; but this, like the first attempt, miscarried, and each married another a second time. He assured me in 1747, that " he loved her better than any woman he ever " saw." In 1753 I first saw her, and became acquainted with her; she appeared to be a person of good sense. By this time she had had three husbands, and he three wives. I asked her if she had loved my father, and why the match did not take effect? She assured me he had her whole heart; but gave me to understand that her father's consent, in the first instance, had been wanting.

My mother being gone, and my father's talents no way adapted to house-keeping, he immediately sold up, spent the money, and, with his three remaining children, took lodgings with *Mary Sore*, a widow, who also held the freehold of three young sons and one daughter; and now his three forlorn children suffered all those evils which naturally flow from the neglect of a parent. Though my brother and I laboured daily, we experienced the want of bread, of apparel, and seemed little beings whom nobody owned. But the poor child Anne fared much worse. Unable to use her feet, she lay neglected upon the floor, or fixed in a chair during the day, till I returned from the silk-mill in the evening, when she rejoiced to see me; for the little remaining time was devoted to her amusement. But, alas! it was of little avail, for in five months she died through neglect. My father loved her, and wept sorely at her death, as I weep now at the remembrance; but, overwhelmed with poverty, he lost all command over his conduct.

Mary Sore, I thought, rather rejoiced at the death of my poor little sister; perhaps for two reasons, to divert my father, but chiefly, because one obstacle was removed which might retard a future union.

With Mary Sore, who was a fine figure, tolerably handsome, and intolerably ignorant, completely vulgar, and completely filthy, he continued ten years. It may fairly be supposed, that a man and woman thus situated would become lovers. He faintly courted her, she strenuously courted him, and, which is a common case, the more she advanced the more he retreated. However, matters, I believe, would have terminated in a matrimonial issue, had not half a dozen children stood in the way. Love, if not founded upon the purest principles, will, like your coat, wear to rags. This was the case before us.

We might reasonably suppose, a man of forty-three, who had lost an eye, and was encumbered with four or five children, would stand upon the lowest terms of favour with the fair sex. But the very reverse was the fact. During the ten years of his being a widower he courted several women, both maids and widows, and governed them all, yet all loved him.

Mary Sore was extremely jealous of these women, often dreamed on the subject, and sent for the old damsels of the neighbourhood, skilled in dreams, to interpret them. Coffee-grounds were most earnestly wished for, but they were out of the reach of the pocket. However, a rusty pack of cards was procured, which was the grand *urim* and *thummim*. These, by cutting, shuffling, and placing in various directions, were to solve every question in love. They were to tell what he would say to Mary, and if out, whether he was gone to one of her rivals, and what would be the result. Though the sorceress, for a pipe of tobacco, chose to prophesy favourably, yet the queen of hearts and the king of spades were often in malign aspect.

My father was informed in the beginning of 1743, that *Benjamin Gudger*, a person he had well known forty years, was taken ill, and could not recover. His wife entering a public house one morning where my father was drinking, he behaved to her with uncommon civility, pressed her to stay, and he would treat her with a glass of whatever she should chuse. She was surprized at this singular attention, which followed former cold civility. *He* understood it, and so did *she*, six months after, when the husband was dead, and he offered her another.

He married her at Michaelmas that year, and she paid him good interest for staying ten, for she was a most excellent woman. I am sorry I cannot bestow the same epithet upon him. He observed at her funeral, " She might have "human infirmities, but she had not one fault." We may reasonably conclude, if a wife has no faults, a husband ought to *behave* as if she had none. Two amiable wives are more than one man has a right to expect, especially if he ventures upon widows, the remains of whose first love are not extinguished. They lived together five years, and he lost her in November 1748, after giving her many a bitter pill.

Losing his second wife, he continued a widower four years; when, in 1752, he ventured upon a third wife, another widow; but, alas! his authority began to fail; diseases began to approach, particularly the stone, attended with a paralytic affection, which entirely broke up his constitution. And now the tables were turned; for, instead of that attention which he experienced from his two former wives, this treated him with great unkindness; and, as he could not make resistance, he often felt the weight of her hand. This ought to be a lesson against marrying in advanced life, for love is not apt to take root after forty, especially in a second venture. After a miserable life, pressed down by affliction, he departed Dec. 13, 1758, at the age of sixty-seven. Five feet seven, corpulent, weighing about sixteen stone.

The powers of his mind were strong. His memory was tenacious, and his head well stored with knowledge. His judgment was frequently sought after in critical cases. I remember at Christmas 1738 being in his company, when a dispute arose concerning a point of law. He decided the question, and, as I thought, fairly; but was contradicted, which always hurt him. He remarked, "From a gentleman the decision "would have passed, but not from a poor wool- "comber." It afterwards appeared he was right.

He was fond of reading, but never purchased a book. He supported his literary existence by borrowing, and often forgot to return. He spoke as correctly as if trained to letters. Had he been born in affluence, he might have figured in the world, but penury damps every rising idea.

He was by far the most eloquent speaker I ever heard in low life, and nearly the best in any life. His manner was decisive, his words were well adapted to the subject, and flowed with ease. Perhaps this was a loss to his family; for his company was coveted by all who knew him. But with all these accomplishments he had no idea of business or economy. Severity to children was one of his maxims, which I have since found erroneous;

for reason opens in a child at a very early period, and he is easier *drawn* than driven. But, with all my father's errors I cannot forbear revering his memory.

He was of an even temper. Not addicted to laughter himself, yet could, when he pleased, make others laugh. He said many smart things, and knew how to set the company upon the tip-toe of mirth.

Like his ancestors he was an advocate for religion, and he attended public worship when liquor suffered him to take care of his person. He read, and taught his children to read, religious books; and made many resolutions against intemperance, which were dispersed by a pot of ale.

I went from Nottingham, March 6, 1742, to see a contested election between *Pole* and *Duncannon*, and, looking into my father's pocket-book, I found this resolution written a month before: " O Lord, by thy assistance, " I will not enter a public house on this side " Easter." This proves how heavy his conduct hung upon his mind. This resolution, like many others, was forgotten. He was intoxicated during the whole of my stay, which was from Saturday morning till Sunday night. When in liquor he was good-natured. His children knew his weak side, and omitted to ask a favour till the barrel worked.

GEORGE,

(The third son of the third Thomas, my grandfather.)

I have now a shorter life to write, but a most amiable character to draw. Of the three brothers, the eldest and the youngest were among the best of the human race, the middle one excelled in mental powers. The two former might be held up to guide the passenger in the right way, and the last to avoid the wrong.

George was born March 11, 1695. I never heard that he entered upon any employment till put apprentice to a stocking-maker.

During his apprenticeship, the rebellion in 1715 broke out, when he entered as a dragoon in the service of the crown, under General Carpenter. The regiment was at the battle of Preston, but he, with the rest of the recruits, was left to guard the baggage.

The rebellion being quelled, he, with many others, was discharged, without having been long enough in the service to assume the uniform. This flimsy contest being over, he returned to his master during the remainder of his time, which was two years, and attended so closely to business that he earned near ten pounds over-work. At his out-come, the master, sensible of his merit, declared " he would " walk one hundred miles for a servant as va-" luable."

This worthy and industrious son and brother then entered upon house-keeping; and, as his eldest brother was dead, maintained his sister till she married in 1726, and his mother till her death in 1727.

Although he had no pretensions to a handsome person, I am apprized of three amours which he had upon his hands while a bachelor. The first was with a country girl, of very plain manners. Those who are adepts in courtship are well acquainted with the little arts of winning; as, the pleasing smile, the meaning look, the gentle tap, the soft squeeze of the hand, the endearing word, the embrace, and the harmless kiss. She, however, would suffer none of these, but ordered him to keep his distance, " for she could hear him if he " stood two yards off." The prohibitions of the fair are sometimes disregarded. George forgot to keep them, and made his approaches beyond the line, but met reproof in the following dialect: "Luc yo now, conna *yo* ston there, and *I*

"ston here, I con hear wot yo han to se."
George, disliking the distance, dropt the pursuit.

A person of the name of Abraham Taylor, whom I well knew, had observed George's conduct, and wished him to marry his daughter, but did not know how to open the affair, for they were no farther acquainted than a bow, as attending the same place of worship. He watched an opportunity of opening a conversation, accompanied with a smile, and, in the course of chat, told George he was going three miles into the country, and should be glad of his company. The offer was accepted. While on the road, words seemed to labour in Taylor's breast, from which he knew not how to deliver them. This being observed by my uncle, " You seem, sir, to have something to " say to me." This broke the ice, and concluded with offering his daughter and a fortune many times larger than his own. A courtship opened, which soon closed, when Mr. Taylor quarreled with my uncle, and was near striking him for ill-treating his daughter. But George modestly told him, " if he did strike, he would " not return the blow, that he had no disre- " spect to the girl, or any of the family, but " that he thought the first requisite in a mar- " ried state was love, and, as he could not fix "his affections upon her, he had too much "regard for her to be the author of her misery."

The third (exclusive of Catherine Magson mentioned in the life of Thomas) was Miss Betsey. Whether she was handsome I cannot say. At the age of forty-five I knew her well, but the time to decide the question was past. She had many lovers besides my uncle, and, like a miser, was still grasping at more. She was a wholesale trader in human beings. Vanity prompted her to form a muster-roll of her lovers. Vanity then did a worse thing, for it tempted her to shew the list. The circumstance reached the ears of her parents, who demanded a sight of the roll. It was found to contain exactly twenty names. Her parents shewed great displeasure, ordered her to quit this vile recruiting trade, and instantly fix upon the man she preferred to the others for a husband. She named George Hutton. My uncle was then given to understand that he might marry Miss Betsey; but, by this time, the list had been handed about, and my uncle, who had heard of it, was afraid of being one of twenty, though the first. He thought, if she retained twenty men while single, one might not satisfy her when married; he, therefore, declined the blessing.

Being unfortunately reduced to nineteen lovers, Miss Betsey was now required to name the next upon the roll. She fixed upon John Hall. He gloried in disappointing eighteen anxious expectants, and eagerly seized the prize. The little loves that wait upon marriage flew around the happy pair; but it was soon found they were birds of passage, for they flew away. She often struck fire, and he quickly caught the flame. Each passed through life with a clog at the heels, and both ended their days in the workhouse.

In 1728, George Hutton married Elizabeth, the daughter of Thomas Spiby, of Nottingham, who brought him neither money nor children. This union induced him to quit Derby, and reside there. Notwithstanding these female taxes upon his industry, of a mother and sister, he had acquired, by the year 1732, nearly £.100.

One Tortoishell, an intimate acquaintance, entered into the hosiery line in London, and having purchased goods of George and others of his friends to a large amount, he decamped with the whole, and defrauded them all. I believe my uncle got nothing in return but two useless journeys to London. Thus, at one blow, went his little capital, which had cost him many years in accumulating, and he was left totally unable to satisfy his creditors.

Honest in principle, and not accustomed to be dunned, he laboured night and day at the most unproductive of trades till he had paid all their demands. Fourteen years after, he remarked to me, while on his death-bed, that Tortoishell had left him fourscore pounds worse than nothing, but that he had paid it, and acquired fourscore since.

I served seven years as an apprentice to this worthy man, whose person I loved, and whose memory I revere, notwithstanding he once beat me to that degree, and with an unmerciful broom-stick of white hazle, that I thought he would have fractured my bones and dislocated my joints, and for a trifling error, scarcely deserving a reprimand; but he was influenced by passion, and possessed of power, and I was obliged to submit. I shall relate this more at large in my own life. Notwithstanding this circumstance, I never knew a better husband, son, brother, or master.

There has been something peculiarly melancholy in the latter days of the existence of the members of the Hutton family. The little good fortune experienced through life, if any, has vanished, their remaining moments have been embittered, and they have departed in wretchedness, want, and distress. Their weekly earnings being small, and consumed as soon as earned, nothing has remained for sickness, age, or accident. Deprived of the benefits of their own labour, they have been dependant on the scanty succour of others. My Grandfather, the third Thomas, sustained a long decline, and, as the maintenance of his wife and children chiefly arose from the labour of his hands, distress and dependance followed. His son, my father, during the last six years of his life, groaned under the palsy, the stone, severe poverty, and the greater severity of a cruel wife. His brother, my uncle George, the present subject, was a man of a cheerful temper, who, in his passage through the world, did all that prudence could suggest, to keep things together, and secure independence. Two years prior to his death, disorders began to rise, and Nature sink. He had five apprentices, meant to assist in family support. During the first six months two became out of their time, whom he could not replace; and a few weeks after, the other three ran away without cause, and never returned, but to harass him. I could enumerate other instances.

My uncle George died Sept. 19, 1746, owing to the breaking of a blood-vessel, by straining to vomit, in a fit of the gravel, at the age of fifty-one, and thus escaped the poverty which began to stare him in the face. He was about five feet seven inches, of a thin habit, and dark complexion.

CATHERINE (my aunt),

The only daughter and youngest child of the third Thomas, was born in 1699, in the same house as her brother George, at the bottom of St. Helen's walk. She was supported by her brother, as observed above, till mature age, when she was employed at the silk-mill.

She possessed a large share of sense and beauty; and her brother still maintaining her, gave her an advantage beyond her equals; for while other girls divided their daily earnings between their back and their stomach, she laid all hers upon the former. This made her fortune; for as the best in every sphere holds a pre-eminence, she was singled out by a master of the works, Samuel Fletcher, who married her in 1726, and retired to his estate at Standbach, in the county of Hereford. Here she enjoyed affluence and happiness. She died of an asthma in 1768, at the age of sixty-nine, leaving two sons and two daughters. Her son now enjoys the estate.

Her person was of the larger size, brown and ruddy, with dark eyes; her gait and manner were majestic, her judgment just, and her sense masculine. She spoke with fluency, and much to the purpose. Yet with all these qualifications she was tinctured with a most unaccountable species of paltry pride. Thus one scabbed sheep spoils the flock. She was so ashamed of her mean origin, that it was kept a profound secret from the world, and particularly from the neighbourhood where she resided. Nay, her children knew no more of her life before marriage, than the children born in Egypt. The more she endeavoured to conceal it, the more the neighbours tried to make the discovery. This proved a continual worm upon the mind. As poverty is no crime, she ought not to have been impressed with shame. Her smile would have disappointed malignant reflection. She secretly prohibited a visit from her relations, except they could appear in a creditable style, and even then they were enjoined silence. My father, in the momentary effusions of love, mentioned a visit. " She " wished he would come well dressed, and on

"horseback, because all her husband's rela-
"tions were genteel." My brother visited her
on foot: his reception did not strike him with
joy. She understood I kept a horse. "Why
"did not William come?" Had I visited her
in my own carriage, I must have been received
with open arms.

Thus we have drawn our line through four
descents. As Thomas, the eldest son in this
generation, died a bachelor, and as George,
the youngest, never had issue, we are again
reduced to one stem, William (my father),
which shews we are not a prolific race, and
that we can barely keep the name alive.

William, by his first wife Anne, had nine
children: Catherine, Anne, who died young,
Thomas, William (myself), Matthew, George,
a second Anne, and John, who all four died in
infancy, and Samuel. Of the four surviving
children, in order.

THE FIFTH GENERATION.

From 1718, and not yet defunct, May 15, 1798.

CATHERINE (my sister),

The daughter of William, born Dec. 11,
1718, was early bred by her mother to indus-

try, and in infancy acquired a character for sense and conduct. At ten she left her mother, whom she ardently loved, but saw no more, to reside with two cross aunts at Swithland near Mountsorrel, who carried on the tripartite calling of mercer, grocer, and village milliner.

Being handsome, Catherine was, at twelve, singled out by William Perkins, a neighbour, and a taylor, a personable figure with a slender capacity, of astonishing industry and complete economy, who for thirteen years adhered as closely to her as to himself.

At twenty she chose to enter into service, and lived with a Dissenting minister at Reresby in Leicestershire, about five years, when he died. In this servitude she gave the utmost satisfaction, for she was never bidden twice to do the same thing. As the family declined house-keeping, they recommended her to the service of Mr. Ambrose Rudsdall, another Dissenting minister, at Gainsborough.

During the interval between quitting one service and entering upon the other, William Perkins had the address to gain her consent to a private marriage, which she granted upon three express conditions: that he should resign the office of clerk of Swithland Church; that she would reside wherever he pleased except

Swithland; and, as she had promised to serve at Gainsborough, she would not break her word, but would serve one year. All which were readily granted on his side, and the marriage on hers, in August 1743.

She resided two years in this service, when her mistress died; the master quitted the place, William took a house in Mountsorrel, and they resided together three months.

In January 1746 she came to Nottingham to see her friends. My uncle George, among other remarks, hoped she was happily married. She replied in a tone of dissonance, and shook the head, though I cannot, after fifty-two years, give the expression. And now opened a sorrowful scene; disagreement followed disagreement for more than three months, without any alledgment of consequence on either side; but it was easy to see the heart was wanting.

Her friends promoted a reconciliation, in which I took the lead; and William Perkins *purchased* a house in Mountsorrel, where they were to be happy during life. Still matters returned to their former untoward state. An unwillingness for the house began to appear on his part. The title was defective. He would reside no where but at Swithland, where she would not. The separation continued, without plan, without design. She never quitted Nottingham, nor did they ever after live one day together. This disagreement upon nothing, astonished the friends of both.

Her aversion seemed to increase. He approached her with a small degree of fear, and I have seen her turn sick at the sight. From 1746 to 1750 she resided in Barward-lane, laboured hard at the spinning-wheel, and my brother Thomas and I resided with her as lodgers. All thoughts of a union were given up.

In March 1755 I paid her a visit at Nottingham, after an absence of five years. One evening when she and I were left alone, the unfortunate marriage was brought up. I could not forbear expressing my surprize that two prudent people, who could agree with every one else, could not agree with each other. She told me she never had an affection for any man; that she had thought so little upon the subject of love, that she scarcely deemed it necessary in marriage, and could not conceive how she was persuaded to give her hand. That the cause of disagreement between her and William Perkins (for she could not call him husband, as she conceived they were not lawfully married,) lay within her own breast, and never was or should be revealed to any one. That she had written down her sentiments, and at her death a writing would be found, specifying the reasons of her conduct.

She lived thirty-three years after this declaration, followed in retired life the drapery business, and acquired a fortune of more than £.1500, although she passed a life of bodily affliction, which proved expensive.

She died Feb. 26, 1786, at the age of sixty-seven, much lamented, when the writing alluded to thirty-three years before was found, containing nearly these words: " I never could " consider William Perkins as my husband, " by any law divine or human; for the design " of marriage is to increase and multiply; there- " fore I cannot be deemed his wife, because " *I never knew him as a husband.*"

Thus the fatal secret was disclosed, which modesty had concealed forty-three years.

Her person was tall and slender, her complexion fair, her hair light. In youth she was very handsome. Her conduct in domestic life was a perfect pattern of prudence, her temper even, her manner commanding. Her judgment, in difficult cases, was solicited by all who knew her. She was fond of retirement, and of reading, had a most retentive memory, was punctual in her dealings, extensive in her charities, to which she appropriated the daily sum of sixpence, exclusive of charities of the larger kind, such as £.20 towards erecting a Meeting-house, &c. I apprehend she left the world without an enemy, except it was those who, in the line of business, had cheated her.

The following is her character, drawn by my daughter Catherine Hutton:

My aunt had a spirit of dominion which drew every human being round her into its vortex. Born with talents to command an empire, she governed every creature that approached her. But as this spirit of domination was directed by a judgment that was always right, and accompanied by a benevolence that was always sincere, she was more beloved than feared.

After she had determined not to live with her husband, she was left without friends, except her two brothers, something younger than herself. To these one would naturally imagine she would have looked for protection and assistance. No. She took a house, maintained herself by spinning, lodged her brothers, and though both are the most sensible men ever found in that station, and my father one of the most sensible ever found in any, she prescribed to them their way of life, regulated their expences, dictated what they should pay to her, and governed them like children.

When my father found the stocking-frame too narrow for his talents, she was the only one of his friends who encouraged him to quit it, and settle as a bookseller in Birmingham; every one else threatened him with ruin. Her comprehensive mind took in his capacity and frugality, and the probability of his success. But she not only encouraged him by her advice, she assisted him with money to purchase his stock, and defray necessary expences, and without her ever possessing any other means of accumulating money than servitude and spinning. He left Nottingham fifteen pounds in her debt. She also lent him a uniform set of the Spectator, Tatler, and Guardian, which Mr. Rudsdall, her former master, had made her a present of, like the monsters in the shop of Shakespeare's apothecary, *to make up a show;* but, like the guineas in the pocket of the Vicar of Wakefield's daughters, with strict orders *never to part with them.* In this, however, he ventured to disobey her, and was severely chidden for it.

After my Father had left her, May 24, 1750, my uncle Hutton still continued to lodge with her, and she took an illness in consequence of removing to a damp house, as extraordinary as the subject of it. The circumstances cannot now be remembered, but I think I recollect her saying she had no evacuations for six weeks. She kept her bed nearly a year, during which time she subsisted upon her former earnings. She was attended by Dr. Davison, the first physician in Nottingham, who at last said to her, " Madam, I confess I do not understand " your case, and I can do nothing for you."

She then procured Owen's Dictionary, read night and day in bed, sent at times my uncle, and a woman who attended her, and who both obeyed her orders with the greatest punctuality, for different remedies, which she thought might suit her complaints. At last she cured herself, to the great astonishment of her physician, who occasionally visited her as a friend. In the course of her illness there was one night on which she thought she felt death approaching, and believed she should not live till morning. She directed her brother where to find her money, and delivered it to him, bidding him keep it; and, in case his brother Samuel should ever return from the army, share it with him.

It was ten pounds, all in silver. He kept it about five weeks, when she was recovering, and he returned it.

The first time she went out was in a sedan chair, and she could not bear the light of day, but was obliged to draw the curtains. This illness happened in 1756. On her recovery she laid by spinning, and commenced draper and haberdasher; kept no shop, but sold her goods in a private manner at her own house to those who knew her; and at a covered stall in the market on a Saturday to all comers. Here her ascendancy again shewed itself. She got a set of customers, chiefly of the poorer sort, to whom she dictated *what* they wanted, *how much* they wanted, and by what instalments she would be paid. And in this latter part of the convention, such was the love they bore her, and such the awe in which they stood of her, they seldom failed. To chance customers there was something of dignity in her manner, and, if they gave unnecessary trouble, of haughtiness.

In 1758 my father, established in business, thought he could do better for his brother than his own slow motions, though counteracted by industry and frugality, could do at the stocking-frame; and he sent for him to Birmingham.

It was now that my aunt Perkins fitted out her eldest brother for his launching into the world, as she had before done her second. She furnished him with necessaries, and made him out a bill which came to three guineas. "Brother," said she, "this is what you owe me. If you are ever able to pay me, I expect you will; if not, I forgive you." She then made him a present of half a crown, and bade him farewell. It is needless to say he paid her, as my Father had done before. This circumstance my uncle told me to-day, June 10, 1798, while the tears ran down his cheeks, and his voice was interrupted by his emotion.

Her youngest brother, Samuel, alone now remained to be provided for. He who had relished a soldier's life while a bachelor, grew weary of it when encumbered with a wife and two children. In 1763 she bought his discharge, bore his expences out of Scotland, supported his family, and set him up in his trade of whip-making. Thus did this extraordinary woman throw the golden ball into the lap of each of her three brothers; but the youngest had neither the spirit and activity of my father, nor the patient endurance of labour of my uncle, nor the frugality of either. He was a tax upon her bounty as long as she lived.

During the last twenty years of her life my aunt lived alone. She would not be troubled with a servant, and no friend, or even customer, dared to call at certain hours. Indeed her habit of body, since her illness, would not always allow of interruption. One of her nieces, Samuel's daughter, was let in at a regular hour to do the daily work of the house, and go on errands, and dismissed when these were over.

My aunt was naturally devout, and for the first fifty years of her life, was a rigid Calvinist, believing *that* religion alone right, though not condemning those who went wrong. She then became a zealous Sandemanian, a sect who form themselves on the example of the Apostles, without considering that the brotherly love and common right of property, which were necessary in an infant church, would be absurd in an extensive one. How far my aunt conformed to these principles I know not. She was above deceit. No doubt the brethren were satisfied with what she distributed, and what she withheld. I am sure that her own conscience would be her sole director, and I know that her sense and fortune made her one of the chief pillars of this little church. (Thus far my daughter, Catherine Hutton.)

Thomas (my brother,)

The eldest son of William, was born June 20, 1722, and, during infancy, and his Father's misfortune in trade, was taken under the protection of his uncle George, who behaved to him with the greatest tenderness.

He was put to school, but had no need of being taught his book, for he seemed, by a kind of instinct, to learn without. By the time he was seven, he was master of the Jewish history, as recorded by Moses and the succeeding rulers of the Jewish empire. He then began the Latin tongue; but, alas, fortune was unfavourable to letters, for at eight he was obliged to forsake every pursuit for bread, and was forced to attend the Silk-mill as an apprentice for seven years, from five in the morning till seven at night. Thus a rising genius was cramped, and every prospect of future life clouded.

I well remember, at this early period he was singularly well acquainted with the History of England, had imbibed a set of political opinions, and frequently, in conversation with the masters of the mill, with the utmost modesty in some cases, he set them right, and in others, set them fast. He bore the character of a boy of peace and knowledge, but never had the art of putting himself forward. During eight years attendance upon that place, remarkable for ignorance and vulgarity, I do not recollect that he ever had the least difference with any one.

In 1738, he quitted the mill, and was bound apprentice to his uncle George Hutton, a stocking-maker at Nottingham. These seven years he served with the same steadiness and peace as he had done the former seven at the mill. Slow in action, constant at his work or his book, but clumsy at his play, which he never courted, and in which he never shone, his life was a scene of clock-work, and, like the clock, he had but one pace.

His servitude being expired on his birth-day, June 20, 1745, at the age of twenty-three, for he was sixteen before he was placed out as an apprentice, another instance of family neglect, he commenced journeyman, and lived upon the frame, or rather starved, during thirteen years. From the steady stroke he kept up, of rising, working, eating, resting, this long interval does not afford me one incident to record. How difficult then is the historian's task, to write upon nothing!

In 1758, I invited him to reside with me at Birmingham, in quality of an assistant. He has now, July 1, 1798, his birth-day, been my faithful servant forty years, my staunch friend seventy-one, and my worthy brother seventy-five. Out of the above seventy-five, we have resided together sixty-seven.

Life in him is slow in all her motions. I do not recollect that he was ever in a hurry, or performed one quick action. In 1772, at the age of fifty, an age when the generality of men decline matrimony, he entered into it. But though his actions differed from those of the world, they rarely differed from prudence. After the moderate courtship of *twice seven years*, he married Martha Parkes of Wordsley, in the county of Stafford, who perfectly answered his wish. By her he had two sons, George, who died in infancy; the other, Thomas, who is extremely handsome, and extremely idle, will be reserved for the sixth generation.

This amiable, but most uncommon character, my brother, has much the size and temper of his Grandfather. Like him, I believe he would not have ventured to Northallerton for the same estate. He never thought riches contributed to happiness; therefore, though an economist, he never wished for them, but often weighed his own portion of content against the affluence of others, and found his scale preponderate.

Man's life is said to be chequered. His has been as even as a fine-spun thread; an extended age without novelty. The history of a day is the history of his life. It may be said of him,

> He work'd and ate, he read and slept, unknown to sorrow,
> Will work and eat, will read and sleep, just so to-morrow.

No man perhaps ever lived 76 years in a narrower circle. Inoffensive as an infant, he never said, or did harm, except by mistake. He is a man of thought, and possessed of a most astonishing memory. Every incident, date, and character of moment, in the History of England, during the last seven hundred years, he retains without trouble to himself.

One of the singular traits of his character proceeded from his own mouth. He remarked, while standing at the fire with my son, and Samuel Hutton, a child of eleven, Grandson to my brother Samuel, that he had lived 76 years, and had never been asked for money! neither had any man, probably in his station, accumulated a Library equal to his! This consisted of about 200 volumes*.

WILLIAM (myself,)

The second son of William, born Sept. 30, 1723. As my life differs materially from the lives of my ancestors,—as rising to greater elevation, conducting a Court of Requests during nineteen years, and being an Author, have

---

* May 2, 1800.—I have now the melancholy task of recording the last event of this worthy brother.

After enjoying a series of health during seventy-six years, a decline gradually approached, but equanimity never forsook him. His rational and animal powers sunk together, till they fell even beneath those of an infant. No physical art was administered, because he knew he was beyond its reach.

He daily attended the *scene* of business, through an ardent wish and long habit, though unable to act, till Dec. 18, 1799, but continued to sink under the farther pressures of decay nineteen weeks, till yesterday, May 1, 1800, when he departed at the age of seventy-eight.

His portrait, which is an admirable likeness, was drawn in April 1799, in the dress he wore, and may be said to have been taken in the last hour in which his visage was his own, uninjured by decay. It is one of the illustrations of this History of the Hutton family, in my own handwriting, in my son's library.

brought me upon the public stage,—the insertion of my History, in its proper place, would, by its length, have broken the line of descent.

Samuel,

(The third son of William, my Father,)

Born Feb. 2, 1733. That day at noon, Friday, my mother said to me, " Perhaps you " will have a little brother by the time you " return from the mill at night." This happened accordingly. I was so pleased with the sight of the little red-faced dear, that I declared " he should never want money while I " had any;" but I have since seen reason to repent the promise. My mother died the day five weeks after her delivery, of a cold caught by rinsing clothes in cold water during her lying-in.

As she saw her end approaching, she cast a melancholy eye upon her two babes in arms, Anne and Samuel, and wished, with a sigh, they might go before her, for they would be neglected if left. Her remark, without the aid of prophecy, was ratified, for Anne was carried to the grave five months after, through bad, or rather *no* nursing; and Samuel, the subject of my pen, who has now lived 65 years, has seen many sorrows. The parent's favourite is usually the youngest, but the reverse was his lot.

My Father had no violent love for any of his children, but the least of all for the last, although deprived of the tenderness of a mother, which ought to have excited compassion. I have reason to believe he never gave him a kiss during his whole life, and I have the same inducement to believe he never gave me one, till I was 23 years of age, nor should I have been favoured with that, though the favourite son, had he been sober, but we all know liquor inspires the man.

Samuel was sent to nurse with Joseph and Sarah Knowles, at Mackworth, and was treated with all the tenderness humanity could wish during three years, for eighteen pence a week.

My Father courted Mary Sore, a selfish widow with whom we lodged, and as he thought eighteen pence too much, she, the better to secure his affections, offered to board him for a shilling. Bargains between lovers are smoothly contracted, and my brother Thomas and I were sent to Mackworth, to bring Samuel back. Nothing could surpass the bitterness of soul in the afflicted nurse, at parting with him. She saw the result, offered to abate her price rather than part with the child; but tears are vain when profit steps in. We brought him from a state of perfect happiness to complete misery. His Father treated him with severity; the widow, with the worst of food that could be bought or begged, with lodging beneath that of a dog, and with punishment whenever she pleased. His father's hand was in her power. This scene continued seven years. If ever love subsists between a parent and child, the parent must begin first, then the building rises from its proper foundation.

In 1743, at the age of ten, he was placed as an apprentice to his uncle George Hutton at Nottingham. Thus through the indolence of my father, in not procuring proper trades, all his three sons were brought up in one house to that starving business, weaving of stockings.

It soon appeared that this dull occupation was very unsuitable to the active spirit of the child. He followed it three years, during which period he ran away about ten times, and in 1746 for the last.

The conduct of many fathers and masters in training up children is very censurable. The child's temper is seldom attended to, and the *rough* hand is employed to force, instead of the *smooth* tongue to guide: hence we take ten times more trouble to *ruin* than would save.

When a teacher *draws*, he treads upon sure ground, but when he *drives*, nineteen wrong ways are taken for one right. Nay, as every human being wishes to be master of his own actions, the best mode of education is to guide without *seeming* to guide.

Samuel did not return till 1751. During these five years his adventures and hardships were innumerable and astonishing, such as would well become a circulating library, but they are too voluminous for admission here. He appeared an animal cut off from the only world in which he was made to exist.

At the above date he was bound apprentice to a collar and whip-maker, at the advanced age of eighteen, but it was now too late to begin a new life, and correct those wandering thoughts which had strayed for seven years. And as the master was as great a rover as himself, they both went into the army, the man first in the 12th regiment of foot, and the master into a regiment of dragoons. They met in Germany in the war of 1756, under Prince Ferdinand. The master lost his life.

At the battle of ——————— the grenadiers were marching three deep up a hill, Samuel in the rear rank. The front man, directly before him, was shot dead. The centre man, marching to the spot, took up the dead man's knapsack, and, at that instant was shot himself. Samuel, in three seconds, arrived at the same spot, and expected the same fate.

During Samuel's stay upon the Continent, he married the widow of a soldier who had fallen in battle. By her Samuel had two sons and two daughters, who will compose part of our sixth generation. After marching in the regiment twelve years as a grenadier, and part of that time as a petty officer, he quitted the service in 1763.

Family consultations were now held relative to his future mode of life. Whip-making was adopted, and followed in a desultory style during some years; but it appeared the soldier had spoiled the tradesman, for now he found no way but that of retreating. When commercial talents have long lain dormant, it is difficult to revive them, and more difficult to *create* what never existed. I cannot forbear considering that man's case as most unhappy, who is *able* to labour, unwilling, yet must subsist by labour *.

* April 13, 1801.—I have now to record the termination of existence of this, my youngest brother, who died the 14th instant, at the age of sixty-eight, after an indisposition of ten days: worn out after many scenes of adver-

We have now drawn the line through five descents of the Hutton family. These generations were continued by a single stem. Only one in an age left descendants. But now the family divides itself into three branches, as all the three sons have issue.

THE SIXTH GENERATION,

The issue of Thomas, the first son of William (my father.)

The first of this generation is Thomas, the son of Thomas, my elder brother, an only son, a spoiled child, master of his parents before he ought to have been master of himself. From his birth to the age of seven he did as he

sity, and only one of prosperity, which he did not know how to improve, that of a legacy of £.500 bequeathed by his sister. An inclination to ramble in early life, and having spent the prime of his days in the army, rendered him unfit for the acquirement even of a livelihood. Like others of his family he was sensible and peaceable.

Of the nine children proceeding from William (my father), I am now the only survivor. Catherine and Thomas were generous economists, I more frugal; Samuel knew but little how to get, and less how to keep money. His portrait in the great folio manuscript is an excellent likeness.

listed, from thence to fourteen as he pleased, and from fourteen to twenty-one there has been no health in him *.

The issue of WILLIAM (myself),
the second son of William.

I perceive this work, contrary to expectation, will be extended to a considerable length. But of all its parts I am now entering upon the most difficult, the delineation of my children. Faithfulness ought to be the guide of the historian, but prejudice will be suspected. I confess my children are my treasure, my happi-

---

* Nov. 26, 1808.—This day the above Thomas Hutton finished his earthly career, at the age of thirty-two. He had a handsome person, a modest deportment, an engaging manner, and an excellent understanding, but he was nursed into more than the inactivity of the Hutton family. Apprenticed to one of the manufactures of Birmingham, he wanted application to pursue his trade. With a taste for the stage, and possessing the requisites to ensure theatrical success, he wanted resolution to become an actor. He lived with his parents a life of idleness, dissipating their fortune, and preying upon their constitutions, till they both sunk under the burthen; and the money, which was considerable, owing to a legacy from my sister, was nearly consumed. A dram-bottle finished himself. Had he possessed a moderate share of prudence, the fortune of the family would have been his.

ness. I have ardently wished I might not be separated from them. I have hitherto had my wish. The world would only exhibit a barren desert without them. That I may not split upon the rock I see before me, I shall, as far as I am able, confine myself to facts.

CATHERINE,

the daughter of the second William (myself),

Came into the world before her time, and perhaps was the smallest human being ever seen. She was so very diminutive, that even a pregnancy in her mother was scarcely discernible. Curiosity led me, when a month old, to shut her up for a moment in the small drawer of a bureau, with all her habiliments: nay, I should have put her in my pocket and shut the lid over her, but through fear of her sustaining some injury. Though she afterwards grew to a proper size, yet she always carried a delicate frame.

This dear little animal had been two days in the world before I took the least notice of her. So intent upon the mother whom I knew and loved, I disregarded the daughter who was a stranger.

It soon appeared that what she wanted in body was given in vivacity. Her spirit was so animated, that the body seemed to be no clog. An astonishing capacity opened, which might be said to take in knowledge without instruction. One instance among many was, that she never was taught to read. She went to a writing-school at nine, where her fame had gone before her; for when she first stood up with the History of England in her hand, Mr. Baker the master said, " Now let us hear a " Bishop read."

In temper she is most amiable. Her wish is to do good to all, and she gratifies that wish as much as lies in her power. Her domestic economy is equal to her other qualities. Her filial love was exemplified in attentively watching over a declining mother during seventeen years, the last five of which she was her constant nurse. Whatever lies within the bounds of female reach, she ventures to undertake, and whatever she undertakes is well done.

I cannot refrain from inserting in this place a copy of her Dedication of " The Miser Mar- " ried," a Novel published by her in 1813. Though its insertion here will have the appearance of Paternal Vanity, I give it as a proof of Filial Affection.

DEDICATION.

TO MY FATHER.

My beloved and respected Father,

To you, from whom I inherit the Faculties which have enabled me to compose a Book, to whose Industry I am indebted for the means of leisure, and by whose Kindness I am permitted to enjoy it, do I dedicate that Book, as I have dedicated my life.

Of your Talents, which have broken through the Fetters of Ignorance, I will say nothing. They are before the World, and the World has judged favourably of them. Of your Conduct, I may be allowed to say that its tenor is Independence for yourself, and unlimited Indulgence to all around you. I trust mine has proved that I am not insensible of the Blessing.

To you it is unnecessary, but in this place it is proper, to add that

I am,

Your most grateful

And affectionate Daughter,

CATHERINE HUTTON.

THOMAS,

Son of the second William (myself.)

A dreadful tumour in the right breast of his mother, during pregnancy, which threatened to become a cancer, broke at his birth, and denying that nourishment necessary for the child, he dwindled, became rickety, and his life seemed in danger.

My affections were engrossed by the dear little Catherine, who played about me like a puppet. It was some time before I could take my boy into favour. The first emotion of the heart was pity, and this was soon followed by all the endearments of a father. No care was wanting to set him on his feet. As soon as this can be done a child becomes a better nurse to himself than all the world can be to him. We find him always in action, which soon straightens his legs, reduces his bulky wrists, gives him strength, sets him a growing, and forms the man.

Bathing, sliding, schooling, romping, attended with health, carried him to the age of eleven, when his employments were reduced to business and play. He was soon master of figures, and kept his father's accompt-books, till they, and the trade, in 1793, became his own.

Rising towards manhood, my son was first a reader of books, and then a purchaser. His library is now such as few men in his station ever possessed. It contains the best editions of all the best English authors, in the best bindings possible. His collection of prints is no less remarkable, and his book-cases are of a piece with what they inclose. Thus, of a family fond of books, Thomas surpasses all. None of his predecessors have had either the spirit, the taste, or the means, to accomplish what he has done. No day passes without reading, but the necessary duties are not infringed upon by the book.

He married, September the 5th, 1793, Mary Reynolds, of Shiffnall, in the county of Salop, by whom he has no issue.

We are told that a candle ought not to be hidden under a bushel. My son has not attended to this precept. Excellent in principle, sound in understanding, rapid in execution, he is calculated to make a shining character. His internal powers are well adapted to please, if they were not forbidden.

I think the supineness of the Hutton family has not descended to my children.

The children of Samuel, my youngest brother.

Samuel as before observed, married in Germany a widow, whose husband had fallen in battle. She had no children. Samuel was pleased with the prospect of not being encumbered with a military family himself; but our well-laid schemes are often frustrated. His wife quickly brought him recruits, ill adapted to a soldier's life. The eldest,

Thomas,

Was born in camp at Earph in Germany. He was upon the verge of falling, by the fate of war, soon after he was born. While on his mother's knee, by the fire in the tent, a cannon ball flew so near the child, as to carry him several yards by its force.

Thomas was brought up a cabinet-maker in Nottingham, which occupation he now pursues. He is full of vivacity, humour, and, what is better, good sense, good nature, and humanity. While he passes through life, he enjoys it. He supports the characters of a kind son, husband, and father, is respected by all who know him, and carries that rotundity of figure which betokens a plentiful table, and a mind at ease. His talent at cutting and uniting timber may be seen in the magnificent book-cases of his fabrication in my son's library.

Catherine, the eldest daughter of Samuel, was born at Edinburgh. She is a sensible woman, and a prudent wife.

Anne, the second daughter of Samuel, was born at Nottingham. She is open and undesigning.

These three children, Thomas, Catherine, and Anne, had each a legacy left by their aunt Perkins in 1786. Each married a few months after her death, and in eleven years they have jointly produced about twenty-two children.

Thus we have gone through the sixth generation, consisting of three males all named Thomas, and three females, two of them Catherine.

THE SEVENTH GENERATION,

Consisting solely of the descendants of the children of Samuel, my youngest brother.

Though the present generation is numerous, its history will be short. I must give up anecdote and character, for, as infants, they produce neither. I must leave their various histories to be recorded by my successor to the pen, and shall only notice

SAMUEL, the eldest son of Thomas,

Who, at the age of eleven, came from Nottingham to Birmingham, with the view of being trained to my son's business, and inheriting our fortune. He appears, at this day, April the 10th, 1799, to be worthy of both. His behaviour, as a child, is excellent, and seems to promise an amiable and wealthy man.

THE END.

www.ingramcontent.com/pod-product-compliance
Lightning Source LLC
Chambersburg PA
CBHW081913170426
43200CB00014B/2716